ERIC LINK[illegible]

Orkney and Shetland

AN HISTORICAL, GEOGRAPHICAL, SOCIAL AND SCENIC SURVEY

FOURTH EDITION REVISED BY
JAMES R. NICOLSON

ROBERT HALE · LONDON

First published in Great Britain 1965

Second edition 1971
Reprinted 1973
Third edition 1980
Fourth edition 1984

Robert Hale Limited
Clerkenwell House
Clerkenwell Green
London EC1R 0HT

ISBN 0 7090 2055 4

PRINTED IN GREAT BRITAIN BY
ST EDMUNDSBURY PRESS, BURY ST EDMUNDS, SUFFOLK
AND BOUND BY HUNTER & FOULIS LTD.

CONTENTS

PART ONE

Orkney

PART TWO

Shetland

PART THREE

Modern Islands

ILLUSTRATIONS

MAPS

Picture Credits

J. Allan Cash: 1; Ministry of Public Building and Works: 2; *Notice of Runic Inscriptions in the Orkneys* by James Farrer (1862): 3; William Hourston: 4, 5a, 6a, 6b, 7, 10, 13, 14, 16a, 16b, 17, 18, 22a; Gunnie Moberg: 5b; Phoenix Photos: 8, 11, 20; W. S. Thomson: 9, 19a, 21, 22b; A. D. S. Macpherson: 12a, 12b, 15a, 15b; J. Sinclair, 19b; Dennis Coutts, 23, 24a, 24b, 27, 28, 29, 31, 32, 35a, 35b, 36b, 37b, 38a, 38b, 39a, 39b; J. Peterson: 25, 26b, 30a, 30b, 33b, 36a, 37a; Eric G. Meadows: 26a, 33a, 34; British Petroleum Co. Ltd: 40a, 40b.

REVISER'S NOTE

When Eric Linklater's *Orkney and Shetland* appeared in 1965 it was hailed as a masterpiece. His love for his native islands, his appreciation of their rich heritage and his concern for their future combined to make it a landmark among books on the Northern Isles. *Orkney and Shetland* was reprinted in 1971 and Eric Linklater was able to bring the story up to date, welcoming the new mood of optimism in Shetland, by adding a new section to which he gave the heading "Modern Islands". Eric Linklater died in 1974 three years after the discovery of North Sea oil which was to have such a profound effect on Orkney and Shetland and make even his reappraisal out of date.

In carrying the story of Orkney and Shetland up to the 1980s I have replaced Eric Linklater's third section with one of my own while retaining the heading "Modern Islands". In it I have sought to place the economic recovery of the 1960s in its proper perspective, to cover the cataclysmic effects of the oil construction phase and to show how the islanders are already looking ahead and making plans for the post-oil era which will come sooner than many people realize. The main body of the book has been left untouched and it is still as valid today as a history of Orkney and Shetland and as a description of the landscape as when it was written twenty years ago. The style is so unmistakably that of the great Orcadian writer that to intrude other than by way of a few brief footnotes would be nothing less than sacrilegious.

James R. Nicolson

To my old friends
Bob *and* Hester Scarth
of Binscarth

PART ONE

ORKNEY

I

The Sea Road

The traveller to Orkney can choose both route and vehicle. He may fly at speed, and in tolerable comfort, from London or Glasgow, Edinburgh or Inverness; or take ship from Aberdeen. But the most pleasant approach, and the most enlightening, is by road from Inverness to Thurso and its little port of Scrabster, and thence by the mail-boat *St. Ola* to Stromness in the West Mainland of Orkney.

The road skirts the three great firths that, from the east, invade the northern counties of Scotland—the Beauly, the Cromarty, and the Dornoch Firths—and turns narrowly through the small town of Dingwall. When Orkney under its Norse Earls was a warlike power with expansive tendencies, these parts were intermittently subject to the Earldom, or debatable land, and Dingwall must have been a frontier post of some authority: the place where a Norse *Thing*, or parliament, met at the inner end of the long *voe* of Cromarty. A little farther north, beside the Dornoch Firth, is the burial mound of one of its early rulers, and as the road marches by a *corniche* above the pale blue sea, it bears the traveller out of a genial, well-farmed, or wooded landscape on to the bare nobility of rising hills. It strides across the Ord of Caithness, dips steeply to hidden Berriedale, and threads a long moor, untenanted and lugubrious under rain, where now it is curiously partnered by the tall pylons carrying power bred in the atomic pile at Dounreay. Then, suddenly, there is Thurso by the Pentland Firth, and the Pentland Firth is to Orkney what the Channel is to England: a defensive moat, a turbulent forecourt, and the entrance to larger lands.

Its proper name, distorted by cartographers, is the Pictland Firth. That is what the earliest of the Norse intruders called it, who presumably found Picts on either side. The dividing distance is no more than eight or nine miles—less than that from Duncansby Head to the nearest point of South Ronaldsay—but it is formidable water through which the Atlantic tide, pouring into the narrows from the north-west, may run at more than ten knots; and against a contrary wind the returning stream can raise a tumultuously broken sea. Between the Caithness cliffs and the archipelago lie the small islands of Stroma, Swona, and the Pentland Skerries. A little west of Stroma, on the Scottish shore, the tide erupts into a peculiar, pointed violence, a glinting dance of wild abandon, called The Merry Men of Mey; and off the north-western corner of the island is the dangerous whirlpool of The Swelkie.

This was a real peril in the days of sail, and the Norsemen who trafficked in these waters in their narrow ships were so impressed by its roaring menace that they concocted a legend which is preserved in the Elder Edda of Iceland. According to it a magic quern, or grinding-stone, belonged to a King Frodi, for whom it would grind either gold or peace. But the stone—it was called Grotti—was stolen by Mysing, a sea-king, who used it to grind salt. It ground so much that his ship sank beneath its burden in the Pentland Firth. But Grotti went on grinding till all the sea was salt, and as the tide rushes through the eye of the quern the roar of its movement can still be heard.

The traveller, however, need not be unduly alarmed by the Firth's horrendous reputation. Though gales are common in winter, they are infrequent in summer, and I, who cross it every year, have not met one for many years. I have, on the contrary, been rewarded for going this way by the most majestic view that Orkney has to offer: a view of tall, rose-red cliffs freakt with green, channelled by the sea and sculptured by storm, of a grandeur that familiarity cannot diminish.

The mail-boat crosses in two and a half hours, or less, and for its passengers the cliffs of Hoy are their introduction to the islands, and a very misleading introduction except in one respect: their architecture is superb, and architecture of subsequent and different sorts is one of the unexpected but characteristic features of Orkney. But the aspect of Hoy from the Pentland Firth is huge and romantic, its riven cliffs rise to the vast bastion of St. John's Head, more than 1100 feet high, and above them the rolling, barren top of its tallest hill stands 400 feet higher. Nothing of this sort lies beyond. The other islands are fertile and inclined to flatness. There is sufficient hill-ground to prevent monotony, but the hills are fluent, their contours suave, and they seldom exceed 500 feet. The typical country scene is not romantic but domestic, with prospering, well-tended fields and the reflecting surface of large, shallow lochs to repeat the brightness of enormous skies. The island of Hoy is a rampart for the others, concealing them from view, and like a sentinel before its cliffs, isolated by the waves that break to whiteness on its base, is the tall and brooding stack, ruddy of hue, called The Old Man of Hoy.

Eight miles of cliff face the south-west, broken only by the stony bay of Rackwick, and round the promontory of Rora Head, on a line that now runs east of north, are another four miles of red rock-face variegated in high summer by a lush growth of grass that thrives in the salty air. It is here, beyond Rora Head, that the Old Man stands noble and aloof, and beyond him are St. John's Head, and the tunnelled Heel of Hoy, where the Atlantic and the mail-boat turn east into Hoy Sound.

North of that broad entrance are the cliffs, a lesser rampart, of the West Mainland, and ahead is the green and comely shape of Graemsay, a little island decorated by the white stems—one high and one low—of two lighthouses. In Hoy Sound the tide runs almost as fast as in the Firth, and the surface of the sea may be shouldered into ponderously moving dunes and ridges, or strangely scored by the smoothly intersecting circles of many small whirlpools. But presently the tide loses its force, and as the boat turns sharply into the sheltered harbour of Stromness, closed by two minute islands called the Outer and Inner Holms, there is a view from its starboard side of the great land-locked sea of Scapa Flow.

2

Scapa Flow

In the momentous years of this century Scapa Flow has become the most widely known, the most famous or notorious part of the whole Orcadian archipelago. Seventy years ago Orkney lay under the horizon of the world's consciousness. It was a geographical name, and except for its own natives, and some hundreds of deep-sea fishermen, few people knew anything of it; not even—with any exactitude—where it was. But when the old world started to break asunder in 1914, Orkney was re-discovered and history moved again to use it. From 1914 to 1918 the Grand Fleet lay in the strategic shelter of Scapa Flow, waiting for its chance, which came but rarely, to steam out and intercept the German High Seas Fleet; and when the German fleet surrendered, it was shepherded to its last anchorage in the Flow. There, in 1919, its remnant crews, in a superb and dramatic defiance of ignominy, scuttled their many vessels—battleships, cruisers, and destroyers—and sent them plunging to the dark neutrality of its sandy bottom.

When war was renewed in 1939 the Royal Navy returned to Scapa Flow, with fewer ships than in 1914, and within a few weeks was attacked from the air and the depths of the sea. About midnight of Friday, October 13th, the U-boat commander, Gunther Prien, brought his submarine into the Flow by the channel called Kirk Sound, which was thought to be blocked, and sank the battleship *Royal Oak*, at anchor by Gaitnip, south of Scapa Bay; some 800 men died in her. Four days later, on the 17th, the Luftwaffe raided, and the old battleship *Iron Duke*—Jellicoe's flagship in the earlier war—was straddled by bombs and beached to prevent her sinking. The Flow was deserted until it could be more effectively defended, and after the German invasion of Norway, early in 1940, both Orkney and Shetland, then

vulnerable to military attack, were heavily garrisoned. As well as the sailors who already knew its anchorages, many thousands of soldiers and airmen made acquaintance with the shores of Scapa Flow and the adjacent islands; and in the circumstances of the time, few enjoyed their service there.

In shape the Flow is roughly quadrilateral, bounded on the north by the Mainland parishes of Orphir and Holm, which form its north-western and north-eastern walls; and more irregularly on the south by Hoy and the small islands of Fara and Flotta—its south-western side—and South Ronaldsay and Burray to the south-east. Its southern entrance is by Hoxa Sound, between Flotta and South Ronaldsay; its western gate is Hoy Sound, Clestrain Sound, and Bring Deeps between Hoy and Houton Head on the Mainland. In area approximately 50 square miles, it gives shelter against the destructive rage of Atlantic gales and North Sea storm, but is always open to the buffeting of hard weather. Though now abandoned by the Royal Navy, its physical condition—its material boundaries—owe much to the Navy's use of it and to Winston Churchill's perception that our ships could lie more safely if the island walls on its eastern side were made continuous. A ponderous embankment—the Churchill Barrier—now crosses the several channels between the southern corner of the East Mainland and Burray, between Burray and South Ronaldsay; and a continuous, island-hopping road runs from Kirkwall to Burwick near the lower end of South Ronaldsay.

Here, in a naval environment, it is appropriate to quote from the *North Sea Pilot*, published by the Hydrographic Department of the Admiralty, the statement that Orkney comprises "about 56 islands", many of them very small. Even the authoritative *Pilot* will not commit itself to a more positive enumeration, but by common consent the archipelago is divisible into three parts. The islands that lie south and east of the Flow are the South Isles; the principal island, dominated by Kirkwall on the waist that divides it into East and West, is the Mainland; and beyond the Mainland hills, and separated by fierce tides, are the North Isles. Of the whole 56 recognized, with some hesitancy, by the *Pilot*, 18 are now inhabited, and a couple of others tenanted by lighthouse-keepers. As standards of living have risen, the population has fallen from over 30,000 in 1891 to some 18,000 in 1963; and nine of the lesser islands, each of which within living memory supported a few households apiece, are now grazed by sheep and only occasionally visited. The recent movement of people—away from Orkney or from its outer isles to the Mainland—has been due, on the whole, to prosperity, not to want. When the Navy finally cut through its association with Orkney, it brought to an end a companionship which had been of much material benefit to the islands, and by closing its base at Lyness in Hoy, it deprived Hoy of a major source of revenue.

Lyness, now a half-dismantled, shabby little ghost-town, came into being as a naval base and had no other purpose or function. It never had any visible dignity or attraction for the eye—it was, in its heyday, something between a mining village, a dockyard, and a Whitehall slum—but for a few years it was dignified by the large endeavour which animated it, and by the heroic visitors who walked its windswept lanes. It was, moreover, closely related, in a historical sense, to other structures on the shores of the Flow.

A couple of miles south of Lyness, on either side of the entrance to the old sailing-ship anchorage of Longhope, is a Martello tower built for protection against roving French frigates in the Napoleonic wars; and elsewhere are the ruins of a dozen brochs, those mysterious stone towers, not unlike the Martello sort in size and function, that were raised two thousand years ago by an unknown people at war with unknown enemies.

On the east side of Hoxa Sound, in South Ronaldsay, is the bay called St. Margaret's Hope, where in 1263 Hakon Hakonsson, King of Norway, lay for some days with the great dragon-prowed fleet that he had assembled for his ill-fated expedition to recover the Hebrides. For four hundred years the longships of the Norsemen—their striped sails plump with the wind, or their long oars thrashing the water white—were summer visitors to the Flow, and here and there are memories of sudden battle and some small but savage reversal of fortune.

Over much of the Flow the memory of St. Magnus broods, for the spire of his cathedral is visible from afar: a cathedral that was founded in 1137, when David I was King of Scots, and in England the rival claims of Stephen and Matilda fomented anarchy. In Orkney the last of the great vikings, Sweyn Asleifsson, still plied his trade while the pious cathedral-builders were at work, and Earl Rognvald, most genial of Crusaders, ruled the land; or some part of it.

History has marked Orkney almost as decisively—and in some places as visibly—as geography; and for a proper understanding of what is visible, a journey in time is necessary before undertaking a physical progress. It was in 1957 that the Admiralty declared it had no more use for Scapa Flow, and so concluded the half-century in which Orkney became part of the modern world. But half a century is only a moment in time when set against the long story of the islands, and it is hardly possible to describe them without, as a beginning, recounting something of that story; since many of their most conspicuous features are illustrations of their history and pre-history, or monuments to it.

History, and the distant years before history began, have the prior claim; and when that has been acknowledged, it will be convenient to return to Scapa Flow and consider the landscape.

3

Orkney Before History

Orkney has been inhabited for more than 3,000 years—perhaps, more nearly, 4,000 years—and the relics of its earliest colonists are so numerous that they may have numbered almost as many as the last census. It would, moreover, be erroneous to think of them as people who lived in extreme discomfort on the windy edge of a cold, hungry, hostile environment. They were well fed, and their world was warmer than ours.

The first arrivals came in the sub-Boreal period, which began about 2,500 B.C., and is thought to have lasted for nearly two thousand years, during which time the climate of Britain was relatively mild; and the two northern archipelagos were the terminus of a migration which had had its beginning somewhere in the Mediterranean. When it began is not known, nor why. It may be that early man, born free from the psychological and physical confinements of civilization, was by nature a wandering creature. While the scent of game led him by the nose, a native curiosity may also have lured him on: the appetite of the mind was, perhaps, as compulsive as that of the belly.

However that may be, a race of Stone Age men moved slowly west and north—out of the Mediterranean, by Spain and Portugal to Brittany and Ireland, and up the west coast of Scotland—leaving, as evidence of their culture, the megalithic tombs by which archaeologists have traced their progress and proved their consanguinity. These people were gifted in more ways than one. As well as the art of building in stone, which came to its finest expression in Orkney, they must have learnt how to build boats and from observation have discovered the working of the tides. They were cattle-men and shepherds, they drove their flocks and herds before them, and from recent investigation it seems that they also brought seed-corn; for which in Orkney they found a kindly soil.

Geologically considered, Orkney consists—almost uniformly, with the exception of Hoy—of flagstones from the middle deposits of Old Red Sandstone, with deposits of boulder clay over much of the land. The gentle look of the islands, the fluency of their characteristic low hills, was created by the double glaciation to which they were subject in the Ice Age: the movement of the Scandinavian ice-sheet and the incursion of another from the Highland parts of Scotland. When the ice receded, perhaps 15,000 years ago, there was a long period when Orkney enjoyed a continental climate, and trees grew. Then the weather deteriorated, and in a wet and stormy Atlantic period the forests of birch and rowan, elder and hazel, died and decomposed into peat: great, abundant blankets of peat. So when the megalithic visitors arrived, there was fuel in plenty though the islands were treeless.

There were other advantages which made Orkney a more agreeable land, for settlers, than the neighbouring hills of Scotland. Over much of Scotland the Caledonian forest was impenetrable to men who had no better cutting instruments than a stone knife; and where trees did not grow, there was swamp. But Orkney was open country, and its sandy soil was dry, and light enough for primitive cultivation. It was, moreover, far from being barren. All its cliffs were loud with a multitude of sea-birds, and its shores abounded in shell-fish. Fresh water and salt were teeming with fish of a livelier sort, there were red deer on the hills, there was good pasture for the migrants' sheep and cattle.

In these conditions the Stone Age people flourished, and for posterity left proof of their creative energy, their prevailing concern with death, and their relative wealth. Until some thirty or forty years ago, all the surviving or recognized work of their hands consisted of the chambered cairns in which they buried their dead. Some of these are of so elaborate a structure that any consideration, not merely of the ingenuity that went into their building, but of the man-hours expended, compels an acceptance of the fact that there was a good deal of leisure in the Stone Age: the sort of leisure, that is, which can be abstracted from the daily task of gathering food, and devoted to such unprofitable—or, at any rate, unproductive—labour as building tombs.

It was a major occasion when, in 1928, at the Bay of Skaill on the west coast of the Mainland of Orkney, the late Professor Gordon Childe began to open a series of basin-shaped hollows, cushioned by short, sheep-nibbled green turf, and presently uncovered the astonishing village of Skarabrae. It lay on the steep edge of a broad, sandy bay, and much of it, quite obviously, had been broken and swept away by the long erosion of the sea; but what remained was seven huts or chambers, or portions of them, which were of the same period and connected by passages; and four buildings of a somewhat earlier period. To the unacademic eye—the eye untaught by archaeology—the most remarkable and rewarding feature of the village was its manifest domesticity. Here was a place built to be lived in, that had been lived in, and its habit of life was immediately familiar: there were bed-places and fireplaces and cupboards, and little paths from one house to another. Suddenly, and in the most delightful fashion, the Stone Age was discovered and became real.

But was Skarabrae truly so old? Was it possible that nature, with the convenient help of a sandstorm, had preserved these simple dwellings for, perhaps, three and a half millennia? To begin with, Professor Childe was cautious and doubtful. There was no certain evidence of so great an age, nor in all Britain were there similar buildings with which he could compare his discovery. But the singularity of Skarabrae vanished when excavation at Jarlshof, in Shetland, uncovered a group of huts, like those at Skaill though less well preserved, which included a smithy; and from the evidence of the smithy it appeared that the smith had come from Ireland and worked in bronze. No metal implements were found at Skarabrae, and therefore it looked as if Skarabrae was older than the Bronze Age; for bronze implements, and the skill to make them, could hardly have been introduced to Shetland before being known in the more accessible islands of Orkney.

Subsequent discovery at Rinyo, in the island of Rousay, confirmed the deduction. Excavation begun in 1938 and continued, again by Childe, in 1946, uncovered a hutted settlement of the same sort as that at Skaill, in which were found part of a "beaker"—a sort of pottery that the widely wandering Beaker Folk first brought to Britain not later than 1800 B.C.—and later, among a great accumulation of coarse pottery such as that used by the Skarabrae inhabitants, some fragments of Unston pots. These are pots of a kind found in large numbers in the chambered cairn of Unston, on the Loch of Stenness, from which they got their name; and the manifest inference is that the people of the Rinyo settlement, who were contemporary with the people of

Skarabrae, lived in the late Stone Age when the megalithic nomads from the Mediterranean buried their dead with ceremony and provision for their future life. The village by the Bay of Skaill is as old as the burial cairns which illustrate the first chapter in an Orcadian history of architecture.

The cairns are, in the main, of two sorts. There are those which roughly resemble a subterranean cow-shed, being long and narrow, and divided on either side into stalls separated by upright slabs of stone; while those of the other sort are entered by a tunnel which leads to a central chamber, in the walls of which are cells or lesser chambers. The most impressive of the cow-shed kind are in Rousay, where the richness of antiquity's remains and the elaborate preparations for death have made something like a little Egypt.

In the years before the last war Rousay was so fortunate as to have a resident laird—he owned much of the south-western part of the island—who was rich and slightly eccentric. His name was Walter Grant. His forebears came from Moray, where the art of making whisky has long been seriously studied, and built near Kirkwall the distillery called Highland Park, which still produces from barley an *eau de vie* of great merit and singular charm. Walter Grant appreciated the whisky he made, and acquired also a great reverence for the works of antiquity, and a remarkable faculty for discovering them. It was he who found and, under expert supervision, first opened the great stalled cairn of Midhowe, on the cliffs that overlook Eynhallow Sound.

Before excavation there was a long grassy mound from which protruded the edges of several flagstones. When uncovered, a narrow chamber was seen to be enclosed by walls of extraordinary thickness, and divided by vertical flagstones into twenty-four stalls. The whole structure was 106 feet long by 42 feet wide, the walls being 18 feet thick. The chamber was 76 feet long by about 7 feet wide, and the tallest of the vertical slabs was nearly 8 feet high. The walls had an outer facing of stones so tilted that they made a herring-bone pattern: an ornamental effect which, presumably, was meant to be seen and admired. It may therefore be inferred that the turf which covered the tomb was the accretion of time.

Twenty-five disarticulated skeletons were assembled—seventeen adults, six adolescents, and two young children—together with the bones of sheep and cattle, the antlers of a red deer, a

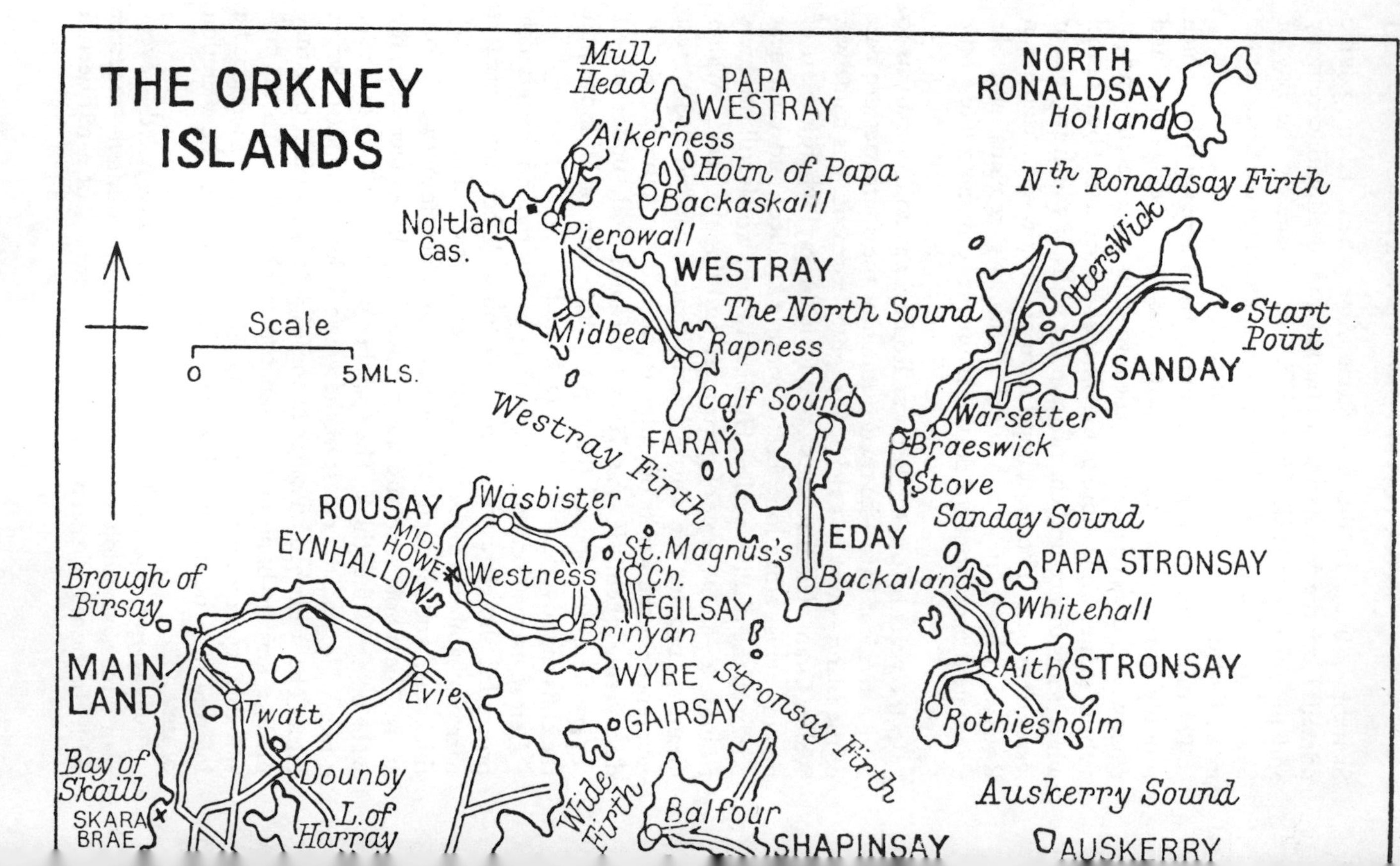
THE ORKNEY ISLANDS
Scale
0
5 MLS.
Mull Head
PAPA WESTRAY
Aikerness
Holm of Papa
Backaskaill
Noltland Cas.
Pierowall
WESTRAY
Midbea
Rapness
The North Sound
Calf Sound
FARAY
Westray Firth
NORTH RONALDSAY
Holland
Nth Ronaldsay Firth
Otterswick
Start Point
SANDAY
Warsetter
Braeswick
Stove
Sanday Sound
EDAY
Backaland
PAPA STRONSAY
Whitehall
Aith
STRONSAY
Rothiesholm
ROUSAY
Wasbister
MID-HOWE
EYNHALLOW
Westness
Brinyan
St. Magnus's Ch.
EGILSAY
WYRE
GAIRSAY
Stronsay Firth
Brough of Birsay
MAIN LAND
Twatt
Evie
Dounby
L. of Harray
Bay of Skaill
SKARA BRAE
Wide Firth
Balfour
SHAPINSAY
Auskerry Sound
AUSKERRY

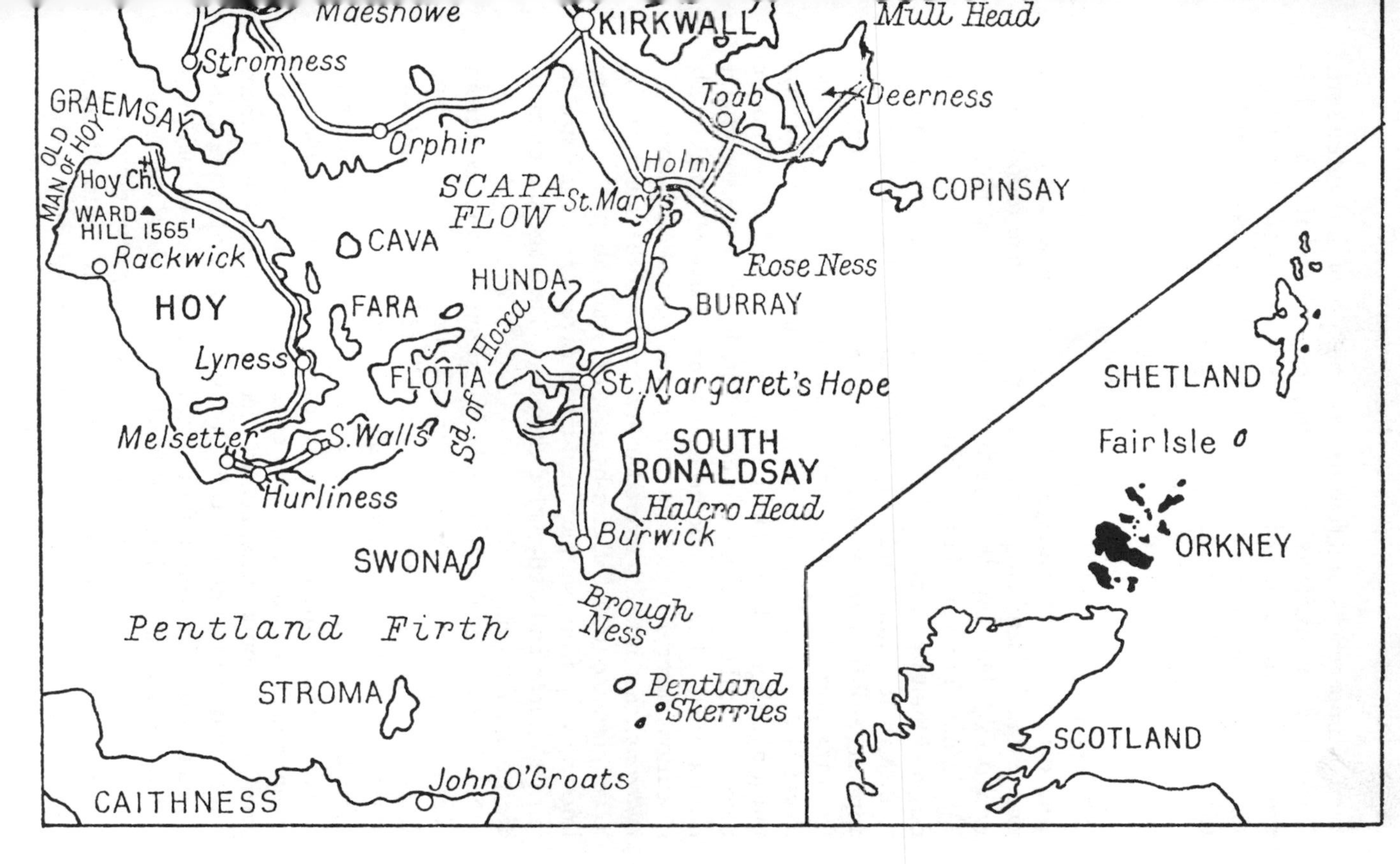
Maeshowe
KIRKWALL
Mull Head
Stromness
Toab
Deerness
GRAEMSAY
Orphir
OLD MAN OF HOY
Hoy Ch.
Holm
SCAPA FLOW
St. Mary's
COPINSAY
WARD HILL 1565'
CAVA
Rackwick
Rose Ness
HUNDA
HOY
FARA
BURRAY
Sd. of Hoxa
Lyness
FLOTTA
St. Margaret's Hope
SHETLAND
Melsetter
S. Walls
SOUTH RONALDSAY
Fair Isle
Hurliness
Halcro Head
Burwick
ORKNEY
SWONA
Brough Ness
Pentland Firth
STROMA
Pentland Skerries
SCOTLAND
John O'Groats
CAITHNESS

heap of limpet shells, and fragments of pottery of the Unston sort. There were no artefacts of any importance, and the most impressive feature of the whole building is the labour-devouring, massive scale of the walls built to protect the bones—or enclose the souls—of so few people and their children. When it was first opened the cairn produced an impression of fabulous age, but this has been somewhat diminished by the building, erected by the Office of Works, which now protects it.

There are seven other stalled cairns in Rousay, two of them with decorated outer walls, while in one, at Yarso, the bones of twenty-one human beings and thirty red deer were found. More remarkable than any of these is the double cairn at Taiversö Tuick, near Trumland House. This is a structure of two storeys, dug and built into a ridge, the lower storey having entrance by a tunnel 19 feet long and 2 feet high at the outer end, which approaches it from the south; while the upper storey was entered from the north by a passage about 11 feet long. Except for the lower part of its walls, not much now remains of the upper storey, but it was slightly larger and built upon the rim of its neighbour below. That the structure was composite in origin—planned and built as such—there can be no doubt; and Taiversö Tuick, with its curious name, has the added interest of a small earth-house, or *souterrain*, that was discovered a few yards to the south of the lower entrance tunnel. Earth-houses, of which about a score are known, vary from simple, man-made caves of meagre size to fairly elaborate and well-walled chambers. Their age and purpose are both unknown.

North of Rousay lies the island of Westray; north and east from Westray is the lesser island of Papa Westray; and east of Papa Westray is the minute Holm of Papa, about half a mile long. But in this remote scrap of land, never inhabited, there is a chambered cairn more than 100 feet long by 40 feet broad, with walls as thick as those at Midhowe. The narrow chamber, with walled-off compartments at either end, is not stalled, but opening from it are small, round, mural cells, about 4 feet in diameter: ten of them single, two of them double cells. It was first opened in 1849, and no human remains were found in it; but in "a series of markings rudely engraved upon the stone work of the chamber" the learned authors of the *Inventory of Monuments* in Orkney have discerned a decorative motif with "continental and Aegean affinities". This adds appreciably to the mystery of the Holm of Papa Westray.

The Holm is not easily accessible, and there are chambered cairns on the Mainland, of the sort that has a central chamber, which can more easily be reached, and without discomfort will satisfy curiosity. There is a good one on Wideford Hill, not far from Kirkwall, and Unston, where the distinctive pottery was found—decorated, shallow bowls with round bottoms—is near the Bridge of Waithe and only a few hundred yards from the main road between Kirkwall and Stromness. Another is on the slope of the hill of Cuween, rather more than a mile south of Finstown. The island of Sanday is easily reached; and there is a dilapidated cairn, of this sort, at Quoyness; another on Vinquoy Hill in Eday.

But the master-work of all, magnificent in construction and unique in its truly megalithic grandeur, is, of course, Maeshowe in the parish of Stenness. To the outward view a green, inverted, shallow bowl, it is only a short way off the Kirkwall road, where the Staney Hill road meets it, and a little distance from the southern end of the Harray Loch. Across the water, on the narrow land between the Harray Loch and the Stenness Loch, is the great circle of Standing Stones—or rather, the remnant of the circle—called the Ring of Brodgar.

Entrance to Maeshowe imposes humility, at least in posture, for the visitor must stoop and bend in a passage 36 feet long and not much higher than 4 feet. The walls and roof of this passage are formed of vast slabs of stone about 18 feet in length, 4 feet in breadth, and some 7 inches thick. It leads to a central chamber 15 feet square, the original walls of which are more than 12 feet high, above them being a modern dome-shaped roof which was built on to cover the square opening left by excavation in 1861. In the walls, a yard above the floor, are the square entrances to three mural cells, each of which is more than 3 feet high with a floor of about 25 square feet. These cells, roofed by single slabs, have good, carefully built walls, and on the floor of the main hall lie three massive blocks which originally closed the entrances.

Above the roof-level of the cells the walls of the central chamber are so built that course overlaps course, and the successive, slight protrusion of massive stones produces a convergence that, in the original ceiling, may have left a gap narrow enough to be bridged by a single slab. To support the converging roof there is, at each corner of the chamber, a projecting pier faced by a splendid monolith. In the candle-lit darkness of the tomb these smooth, enormous stones stand with imperishable dignity, and the mind of the beholder fills with awe to think of the strength and cunning of the unknown men who built a place for their dead with so majestic a conviction of their dead priests' importance. For the whole ponderous structure was calculated with superb precision to sustain, as it seems, not only the weight of its own masonry, but the thrust and stresses of time itself; stresses it has survived for more than thirty centuries.

Surely it was built as a sepulchre for the priestly kings—or kingly priests—of a people whose knowledge of mathematics was sound, though empirical, and whose society was so organized as to recognize a central authority, and believe in some ghostly or spiritual doctrine of a life that transcended life on earth. The dead are not entombed with such care because they decay, but because they renew their life—or so it is thought—in some other shape or essence; and from Maeshowe one returns to Skarabrae and a realization that the people who slept there, in stone bed-places, had a working knowledge of mathematics, a priest-king to whose teaching they listened, and immortal longings.

Maeshowe has features, inside and out, of adventitious interest. In the twelfth century it was broken and entered by the Norsemen of Earl Rognvald's time, who had returned from a very secular Crusade, and they, presumably, removed whatever treasure its mural tombs may have held; if, that is, it had been left untouched by earlier vikings. They also recorded or celebrated their unmannerly exploit by writing on the walls; on which can still be seen, very clearly, many runic inscriptions. Something more will be said of this adventure in due course; here it is enough to note that what the Norsemen broke into was a "howe"—they saw Maeshowe as we see it, an inverted bowl—and that prompts a question. Did its builders leave, open to view, a drystone tomb, its outer walls as carefully constructed as its inner parts? Did they cover it with earth dug from the surrounding ditch, or is its mantle of turf the work of time and the casual accretion of wind-blown soil? From its shape it might well be a sand-dune, immensely old, and at long last carpeted with grass; it would be interesting to cut an entrance and look for an external wall.

Across the loch, a mile and a half away, the tall stones of the Ring of Brodgar stand within a deep ditch, some 30 feet broad, that surrounds two and a half acres of rough heather. Why this patch of moorland should be so dignified is not known. It has been suggested that the circle of stones is the paling of a grave, but there is no sign of a grave within the enclosed land. Did the Stone Age folk make a temple for the worship of the sun, or a shrine for devotees of the moon? It is not known. All that can be said is that originally there were probably 60 stones in the circle, of which 27 are now erect—some rescued and raised again in recent years—while four lie prone and there are stumps of nine others. The tallest of the standing stones are 10 and 11 feet high, undressed slabs of natural rock daubed with yellow lichen, and though by daylight they have an honest, rural, harmless look, they are very different if you walk by them, alone, under a misty half-moon towards midnight.

A little way from them, across the Bridge of Brodgar, there are four greater stones, the tallest 17 feet high, on the arc of a small circle, and between them a cromlech or altar which has no right to be there. The standing stones are the survivors of seven; and the cromlech is a misguided effort to restore something which never existed.*

Elsewhere in the islands there are isolated monoliths, and many, many minor relics of antiquity: the *Inventory* lists several hundred. Some can be ignored because they duplicate others, and some are of no great interest except to the archaeologist. But there are ruins of one particular sort which demand interest because they exist only in the northern counties and islands of Britain; because they prompt urgent but unanswerable questions; and because they were built on the near edge of antiquity and stand balanced, as it were, between history and pre-history. These are the brochs.

On the authority of the *Inventory of Monuments in Orkney and Shetland* there are 102 brochs or broch-sites in Orkney, and 95 in Shetland. These are distinguished as Certain, Probable, and Recorded: the Probables being scanty ruins believed to have been brochs, while the Recorded are those noted by trustworthy authorities in the past. Of the same three categories in Caithness and Sutherland there are 233; in the Western Isles 44. There are three very good ones on the west coast of Inverness-shire, and possibly half a dozen in the middle and south of Scotland. A map of their distribution shows a scattering of them, widely dispersed, in the Hebrides, a dense cluster on the north-eastern tip of Scotland—the Caithness promontory—and strong concentrations in Orkney and Shetland. They were military buildings—of that there is no doubt—and their distribution must reflect the common determination—if not the concerted plan—of a people or peoples,

*No longer there since archaeologists agreed it had no right to be there.

united by blood, treaty, or common interest, to defend themselves against a common enemy. And, again on the evidence of distribution—a screen on the west, the main strength in the north and east, coast-lines well defended—there can be no doubt that the enemy was sea-borne and came from the north or east, or from both.

The only broch surviving in almost its original shape is on the island of Mousa in Shetland, and its structure will be described in a later chapter. All that need be said here is that the broch was a tall, round tower with a double wall and an interior diameter of, on the average, something between 25 and 35 feet. The outer wall was windowless, the doorway was small and guarded. Apart from stout walls, the prime significance of the building lay in its height. One is faced, then, with two problems: the first being who was the sea-borne enemy? And the second, in what way was the height of a broch significant?

It is generally accepted that the age of the brochs—or rather, of the broch-builders—extended roughly from 200 B.C. to A.D. 100. In the latter part of that period there were Roman ships in the offing, and in A.D. 83 a Roman fleet made a northward reconnaissance in some strength. But no one has seriously suggested that the brochs were built to repel Roman invasion. Who else was on the move at that time?

The Picts are a mysterious people. On the evidence of Roman writers their existence in the north of Scotland, their turbulent character, and the gravity of the menace they offered were recognized features of the political scene in the fourth century. They were sometimes called Caledonians, they were associated with the *Scotti*, and they were hostile to Rome. It has been suggested, though not very persuasively, that the Picts were the broch-builders. This seems improbable, however, when one compares the distribution of Pictish place-names and the well-known, stone-carved Pictish symbols with the restricted distribution of the brochs. Pictish symbols are fairly common in Strathspey, in Aberdeenshire and Angus, and Pictish place-names in Fife; but if the Picts were the broch-builders, why are there no brochs in Aberdeenshire and Angus and Fife?

Who the Picts were, and where they came from, are questions difficult to answer. The historical Pictish period was roughly from A.D. 300 to 850, during which time they consolidated their strength and achieved something like a unified power. Their origin has been much debated, and it may be that their name has little racial significance. Their pre-history may have been prolonged, and an amalgamation of wandering tribes may well have included Celtic elements. It is to be noted that ancient writers—Gildas, Nennius, and the Venerable Bede—were convinced of their northern origin, and according to Bede they came from Scythia, which conceivably is to be identified with Skåne in southern Sweden, where incised stones certainly record the existence of a maritime people.

If, then, the pre-historic Picts—precursors of the vikings—came oversea from Scandinavia and the Baltic, and at a very early date established themselves on either shore of the Pictland Firth, the brochs can readily be explained as the defences raised against them by the Iron Age inhabitants of the invaded north and the threatened islands. Stimulated by the imminence of danger they elaborated a technique already used, though tentatively, in the galleried forts of the west coast, and as wave after wave of aggression came out of the north, the brochs were raised to withstand and repel the persistent enemy. They failed, and the Picts came in and conquered. That may be the answer to one question, but the other remains, and still one asks: Why did the native Iron Age people build their brochs so high?

At Gurness in Evie, on the Mainland of Orkney, there is the considerable stump of a large broch, well preserved; there are the remains of four others on the neighbouring shore. On the opposite Rousay shore there is the impressive ruin of the Midhowe broch, and nearby are the remnants of two others. A couple of miles from this trio are two more, one of which, the Knowe of Burrian—much of it lost by erosion—lies opposite Gurness, with a mile of seaway between them. Both sides of Eynhallow Sound, that is, were strongly fortified, and fortified primarily against a sea-borne enemy.

Now a widely accepted explanation of the military value of a broch is that it offered protection, in the event of invasion, to the people of the district and their movable wealth: that is, their flocks and herds. But in a stone tower with an internal diameter of from 25 to 35 feet there cannot have been room for many people, and certainly not for many animals. There may, however, have been outbuildings, and perhaps a confining wall or ditch within which a large number of refugees, both human and animal, could have taken shelter. But if the wall or ditch gave protection, what was the purpose of a 40-foot high broch in the middle of it? Did the height of the broch enable the defenders to keep their enemy at a distance by giving them a commanding position from which they could shoot?

It has sometimes been suggested that the height of the brochs was useful for observation; but that cannot be accepted as a reason for their elaborate structure by those who know the open country of Orkney, where distant views are exhibited to anyone who stands on his own feet. From the pattern of the defensive works that line Eynhallow Sound—and there are other places which show a similar pattern—it does, however, look as if the brochs had been intended to deter, from a distance, the approach of an enemy: an enemy disembarking from boats on the shore. This, it is obvious, could not have been achieved without the existence of some primitive form of artillery, such as a catapult or *balista*, or the simpler contrivance called a *trébuchet*, which was a wooden arm, working on an axle, with a counter-weight on the outer end and on the inner a sling which might be loaded with one large boulder or a basket of great pebbles. Haul down the inner end, and load it; release it, and the counter-weight pulls it up till it discharges its boulder, or the pebbles, in a long arc towards the enemy.

To some it may seem extravagant to suggest that people of the Iron Age used such an engine. It is indisputable, however, that their knowledge of architecture enabled them to build the brochs, and so sophisticated an ability could surely include the wit to make and use a simple mechanical device? Except as artillery platforms there is no satisfying explanation of defensive towers so elaborately tall.

Maeshowe: interior before the mound was capped

4

Years of Obscurity

The Orkneys are mentioned by the elder Pliny, author of a famous *Naturalis Historia*, who died while watching an eruption of Vesuvius in A.D. 79; and Tacitus, who was the Roman general Agricola's son-in-law, says that in A.D. 83, or 84, Agricola's fleet "discovered and subdued previously unknown islands called the Orcades." They cannot, however, have been wholly unknown, since Pliny knew of them, and there is no evidence of their subjugation. Some other Latin references are equally unreliable. According to Eusebius, a bishop of Caesarea, the islands were annexed by the Emperor Claudius; but Claudius spent only sixteen days in Britain, in A.D. 43, and got no farther north than Colchester. More than three hundred years after the alleged conquest by Agricola, the poet Claudian declares that in an expedition of the Emperor Theodosius "the Orkneys were drenched with rivers of Saxon blood", and it is possible that a Roman fleet, during the regency of the general Stilicho, destroyed a concentration of Saxon pirates in northern waters. In 399 Claudian wrote that the sea was peaceful after the defeat of the Saxons, and Britain safe after the destruction of the Picts: showing an optimism unjustified by events. The Saxons, indeed, may have been recurrent visitors, for Nennius, who wrote a *History of the Britons* in the early ninth century, says that Orkney was "wasted" by Hengist, whom the British king Vortigern invited to England, about 443, to help him against Pictish and Saxon marauders.

The most interesting classical reference is by Diodorus Siculus, a Greek historian of Julius Caesar's time, who calls the northern corner of Britain ὄρκαν ἀκρωτήριον: the Orcadian promontory. His information apparently came from Pytheas of Marseilles, a Greek explorer who visited the coasts of northern Europe perhaps as long ago as 330 B.C. Now early Irish writers call the Orkneys *Inse Orc*, the Islands of the Boar, and if, as it appears, that name

Yesnaby Castle, Sandwick

was known in the time of Pytheas, who turned *Orc* into Greek, the islands were colonized by a Celtic tribe, whose totem was the boar, some time before 330 B.C., and their name has endured for an uncommonly long time. It is even possible that the People of the Boar were the Iron Age broch-builders.

When the Picts arrived is not known. There is no reference to their presence in Orkney before the sixth century, when a petty king ruled the islands and acknowledged allegiance to the king of the northern Picts. It was in or about the year 564 that Columba paid his authoritative visit to the Pictish king, apparently near Inverness, and there "commanded King Brude, in presence of the kinglet of the Orkneys, saying 'Some of us have recently sailed out, desiring to find a desert in the impassable sea; and in case they chance after long wanderings to come to the Orkney isles, command this chieftain earnestly, since his hostages are in thy hand, that no harm befall them within his territories'." So says Adamnan, in his life of Columba.

The missionaries who had ventured into "the impassable sea" were led by Cormac, "a soldier of Christ", and by Columba's intervention and Brude's command he was saved "from imminent death" when he reached Orkney.

Sixteen years after that, according to the Annals of Ulster, a king of Dalriada, called Aidan, waged war in Orkney; and a hundred years later, in 682, on the same authority, Orkney was "destroyed" by another Brude, king of all the Picts, who was later victor in a great battle with Ecgfrith, king of Northumbria.

From then till the time of Harald Fairhair, the king who unified Norway, there is no historical record of events in Orkney—except for an obscure conflict with southern Scots in 709—but it would be rash to suppose that all was peaceful in the north. The viking raids in England and Ireland began about 800, but the Norsemen probably came to Orkney before that.

5
The Saga Age

According to the story commonly accepted until quite recently, the Earldom of Orkney was established by Harald Fairhair, King of Norway, soon after the battle of Hafrsfjord in 872. Harald, who had succeeded in unifying Norway, sailed west over sea to destroy the vikings who harried his country in the summer, and spent the winter in Orkney and Shetland. Harald subdued the northern isles and the Hebrides, sailed as far as the Isle of Man, and laid it waste. He fought many battles, and in one of them Ivar, son of Earl Rognvald of Möre, was killed. Rognvald was a great chieftain who had helped Harald in his conquest of Norway, and to compensate him for the loss of his son, Harald gave him Orkney and Shetland. But Rognvald had his own earldom in Norway, and gave the islands to his brother Sigurd, who was one of Harald's forecastle men: one of his chosen warriors, that is. Before Harald returned to Norway, Sigurd was confirmed in his possession and status as Earl of Orkney.

This story is disputed by Professor Haakon Shetelig, and its implication, that Orkney had only lately been used by the Norsemen, or known to them, is certainly not justified. It is more realistic to say that Norse settlers came to Orkney and Shetland as early as 800, and probably before that: the Norsemen raided Ulster in 797, and geography suggests that Orkney was their advanced base for that and many subsequent attacks on Ireland. Shetelig finds no evidence for Orkney's early dependence on Norway—that came later—but from the *Historia Norwegiae* extracts corroboration of an Irish statement that Rognvald, a Norwegian chieftain, was established in Orkney, with the dignity of an independent Earldom, as early as 860. He upsets the old story still further by his assertion that the battle of Hafrsfjord was not fought until about 900.

It may, then, be closer to the facts to say that Rognvald was the scion of a family that had established its independent power in Orkney; that he assisted Harald in his subjugation of Norway and was rewarded with large grants of land in Möre and Romsdal; that he chose thereafter to live in Norway, and Sigurd his brother became, not indeed the first Earl of Orkney, but the first of whom we have some positive knowledge. Rognvald of Möre owes a posthumous importance to his son Rolf, or Rollo, who sailed up the Seine, got land from Charles the Simple, King of France, and became the ancestor of the Dukes of Normandy.

The *Historia Norwegiae* says that the Norsemen who first came to Orkney found it inhabited by Picts and Papae; and records the fabulous story, which long survived, that "the Picts little exceeded pigmies in stature; they did marvels in the morning and the evening, in building (walled) towns, but at midday they entirely lost their strength, and lurked, through fear, in little underground houses." It denies the ancient use of the name *Orkney*, and declares that the islands were formerly called Pictland, "whence still the Pictland Sea is (so) named by the inhabitants, because it divides the islands from Scotland." And of the Papae—the early Christian missionaries of Columba's church—it offers the explanation: "the Papae have been named from their white robes, which they wore like priests. . . . An island is still called, after them, *Papey*."

At the time of the Norse settlement the islands are said to have been thinly inhabited; and the fact that Orkney and Shetland place-names are for the most part Norse suggests the truth of this tradition. A large and still thriving Pictish population would surely have made its opinion felt in geographical nomenclature, but the islands may indeed have been devastated by the warlike King Brude in the campaign, already mentioned, of 682.

But Sigurd, when he got his Earldom, had at his command a sufficient strength to set about enlarging his dominion. He made an alliance with Thorstein the Red, son of Olaf the White, sometime King of Dublin, and that famous woman Aud the Deep-minded who later settled herself and a large following in the west of Iceland. Aud was the daughter of Ketil Flatnose who won a kingdom in the Hebrides, and Thorstein her son, a great viking, had also established himself in Scotland. He and Sigurd conquered Caithness and Sutherland, but Thorstein was killed in battle, and Sigurd died of a poisoned wound after an engagement, that did him no credit, with a Scotch Earl called Maelbrigte Tusk. A mound on the north shore of the Dornoch Firth, near the farm of Sydera, has been identified as his burial place.

His only son died childless, and in his stead Earl Rognvald in Norway sent his own son Hallad; who made a brief inspection of the islands, was shaken by the dangers of life there, and went home again. The next in line seems to have been that Rolf, or Rollo, who settled down to rule in Normandy, but he was warring somewhere in the Baltic. If he had been given the Earldom the whole history of Europe would have been different, but in his absence the succession passed to another of Rognvald's sons, who had the several disadvantages of being ugly, one-eyed, and base-born. But Einar, who became known as Turf Einar, was a brave and able man, a gifted ruler, and a poet. He was so good a poet that he gave his name to a particular sort of stanza that he invented or used; and on history he left the indelible mark of the fearful revenge he exacted for the murder of his father.

Old Rognvald of Möre—the greatest man in Norway after the King—was killed by two of Harald's rebellious sons, one of whom, called Halfdan Longlegs, fled to Orkney. Turf Einar did battle with him, and having defeated him, pursued him to North Ronaldsay and put him to death. Not only that, but carved—by pulling his lungs through his severed ribs—a blood-eagle on his back. A barbarous revenge, but for a bastard son a signal proof of the veneration in which he held his father.

Earl Einar died, peacefully in his bed, leaving three sons in whose time Orkney had to accept two troublesome visitors: an exiled King of Norway, Erik Bloody-axe, son of Harald Fairhair, and his wicked, beautiful Queen Gunnhilda. Erik took two of Einar's sons to war in England, where all three were killed, and Thorfinn Skull-splitter, third of the sons, remained to rule the islands in a manner that his by-name may indicate. He died and was buried under the great Howe of Hoxa in South Ronaldsay; and left five sons.

Also in Orkney was that *femme fatale* of the saga, Ragnhild, daughter of Erik Bloody-axe and Gunnhilda, whom Storer Clouston has forcefully and somewhat bitterly described as "a high-born woman of the tigress-harlot type, imperious in her desires, a consumer of men, thirsting for the blood of her lovers like a female spider."

Ragnhild married in turn three of the sons of Thorfinn Skull-splitter, and contrived the murder of two of them, as well as of a named lover. Her third husband survived her, killed a younger brother in battle, and was succeeded by Hlodver Thorfinnsson, whose claim to respect is that he became the father of Earl Sigurd the Stout.

From the very beginning, from the time of the first Sigurd, the Earldom had shown its desire for expansion into Scotland, and Sigurd the Stout not only held Caithness by force—Caithness then including much of what is now Sutherland—but sent out his ships to harry in the Hebrides, elsewhere in Scotland, and in Ireland.

There are three notable episodes in which Sigurd plays a part. The first was a battle with the Scots Earl Finnlaech at Skitten Mire, which may have been near Duncansby. Now Hlodver, Sigurd's father, had married Edna, the daughter of an Irish king, Kjarval, who had certain magical gifts; and when Sigurd consulted his mother about the advisability of going to war with Finnlaech, she told him: "I would have brought you up in my wool-basket if I had known that you wanted to go on living for ever! Surely it's better to die with honour than live in shame, so take this flag that I've made for you. It is in my mind that those before whom it's carried will get the victory, though it will be the death of him who bears it."

The flag was a fine piece of needlework in the shape of a raven, and three standard-bearers were killed before Sigurd won his battle. More importantly, the Orkney odallers who had followed the Earl—landowners in the old Norse system of law, whose rights had previously been forfeited—had their full titles restored in payment for their service.

The second episode was dictated by Olaf Tryggvisson, that warlike Christian King of Norway. He by chance, with a superior force, encountered Earl Sigurd in Kirk Hope in Walls, and in the flush of his missionary enthusiasm declared: "It's my wish that you should be baptized, and all under you. Otherwise you'll die on the spot, and I'll spread fire and flame through the isles."

Sigurd tactfully submitted, and all Orkney nominally accepted Christianity. That was in or about the year 995. But a few years later Sigurd repudiated the allegiance he had sworn to Olaf, and made a marriage that was to have large consequences. He had already three sons by a previous wife, and now he married the daughter of Malcolm, "King of Scots" according to the saga, who was presumably Malcolm II. And of that union was born Thorfinn, destined to become the greatest of the Orkney Earls.

The third of the episodes in which Sigurd the Stout played a part was the decisive battle of Clontarf in Ireland, in which Sigurd and an Irish king, Sigtrygg, fought against Brian Boru, King of the Irish, and were defeated on Good Friday in the year 1014. Sigurd again went into battle under the raven banner his mother had made, and was killed beneath it. And Brian Boru died in the hour of his victory.

The three sons of Sigurd's first marriage ruled Orkney, and Thorfinn his youngest son lived with his grandfather the King of Scots, who made him Earl of Caithness and Sutherland. Thorfinn matured early, and in the words of the saga "was the tallest and strongest of men, black-haired, with harsh features and grim of aspect. It was clear, as he grew up, that by nature he was warlike and ambitious."

Ambition and his royal grandfather were to involve him as deeply in the affairs of Scotland as in the government of his native islands, and it is exasperating that there are no Scottish records to supplement the bare statements of the Orkney saga and clarify some parts of it that are puzzling. Scottish records, of any relevancy, do not exist, and the saga is our only authority for Thorfinn's relations with the neighbouring kingdom. What it says may not lightly be discounted, nor accepted without scrutiny of its inherent probability. It is now generally accepted that the author of the saga was an Icelander who wrote it in the early years of the thirteenth century; and in his favour, as an historian, there are indications that he was aware of a changing temper in Orkney. By the time of Thorfinn there was an approach, however distant, to a habit of thought and the kind of behaviour that a modern mind can apprehend. The grim heroism of Turf Einar has become a distant memory, there are no more Thorfinn Skull-splitters in the story; but politics increasingly intrude. The people of the drama, though sometimes a little larger than life as we know it, are not alien to a liberal conception of life. Though their actions may not elicit sympathy, they speak a recognizable language, and in his latter years Thorfinn himself shows a moderation, a politic restraint, that demands the most admiring respect.

His three half-brothers in Orkney were speedily reduced to two by the death of the eldest. The survivors were Einar, a greedy, cantankerous man who spent much of his time on viking cruises; and Brusi who was mild and genial. When Thorfinn, in Scotland, claimed that third of the islands which the dead brother had ruled, Brusi was willing to let him have it, but Einar refused and took it for his own. Einar's rule was oppressive, and bred bitter discontent. A man called Thorkel, of great note in the islands, stood out against his tyranny, but had to flee for his life. He went over to Caithness, where he became the devoted friend and protector of the boy Thorfinn, and got the by-name of Thorkel Fosterer. And there were other discontented Orkney men who joined Thorfinn.

When Thorfinn came to recognized maturity—at the age of fourteen, it appears—he invaded Orkney and offered battle to Einar; but Brusi came between them as mediator, and Thorfinn got his share of the islands without fighting for it. The division brought no peace, however, and continued dissension led to an ill-advised appeal for help from Olaf II, King of Norway. Thorkel Fosterer, again in fear of his life after an unsuccessful mission on Thorfinn's behalf, went to his court and spoke bitterly against Einar, but well of the young Earl; who also was persuaded to visit Norway.

The young Earl was handsomely entertained, and for a parting present Olaf gave him a good ship. Thorfinn and Thorkel returned to Orkney, again prepared for battle with Earl Einar; and again Brusi made peace between them. A formal reconciliation between Thorkel and Earl Einar was arranged, but when they met, at Thorkel's house in Sandwick, it became evident that Einar intended treachery, and Thorkel struck first. He was a reasonable, decent man, not given to casual homicide, but he killed Einar—and fled again to Norway.

Now Brusi, that peace-loving, genial person, disclosed a new temper and claimed Einar's third of the islands.—He could offer legal argument for his claim, and he had a ten-year-old son, called Rognvald, for whom he may have been ambitious.—When Thorfinn challenged his claim, and demanded a full half of the Earldom, Brusi also sailed to Norway and sought King Olaf's help. Thorfinn followed, secure, as he thought, in the friendship that Olaf had already shown him.

This was Olaf's opportunity, and he took it. He asserted his own claim to Orkney, basing it on the allegation that Harald Fairhair had retained the odal rights, and the Earls had since held the islands in fief but not in full ownership. Neither in the Orkney saga nor the saga of the Kings of Norway is there anything to substantiate his claim, but Olaf was in a position of undisputed power: Brusi and Thorfinn sought his favour, and Thorkel Fosterer, who had killed Earl Einar, looked to him for protection. Olaf, a great-grandson of Harald Fairhair, was known in his lifetime as Olaf the Fat, and after his death as Olaf the Saint; but at this juncture he was more obviously Olaf the Politician.

Brusi, at first with great reluctance, accepted the King's claim and "became his man". Thorfinn said that he owed allegiance to the King of Scots, and could not serve two masters; but also submitted. And Thorkel Fosterer paid the fine that Olaf demanded for his killing of Einar.

But dominant in Thorkel's mind was his affection for Thorfinn, and with the young Earl he went back to Orkney while Brusi stayed in Norway as Olaf's subject and his ally. It is pretty clear that Brusi was thinking of his son's future; the boy Rognvald was a golden-haired, handsome, attractive child, and when at last Brusi sailed for home, as the King's vassal with authority over two-thirds of Orkney, Rognvald remained as Olaf's ward.

Thorfinn accepted this division of the Earldom, and for some years lived a viking's adventurous life while Brusi stayed in Orkney to defend the islands against the Norse and Danish marauders who, on their way to booty in the west, paused often to replenish their ships' larders in Orkney or Shetland. It became apparent, however, that Brusi lacked either the will or the vigour for so demanding a task, and with what now seems a remarkable display of realism he let Thorfinn take two-thirds of the Earldom's revenue as the price of maintaining its security.

Conditions in the Scandinavian and Britannic countries were, about this time, so disordered that anarchy was epidemic, and before the long period of peace that came with Thorfinn's absolute domination of northern Scotland there were many years of warfare that cannot properly be mapped or adequately described. In 1028 King Canute of England and Denmark invaded Norway and drove out King Olaf; who died two years later at the great battle of Stiklestad. In 1034 Malcolm II, King of Scots for thirty years, was succeeded by that Duncan whom the genius of Shakespeare—but not his own—was to glorify; and in 1035 the death of Canute was quickly followed by the collapse of all his empire. In Orkney Brusi died, and Thorfinn became sole ruler of the islands.

"A man of great energy, and greedy both for wealth and honour. He was lucky in battle, skilled in the art of war, and of dauntless courage."—So says the saga, and the accuracy of this assertion is not to be doubted. But now appears a great puzzle, for the saga declares that Malcolm, King of Scots, was succeeded by "Karl Hundi's son", who engaged in war with Thorfinn. The war is described in some detail, and the narrative of events is so clear and reasonable that the account must be accepted as factual and largely true. The puzzle is created by King Karl—"Karl Hundi's son"—for in the scanty records of Scotland there is no such person. The saga describes a sea-battle off Deerness, and a great land-battle somewhere on the Moray Firth—possibly Tarbatness, perhaps Burghead—for which "King Karl" had mustered an army from as far away as the southern parts of Scotland, and Ireland too. The Scots were defeated, King Karl was killed or fled, and Earl Thorfinn "went south as far as Fife and laid the land under him." His victories in this great campaign were celebrated in spirited verse by the most gifted poet of the age, Arnor the Earl's Poet—but Arnor offers no clue to the identity of King Karl.

The story of the war is too explicit, and too inherently probable, to be dismissed as fiction; and the saga-writer's apparent ignorance of the Scottish succession does not make him a deliberate liar. The sagas are habitually indifferent to the periphery—of persons or events—of the stories they tell, and "King Karl" may be a vulgar and derisive by-name for Scotland's unhappy Duncan—a medieval precursor of *Kaiser Bill*—or perhaps Karl Hundi's son was the real name of King Duncan's commander-in-chief: Thorfinn's enemy in the field, who gave more cause to be remembered than a monarch far away. It has been suggested that he was, in fact, no king, but some earl or mormaer of Ross or Argyll, contending only for a disputed province; but the sources of his power are too large, the scope of the campaign too broad, to make that acceptable, and the long peace between Thorfinn and Duncan's successor, Macbeth, is suggestive not only of Thorfinn's established strength in Scotland, but of some factor that promoted their alliance. If Karl was Duncan, or Duncan's general in the field, then Thorfinn by so thoroughly defeating him opened the way for Macbeth's advancement to the throne a few years later.

But another story—unprincipled and splendid and tragical in conclusion—must be told before Macbeth comes on the stage, and its hero and victim is the gifted, gallant, fair-haired Rognvald, Earl Brusi's son, who had grown up in the court of King Olaf. He had fought in the famous battle of Stiklestad, where Olaf—soon to be called a saint—was killed, and there he had saved the life of Olaf's brother Harald: Harald Hardrada who was to die at Stamford Bridge. With Harald he adventured into Russia, where he won favour and great renown. After the death of Canute he played a lively part in the troubled politics of northern Europe, and helped Olaf's son Magnus to regain his father's throne. And when he determined to claim his share of Orkney, King Magnus gave him the title of Earl and three warships to assist his venture.

Earl Thorfinn was closely involved in warfare in the Hebrides and the nearer parts of Ireland. He admitted the justice of Rognvald's claim, and with a politic generosity offered him two-thirds of the revenue of the islands in return for an alliance of both strength and friendship. He said, in effect, "Let him take what pleasure he wants from our Earldom, for if I get his loyalty and help it will be worth more to me than a rent-roll."

Then ensued several years of a very happy, successful, and—in our judgment—an utterly deplorable partnership in which the grim and warlike Earl Thorfinn, with the yellow-haired, heroic Earl Rognvald, waged successful war down all the west coast of Scotland, into Galloway and Ireland and the north-western parts of England—they ranged far and wide through England, where two stiff battles were fought—and Arnor the Earl's Poet hymned their bloody victories in stiff and formal verses. It was towards the end of Harthacnut's short, inglorious reign that England was invaded, and the partnership of the two Earls was also coming to an end. It was a domestic issue, a matter of housekeeping, that destroyed it.

A noble refugee from Norway claimed hospitality of Earl Thorfinn, and almost ruined him by the demands of a numerous and hungry following. Now Thorfinn, when Rognvald first came to Orkney, had agreed, with careless generosity, to let him have two-thirds of its revenue, and when he began to run short of meal and ale he asked Rognvald to share the burden of entertainment; and Rognvald refused. The Norwegian refugee was Kalf Arnisson, who had given King Olaf his death-blow at Stiklestad; had later made his peace with Olaf's son Magnus; but now had fallen out with King Magnus. Rognvald felt no obligation to give him hospitality, but Thorfinn was bound by the ties of kinship, for Kalf was his wife's uncle. Scarcity in the larder, the exasperation of having to feed unwanted guests, and Rognvald's unforgiving memory brought a long friendship to its end, and in the intemperate manner of the north provoked battle as the only answer to dispute.

The war-fleets of Earl Rognvald and Earl Thorfinn met in deadly combat off The Berry, the great red cliff that stands out from the rough shore-line of Hoy—some two or three miles north-west of Tor Ness—and for a long time Kalf Arnisson, with his own six ships, took no part in the battle. But when at last he was persuaded to join Thorfinn, the issue was decided. Arnor the Earl's Poet, who was there, bitterly lamented the slaughter of kinsmen by kinsmen, and horribly described, not only the blood that distained the moving sea, but blood—so deep it ran—that oozed from the planks of the straining ships.

Rognvald, defeated, fled to Norway; and Thorfinn held the isles. But war continued. There was much at stake, and an ancient concept of honour kept wounds from healing. Out of Norway, with the help of King Magnus, Earl Rognvald made a desperate foray—in winter time, in a single ship—and took Thorfinn by surprise in a house on the Orphir shore. He set fire to the house, and through the smoke and flames Thorfinn made his bold escape, his wife Ingibjorg in his arms, and with her in a little skiff rowed across the Pentland Firth—that perilous channel—to safety in Caithness.

Rognvald called himself master of all Orkney, and to celebrate his victory went to fetch malt for a Christmas brewing of ale from the little island of Papa Stronsay, that was sometime a hermitage of Culdee monks. But while he and his men were taking their comfort round a long fire—safe, as they thought, in the bitter safety of December weather—Thorfinn came upon them, and a fiercer fire encircled them. In a like situation, not long before, Thorfinn had escaped with his wife in his arms, and now through the flames Earl Rognvald leapt to the darkness beyond with a lap-dog in his hand. But among the rocks on the beach the dog barked and betrayed him, and Rognvald was slain on a cold bed of sea-weed. It was Thorkel Fosterer who dealt the death-blow; or so it is said. Perhaps none other would have dared to kill him.

Within a few days Thorfinn again ruled Orkney, having ruthlessly killed the Norwegian bodyguard that King Magnus had given Rognvald. He now had to account to the King for all but one of thirty men, and fortunately for him Magnus was already busily engaged in preparation for war with Denmark. Thorfinn with two ships sailed east to confront him; found him near Lindisness, the southern tip of Norway; and stepped boldly aboard the King's ship. There was some hardy conversation between them, for Magnus grew angry and Thorfinn conceded nothing. Their quarrel was still unresolved when Thorfinn took advantage of a fair wind to sail west again—and his luck held, for Magnus died before the summer was out. He was succeeded by his uncle, Harald Hardrada, with whom Thorfinn was on friendly terms, and so remained till his death.

And now comes the glory of peace with greatness, peace with unbroken power and no aggression to spoil its magnanimity, that crowns the long rule of Thorfinn the Mighty. On the authority of the saga "he owned nine Earldoms in Scotland, and all the Hebrides, and a large realm in Ireland"; and in his *Celtic Scotland* Skene accepts the probability of a dominion reaching as far south as the Tay. How Thorfinn ruled so large a realm from a seat in Birsay is unknown, but it can hardly be doubted that, to balance his friendship with Harald Hardrada, there was alliance with Macbeth. Macbeth acquired the Scottish throne in or about the year 1040, and for seventeen years—apparently of peace and plenty—ruled a little kingdom that may have reached no farther than from the Grampians to Strathclyde. But in his kingdom Macbeth enjoyed such ease and security that he could afford to go on pilgrimage to Rome. None other of the Scottish kings made that pious journey, and one is tempted to look for some special inducement. Was it his friendship with Thorfinn, who also rode to Rome?

It was probably in 1048 that Thorfinn set out on his pilgrimage. He went first to Norway, where Harald Hardrada was now King—Magnus having died in 1047—and then to Aalborg in Jutland where he was entertained by the lately crowned Danish King Sweyn, a nephew of the great Canute. From there he rode south into Germany, where the Emperor Henry III welcomed him most cordially, and mounted him handsomely for his journey to Rome; where the Pontiff gave him absolution for his many sins.

There was a relationship between these several courts that must have made Thorfinn's journey an easier progress than, from this distance in time, one might suppose it to have been. The Pope was Leo IX, whose father was related to the Emperor Conrad II. Conrad had been crowned, in 1027, in the presence of Canute, whose favour he had won, a couple of years earlier, by the cession to him of certain lands north of the Eider. The son of Conrad, who succeeded him as Emperor, was Henry III who welcomed Thorfinn; and Henry had married Gunnhilda, the daughter of Canute. Her cousin was Sweyn of Denmark who had received Thorfinn in Aalborg.—The Pope and the Emperor were distantly related, the Emperor's wife was a Danish princess, and if either she or Thorfinn had any interest in genealogy, a common ancestor could probably have been found among the Ynglings or in the nearer reaches of Norse mythology. The Earl of Orkney's pilgrimage had some resemblance to a family visitation, and before returning to Scotland he may well have recommended his friend and neighbour Macbeth to the favour of his kind hosts. It was, apparently, in 1050 that Macbeth visited the Pope in Rome.

Till 1065 Earl Thorfinn lived in untroubled power and unbroken peace, and nothing more clearly shows his greatness than his decision to set a limit to conquest, and his ability to enjoy what he had won without yielding to the common greed for winning more. He built a church in Birsay, he fathered two sons of a mild and excellent disposition, and when he died his little empire fell into pieces like a fallen bowl.

6

Magnus the Saint

In 1066, the year of destiny for England, Orkney played a part—on the losing side—in the first of the two battles fought by Harold Godwinsson. The warrior King of Norway, Harald Hardrada, went west over sea with a powerful fleet, put his Queen and two daughters ashore in the islands, and there mustered a large reinforcement for his considerable army. With Thorfinn's sons aboard—the Earls Paul and Erlend—he sailed south to England, and was defeated by the English King in the bloody fight at Stamford Bridge. Harald Hardrada was killed, and Harold Godwinsson was merciful and generous to Hardrada's son Olaf and the Orkney Earls: he let them go home with depleted crews.

For a long time—possibly for twenty years—Paul and Erlend lived peacefully together, and apparently sought no military adventure other than a curious assault on Glamorgan in alliance with a king of North Wales. Their mother Ingibjorg married Malcolm III, King of Scots: Malcolm Canmore, who was Duncan's son. He had to fight for his throne, and won it with the help of Northumbria; presumably he married Thorfinn's widow to regain some of the territories that Thorfinn had ruled. The sons of Paul and Erlend grew up, and differed markedly from their well-behaved and tolerant fathers; for one was proud, greedy, and over-bearing, and another had within him the germ of sanctity.

The mother of Hakon, Paul's son, was the daughter of a great Norwegian nobleman, Earl Hakon Ivar's son, and his wife Ragnhild, daughter of King Magnus the Good: with such a pedigree Hakon thought himself superior to his cousins Magnus and Erling, the sons of Earl Erlend; and a cantankerous temper let him publish his opinion. Quarrels grew more frequent, and when it became apparent that Hakon was a menace to the peace of Orkney, a remarkable thing happened. The habit of peace established by Thorfinn and maintained by his two sons was strong enough to bring together the landed gentry of the islands, whose joint opinion was that Hakon must go into exile. And Hakon, bowing to their stern opinion, went.

Hakon made some curious friends in northern Europe, and Orkney in his absence lived quiet and undisturbed by history. But then Hakon grew friendly with another Magnus, King of Norway —later known as Magnus Barelegs—who was the grandson of Harald Hardrada; and Hakon, misjudging his man and thinking to make use of him, persuaded the King that a life of old-fashioned adventure, west over sea, would suit his temperament. Magnus was a ready listener, an easy convert, and presently put to sea with the enthusiasm of a convert.

He had mustered an army and gathered a fleet; and in Orkney he brought to a violent end a long half-century of peace. The two gentle Earls were sent captive to Norway, where they soon died, and to Hakon's disappointment Magnus set up his son Sigurd, a boy of eight, as governor of the islands with a council of elders to advise him. With Hakon in attendance, as well as Erlend's sons Magnus and Erling, he sailed on the old route through the Hebrides to war and plunder as far south as the Isle of Man and the Menai Strait. There he fought and defeated two Welsh earls whom the saga calls Hugh the Stout and Hugh the Proud, and who can be identified as the Earls of Shrewsbury and Chester. The year of the battle was 1098.

Apart from hard fighting, the battle was notable for the strange behaviour of Magnus Erlend's son; who said he had no quarrel with anyone there, "and therefore I will not fight". King Magnus told him to get into shelter under the poop-deck if he was afraid, but young Magnus stayed where he was, produced a psalter, and sang psalms throughout the battle.

Having taken possession of Anglesey—an idle gesture—the King turned north again, and Magnus, who till then had served him at table, was dismissed from favour. His dissociation from the common purpose of war had been deliberately ostentatious, and in the heat of battle cannot have earned much sympathy. It is, indeed, difficult to admire so contrived, so theatrical a protest, though the impulse may have sprung from a genuine repugnance to bloodshed. The King's anger did not abate, and one night when the ship lay off shore, young Magnus escaped in his shirt, and took shelter in a wood when search was made for him.

The old S.S. St. Ola *(replaced in 1975) in Hoy Sound with Graemsay and Hoy beyond*

The new St. Ola *passing the Old Man of Hoy*

P&O Ferries

A965
A966

He made his way to the court of the King of Scots, who was Edgar the son of Malcolm Canmore and the English princess Margaret, sister of Edgar the Atheling, whom Malcolm had married after the death of Ingibjorg, Thorfinn's widow. Edgar was a young man who inherited his mother's devotion to the Church, and died unmarried. Magnus may have found him a congenial friend, and perhaps stayed with him for some years. He is said to have visited England, and to have lived with an unidentified bishop in Wales. But nothing certain is known of him, at this time, except that he did not show himself in Orkney while King Magnus was alive.

Magnus Barelegs got his by-name from his preference for some form of Celtic costume less straitly confining than trousers; and he showed his affection for Highland scenery and the western isles by returning, on more than one occasion, to harry and plunder them. He lived until 1103, when he fell in battle in Ulster. His son Sigurd, whom he had married to an Irish princess, returned to Norway, and succeeded to a third of its throne; two brothers shared it with him. Hakon Paul's son, who had faithfully followed Magnus Barelegs in his wars, was recognized by King Sigurd as Earl of Orkney, and assumed its government. But his solitary state did not last very long.

In 1106 the erratic Magnus returned, and after some dispute and recourse to the authority of Norway got his title recognized to a half-share of the islands. It appears that he was made welcome, and the saga says "he was popular with everyone". It may well be that his father's old friends were glad to see him, and his branch of the family had won new adherents by the marriage of his widowed mother Thora—who fetched her descent from Iceland—to a landed man of Orkney. But it must be admitted that much of Magnus's recorded behaviour smacks of political irresponsibility rather than saintliness, until death with much nobility resolves all discord.

He married a girl called Ingigerd, very vaguely identified as being born "of the noblest family in Scotland"; but the marriage was never consummated, for one or both of them preferred a wedded chastity, and for a tedious decade maintained it with the help, at times, of cold water. To begin with, Magnus was not indifferent to the necessary business of his Earldom, and for several years he and his cousin Hakon, dividing authority in an amicable spirit, ruled the islands strictly. But then, as though

The Churchill Barrier
Finstown

losing interest in his patrimony, Magnus went off to the court of the English King Henry I, whose Queen was the sister of his old friend Edgar of Scotland. Henry was much abroad, and the Queen —whose mother was St. Margaret—may have warmly welcomed a visitor of distinguished piety. But in Orkney Hakon took advantage of his cousin's long absence to re-assert his single authority over the islands; and was naturally alarmed when, without warning, Magnus suddenly returned with five well-armed ships.

To such a threat Hakon quickly responded; but once again the landed men of the islands counselled peace. At a meeting of their primitive parliament—the Althing assembled in the parish of Rendall—it was resolved that Hakon and Magnus must come to terms within a given time; and they agreed to meet in Easter week on the small island of Egilsay, that lies to the east of Rousay. Both were to take the same number of men in two ships.

Magnus and his followers were the first to land; and when Hakon came they saw that he had eight ships. But Magnus, who can have had no doubt of his cousin's intention, made no attempt to escape and would not let his men take arms to defend him. He spent the night in prayer, in a small church, and when morning came waited for Hakon on the shore. There were two men who stayed with him till the end, one of them a Hebridean called Holdbodi; and according to him the murder was preceded by a strange conversation.

Magnus, in the first place, offered to go into exile, to Rome or the Holy Land, under oath never to return. Hakon and his men rejected this offer at once.

Imprisonment somewhere in Scotland—Hakon to decide where —was his next suggestion. This too was refused.

He would submit, he said, to being maimed or blinded, and to live out his life in a dungeon.—Hakon agreed to this, but the landed men would not permit it. They were willing, they said, to kill either of the cousins; but never again would they tolerate two living Earls at once.

"Then kill him," said Hakon. "I like my Earldom better than death."

Magnus wept, but made no other protest. Hakon ordered his standard-bearer, Ofeig, to kill him; but Ofeig angrily refused. Lifolf, Hakon's cook, was there, and when he was told to strike the death-blow, he also wept; and Magnus comforted him with the promise that he would not be blamed for what he did.

Magnus knelt, commended himself to God and forgave his enemies. "Stand in front of me," he told Lifolf, "and hew a great wound on my head; for it wouldn't be right to put me to death like a thief." So Lifolf struck, and struck again.

For this conversation Holdbodi is the only authority, but there is no doubt about the manner of the execution. In 1919 an oak coffin was discovered in a broad pier in the choir of the cathedral of St. Magnus, and in the coffin were the bones of a man who had been killed in precisely that way: a clean-cut hole in the parietal bones of the skull, and the upper jaw cut from in front. The signature of Lifolf's axe was unmistakable.

The date of the murder was April 16th; the year 1117. Thora, Magnus's mother, got permission from Hakon to take the body to Christ's Kirk in Birsay, that Earl Thorfinn had built, and bury it there. In the following winter—so says the saga—a heavenly light often hovered above the grave, and Birsay became a place of pilgrimage. Men in peril of their lives came to pray for safety, and the sick came to be cured. But all this went on in secret so long as Earl Hakon lived, and the new Bishop of Orkney had no faith at all in the sanctity of the dead Earl.

During his life, and immediately after his death, there must have been deep division of opinion about Magnus: on the one hand a popular view that saw in him the stuff of holiness and regarded his murder as martyrdom; on the other, the ruling or upper-class judgment that he was a menace to the safety of the isles—that Hakon's treachery must be tolerated as being essential to good government—and that anything like a cult of the dead Earl must be discouraged. It is obvious, however, that Hakon was conscious of his guilt, for he went on pilgrimage to Rome and Jerusalem for his soul's sake, and in the remaining seven or eight years of his life he ruled so earnestly and well that he was generally forgiven upon earth, whatever the judgment of heaven may have been. But the cult of Magnus the martyr continued and grew, and to Birsay came the sick and the halt and the blind in a confident expectation of miracles.

Hakon died and was succeeded by two sons, Harold and Paul, who in the familiar manner divided the Earldom and quarrelled. Harold's mother was Helga Moddan's daughter, of a Celtic family in Caithness that was addicted to violence and suspected of witchcraft; and in some domestic mishap—there was talk of a poisoned shirt, but the truth may have been worse than that—Harold died in a house in Orphir, and Earl Paul, known as the Silent, ruled alone and was generally popular. No more than his father, however, was he inclined to listen to stories of the miracles wrought at Christ's Kirk in Birsay.

There came a time, however, when they could no longer be disregarded; or perhaps it would be truer to say, when it was no longer politic to disregard them. Bishop William himself was converted—he, the first bishop to be appointed to Orkney, lived long enough to be known as William the Old—and presently the bones of St. Magnus were taken from Birsay to the church in Kirkwall, the little town that was now growing up; and miracles continued to amaze the faithful.

It is perhaps significant that a short time before he gave permission for removal of the wonder-working bones to Kirkwall, Bishop William had visited Norway, where a nephew of Magnus was living. His name was Kali, his father was Kol, and his grandfather—another Kali—had sailed with Magnus Barelegs to battle in the Menai Strait, where he got his death-wound. In compensation for that loss, the King gave Kol a richly endowed wife: Gunnhild, daughter of Earl Erlend and sister to Magnus the martyr. Their son Kali had a claim to the Earldom which was reinforced by native ability, by excellence of mind and body. He was a poet with light chestnut-coloured hair, with an athlete's physique: he could play the harp and shoe a horse, he could read runes and shoot straight. In the custom of young men of spirit he sailed abroad, and had some customary adventures. On a voyage to England he made friends with Harald Gilli, a bastard son of Magnus Barelegs, and when Harld Gilli succeeded to the throne of Norway he gave Kali his title of Earl and nominal possession of one half of Orkney. Kali was then re-christened Rognvald: this, by his mother's wish, in memory of the gallant Earl whom Thorfinn the Mighty killed.

It was a weakness of the Norwegian claim to suzerainty over Orkney that its kings so rarely had the power to enforce their wishes. Kol sent envoys to Earl Paul to inform him of the King's award, but the taciturn Paul refused to discuss it. The envoys then adopted what may be called the alternative plan, and crossing the Pentland Firth went to the dangerous house in Caithness where Helga Moddan's daughter—mother of Paul's half-brother, the dead Earl Harald—had lived. Her evil sister Frakok listened to their proposal and welcomed it: what Rognvald and Kol offered her and her grandson Olvir Rosta was half of the Earldom in return for their help against Paul the Silent.

Complacently Frakok spoke of her recent success in marrying-off her niece Margaret, Hakon's daughter, to Maddad, the powerful Earl of Atholl; and mentioned the claimants to the Orkney Earldom that her own family could bring forward. Earl Harald, who is supposed to have died of a poisoned shirt, had left a son called Erlend; and Margaret had borne a son to Maddad of Atholl. These were both children, and as allies no use to Kol and Rognvald. But Frakok's grandson Olvir Rosta—or Roaring Oliver—was the very man for them: an adventurous ruffian of great strength and stature, with enough influence in the northern parts of Scotland to command a large fighting force.

A plan was made for a two-handed attack on Orkney in the following summer: Rognvald with what ships he could muster would sail to Shetland, while Olvir Rosta and a Hebridean fleet would advance from the south. The plan was ingenious, unscrupulous, and came to utter failure. Paul the Silent tackled each in turn and defeated both: Olvir Rosta was thoroughly beaten in a sea-fight off the Mull Head of Deerness, and in Shetland Rognvald's fleet was surprised and taken at anchor without a struggle.

Depressed by defeat and ashamed of so ignominious a defeat, Rognvald was in no mood to try again; but Kol his father was apparently unperturbed, and encouraged by him Rognvald began to prepare for a second attempt. In the early spring of 1136 he mustered in Bergen a fleet consisting of six warships, five cutters, and three transports; and made ready to sail to Shetland. At a council of war he spoke realistically of the general antagonism to him that he expected to find in Orkney—where the majority were contented under the rule of Earl Paul—but swore to win the islands or die in the attempt.

Then Kol his father made a wise and productive suggestion. Magnus the martyr was more mighty in death than he had ever been alive—and surely he, who was Rognvald's uncle, would help him to his inheritance?

"Look for help where it is abundant," said Kol, "and he who had it by right—that is, St. Magnus your uncle—may grant you your realm. And to bring that about, my wish is that you make a vow to have a church of stone built in Kirkwall, when you have won your realm, in such a way that there will not be a more magnificent in the land, and let it be dedicated to St. Magnus your kinsman. Let it be well endowed, and let his relics be brought to it, and with them the seat of the Bishopric."

That St. Magnus was a more respectable ally than Roaring Oliver cannot be doubted; but one would like to know more about Kol. One knows nothing at all about him, except by inference: he was certainly a man of vision, a man of genius. He conceived a great and glowing idea, and by the exercise of talent, ingenuity, perseverance and ruthless allegiance to his idea, brought it into splendid being: he built a cathedral that to this day is the honour of Orkney and the Norsemen's noblest memorial.

And was that Kol's intention from the beginning? Did he push Rognvald into political adventure so that he, Kol, might have the proper excuse and a sufficient revenue to build a cathedral? Did he summon the hard-working ghost of St. Magnus to help him, and play upon the superstition of simple Orkneymen to reinforce his purpose? On the evidence of what he made—the sonorous evidence of rose-red columns and echoing aisles under a clerestory beckoning to the northern sun—he was an artist; and in pursuance of his purpose an artist has no conscience.

It may well be that Magnus the Saint and Rognvald the Crusader owe the best of their fame to that almost unknown and quite inscrutable Norwegian, Kol Kali's son, who had no desire to be canonized or crowned, but was merely an artist who wanted to build something very large and very beautiful; and could think of nothing that would please him better than a cathedral.

7

Sweyn the Viking

Though Thorfinn the Mighty brought the Earldom to the height of its political power, the most interesting years of its history lie, a little later, within the half-century that follows the return to Orkney of Earl Magnus and the martyrdom that promoted him to the calendar of saints. By his death and its sequelae Magnus conferred on the islands a rare distinction, and within a score of years the foundations were laid of that memorial which, while assuring recognition and remembrance of him and his virtue, was to become, in the right of its own dignity, the wonder and splendour of the north. And the cathedral of St. Magnus, though Kol planned it, so exalted the name of Rognvald whose revenue built it—Rognvald the poet and warrior, most generous and gayest of the Earls, most genial of crusaders—that he too won canonization.

Within half a century a pair of saints, and to the honour of both the rising walls of a Romanesque cathedral at the heart of the archipelago: Orkney had done very well for itself. And that was not all. Running like a scarlet thread through the history of those years—a thread outrageously vivid—is the story of Sweyn of Gairsay, last of the great vikings, a masterly anachronism, and in life as devoted an artist of deeds as was Kol Kali's son in architecture. It may be enlightening—for a first glimpse of him—to show Sweyn in action. . . .

In the previous chapter mention was made of Rognvald's preparation for his second attack on Orkney and its good Earl, the silent Paul. Though Paul had made admirable arrangements for defence, Rognvald circumvented them. He sailed to Shetland, and then moved suddenly to Westray; establishing himself there, he began to win adherents, and on the Mainland Earl Paul summoned a parliament. He was less resolute than he had been the year before, and found opinion more divided. When Rognvald, seizing the initiative, sent envoys to Bishop William, asking him to mediate, the Bishop consented, and Paul agreed to a fortnight's truce.

There was a chieftain in Rousay, Sigurd of Westness, with whom Paul was on terms of close and easy friendship, and when Rognvald, taking advantage of the truce, came from Westray to the Mainland, Paul went from the Mainland to Rousay, to stay with Sigurd. Early one morning he, with a company of nineteen men, went otter-hunting on the shore; and when they failed to return for their morning ale, Sigurd sent others to look for them.

Sigurd's men found on the shore the dead bodies of Paul's nineteen, and beside them the bodies of six strangers. There was no trace of the Earl himself, and no suggestion of what might have happened to him except in the statement of a man called Borgar who lived at Gaitnip on the east of Scapa Bay. Borgar had seen a strange merchant ship come into the Flow through Hoxa Sound, and go out westward through Hoy Sound. That ship—though Borgar did not know it—had gone west-about round the Mainland, turned in by Eynhallow Sound, and on the Rousay shore, not far from the Midhowe broch, surprised Earl Paul and his otter-hunters.

Paul was kidnapped, his followers killed, and the ship returned, by the west coast of the Mainland, to Hoy Sound and Scapa Flow and out by Hoxa Sound, as Borgar observed. Aboard, and in command, was a young man called Sweyn of Gairsay, or Sweyn Asleifsson, who had already shown his aptitude for getting into trouble and out of it.

About a year before, in the battle off the Mull Head of Deerness in which Earl Paul defeated Olvir Rosta, the most notable figures were Olaf Rolfsson of Gairsay, who commanded one of Paul's five ships, and Sweyn Breastrope, a large, uncouth member of the Earl's bodyguard. Olaf of Gairsay cleared three of Olvir's smaller ships, and at a critical stage of the battle Sweyn Breastrope hurled a great stone at Olvir and knocked him overboard. His crew pulled him out of the water, and before he recovered consciousness cut the grappling-lines and fled.

Now Olaf of Gairsay was also steward of Duncansby in Caithness, and in the following winter, after Rognvald had gone back to Norway, he held his corner of Caithness against a possible attack by Olvir from the south. About the time of Christmas, when discipline was often relaxed, Olvir took Olaf by surprise, and burnt him in his house with six of his men. His wife Asleif was visiting friends, and their son Sweyn was fishing in the Pentland Firth. Another son, Valthjof, farmed land on the island of Stronsay.

Sweyn came ashore with two companions, the sons of Grim of Swona, and found his father's body in the ruins of his house. He and the men from Swona put to sea again and rowed across to Orkney, where in his house in Orphir Earl Paul was holding his Yule feast. Sweyn told his story, got the Earl's sympathy and an invitation to spend Yule with him. It was now Christmas Eve, and all the Earl's company went to evensong in the church that stood immediately in front of his drinking-hall.

Having worshipped, they sat down to dine: on one side of the Earl was Sweyn Asleifsson, on the other that sinister and surly creature Sweyn Breastrope, who was said to consort with trolls as well as with his fellow-men. The ale was brought in, and with it more bad news: on his way to the feast, Valthjof, the brother of Sweyn Asliefsson, had been drowned with nine of his men in the Stronsay Firth. "Let no one say anything to annoy Sweyn," said the Earl. "He has trouble enough on his mind already." But when he and the others went off to bed, Sweyn Breastrope sat outside to wait for the trolls.

For all but him divine worship alternated with heavy drinking; but Sweyn Breastrope stayed away from church, grew vindictive with drink, and tried to pick a quarrel with the younger Sweyn. It became evident, indeed, that he meant to murder his namesake, who—forewarned and armed by another of the Earl's sea-captains—struck first and killed Sweyn Breastrope. Then, with one companion, Sweyn Asleifsson rode fast over the wintry moors to the Bay of Firth and refuge on the little island of Damsay; from where he sought help of Bishop William on Egilsay. "A good riddance," said the good Bishop when he heard of Sweyn Breastrope's death; and presently sent young Sweyn to safety on the island of Tiree in the Inner Hebrides.

From this rude adventure Sweyn advanced to the rough politics of his age. In the spring he left Tiree and went to Earl Maddad in Atholl: Maddad who was married to Margaret, daughter of Earl Hakon who murdered Magnus, and that Helga who, with her sister Frakok, had been concerned in the strange death, perhaps by a poisoned shirt, of Paul's half-brother Harald. There Sweyn was told that Earl Paul had declared him an outlaw, and given away the land in Stronsay that his drowned brother Valthjof had farmed.

Now in Scotland were the two children who had a claim to the Orkney Earldom—Margaret's son Harald, and her nephew Erlend, son of the elder Harald who had died mysteriously—and Sweyn entered the political scene by promising his support, when he should come of age, to the child Harald. Then he went north to Thurso, where Margaret's uncle Ottar—brother of Helga and Frakok—paid him the compensation due for Olvir Rosta's murder of his father, and gave him a merchant-ship with a crew of thirty men.

Sweyn crossed the Firth, and on the Rousay shore, where he was otter-hunting, kidnapped Earl Paul and took him to Atholl, where Earl Maddad and his Countess Margaret—Paul's half-sister—gave their prisoner what seemed to be a kindly reception. Sweyn returned to Orkney, but now openly, and the luckless Paul remained in captivity to be blinded and murdered. Whether this happened before Sweyn left Atholl, or after his departure, is not certainly known. It seems probable, however, that Margaret deceived him and had her silent half-brother put to death after he had gone; for the saga says that Sweyn, having pledged his support to Margaret's child Harald, later promised allegiance to her nephew Erlend. According to the saga this happened in Thurso when Ottar gave him a ship and he sailed north to kidnap Earl Paul; but the likelihood is that his second promise was made on his subsequent journey to the north—after the kidnapping, that is—and the reason for it was his discovery that Margaret had lied to him, and instead of keeping Paul in a harmless prison had had him killed.

However that may be, Sweyn came to Orkney again, and going ashore at Scapa with eight armed men, walked to Kirkwall and found a parliament assembled. The situation was dangerous, for Rognvald Kol's son was not yet established in his Earldom, and Paul's adherents were still numerous. But Sweyn was welcomed, and said he would like to speak to Bishop William.

The Bishop heard what he had to say, and asked the parliament for a temporary truce. This was granted, and the Bishop summoned Rognvald and his father to a private conversation. The Bishop, who had already befriended Sweyn, was a remarkable man. A clerk of Paris, and perhaps a fellow-student there with the great Peter Abelard, he was very young at the time of his consecration, and lived to be celebrated for his old age. No less remarkable was Kol, and Rognvald, earl-presumptive, was the most amiable of heroes. But Sweyn, youngest of the four, could stand comparison with any of them in wit and daring and dexterity—and he alone knew what had happened, and how it had happened.

He told them what he had done in the matter of Earl Paul, and said Paul had first asked for money to let him retire to a monastery. Paul had suggested, he said, that a story be put about that he had been maimed and blinded—this to prevent any attempt at rescue—but now, as he had learnt, that story had become the truth, and Paul was dead. What Sweyn told his seniors is not fully known, but it may be assumed that he said nothing of his sequent promises to support the claims to the Earldom of the children Harald and Erlend.

The assembled parliament acknowledged the authority of Rognvald and the Bishop, and dispersed. It was accepted, however grudgingly, that Paul was a faraway, disabled captive, if not dead; and Rognvald, receiving the submission of the people, succeeded him. Kol sent ships to England, to bring masons from Durham, and stone was quarried at the Head of Holland, three miles from Kirkwall. In Kirkwall itself the foundations were laid of a large cruciform church, and a cathedral began to rise from the astonished island. No one knows where Kol, in that treeless land, found scaffolding for his great work, but by the mid-century the choir and transepts were complete.

Margaret of Atholl did not wait long before presenting the claim of her son Harald. In 1138 a Scotch bishop arrived to propose yet another division of the Earldom, and the genial Rognvald made no objection to his suggestion that the boy should come to Orkney, to live under Rognvald's tutelage and receive his due title. With Harald, as his foster-father, came a man called Thorbjorn Clerk, a grandson of the wicked old woman Frakok, who presently married Sweyn's sister Ingigerd.

Sweyn had now succeeded to the lands which his father Olaf and his brother Valthjof had held. Nothing is said of his mother, but the inference is obvious that she was a notable woman, for he was known by her name—Sweyn Asleif's son—and the restless habit of his life may, in part, have been the produce of her heroic temper. It is a characteristic of the northern sagas that their women seldom allow a husband or a son to live quietly at home.

Though Sweyn had got compensation for his father's death, from Ottar in Thurso, he now determined to take a fuller revenge on Olvir Rosta, who had burnt him alive, and on Frakok his evil grandmother. He persuaded Earl Rognvald to lend him two ships, and sailing south into the Moray Firth, he landed and marched to Atholl, where Earl Maddad gave him Highland guides. With their help he turned north again, and from the landward side attacked Olvir's homestead in the valley of the Helmsdale river. There was a short and bloody battle, from which Olvir escaped and fled into the hills, but Sweyn burnt the house, and Frakok in it, and went home again with a rich booty.

Then came word from Tiree, where he had once found refuge, that his former host had been attacked by a Welsh pirate and needed help. Earl Rognvald again gave Sweyn ships and men, and Sweyn set out on the first of his long cruises. For two years or more he harried and fought on both shores of the narrow sea between Wales and Ireland—from the Isle of Man to the Scillies—and found time to woo and marry the rich widow of the chieftain of Man, whom the Welsh had killed; her name was Ingrid. He solved a financial difficulty by selling her estate, and returned to Orkney.

Earl Rognvald, in the meantime, had become friendly with Thorbjorn Clerk, Sweyn's brother-in-law, whose grandmother Frakok Sweyn had burnt. Thorbjorn Clerk had taken nominal revenge for that insult by killing two of Sweyn's followers who had helped in the burning, but Rognvald pacified the brothers-in-law, and when Sweyn proposed another cruise to the west, gave him five ships, one of which was commanded by Thorbjorn Clerk.

The cruise was profitable, and in the autumn the fleet sailed north to Sweyn's estate of Duncansby. There, with deliberate insolence, Sweyn provoked hostility and invited misfortune by insisting that in their division of the spoils he must be given a chief's share. The indignant Thorbjorn Clerk carried this tale of injustice to Earl Rognvald. He soothed the angry man, who promised to carry the quarrel no farther, but promptly divorced Ingigerd his wife, and sent her over the Firth to Sweyn her brother. Sweyn met her with kindness, and replied to Thorbjorn's rudeness by insulting Rognvald: by defying his authority with wanton insolence.

He had an old comrade called Margad who happened, about this time, to kill a friend of Rognvald's; and Sweyn not only accepted responsibility for Margad's misdeed, but garrisoned a stronghold on the east coast of Caithness and prepared to defend him by force. No reasonable explanation can be found for behaviour so reckless: no explanation, indeed, but Sweyn's determination to defy his Earl because there was no one greater whom he could defy.— Rognvald laid siege to his stronghold, and when the garrison were in danger of starvation, Sweyn permitted their surrender. Rognvald, most lenient of champions, laid no punishment on Sweyn's sixty men-at-arms. But Sweyn and Margad were not among them. In the darkness of the previous night his men had let Sweyn and Margad down the high cliff on ropes, and they had swum southward till they found a beach. They borrowed horses, stole a boat, and on the southern shore of the Moray Firth took passage in a little trading ship to the Firth of Forth. In Edinburgh Sweyn found his way to the court of David I, King of Scots.

The saga says that King David tried to win him for Scotland's cause, but Sweyn perversely refused because of his allegiance to the man against whom he had rebelled; and presently persuaded the King to make peace between him and Rognvald. So Sweyn, with a pardon from the magnanimous Earl, went back to Gairsay, but prudently left Margad in Scotland.

Earl Rognvald was preparing for a voyage to the Holy Land, but there is no record of his having asked Sweyn to join him, or of Sweyn having volunteered for the crusade.

8

Rognvald the Crusader

In the spring of 1148 Earl Rognvald went to Norway as a guest of its parti-King Ingi. With him was the boy from Atholl, Harald Maddad's son, and at the King's court was a young man called Eindrid who had served for some time in the Varangian Guard at Constantinople. It was Eindrid who spoke of the pleasures of foreign travel, and planted in Rognvald's mind the idea of a crusade. There were others who promised to join him if he would be their leader.

The decision was taken, and a ship commissioned. Rognvald and his following set sail for home in two lightly built longships that Ingi gave him, and ran before a following gale that wrecked them on the Mainland of Shetland, in the bay of Gulberwick. Rognvald, unperturbed by disaster, spent some time in Shetland, but went south to Orkney before Christmas. At his Yule feast Bishop William was persuaded to join the crusade—though by this time the Bishop may have been well over seventy—and nine others, chiefs or men of substance, also pledged themselves to go. After another winter of preparation Rognvald sailed to Norway, and found his new ship ready for him: a handsome vessel of thirty-five benches, with carved bulwarks, and the figure-head, the poop, and the weather-vanes inlaid with gold. But Eindrid and his friends kept them waiting, and that summer was wasted. When Eindrid came at last, it was seen that his ship also was dragon-headed and as richly gilded as the Earl's. But this ostentation was wasted like the summer, for Eindrid lost his fine ship on a Shetland reef.

The crusaders, Orkneymen and Norwegians, spent an uneasy winter in Orkney—there was a good deal of quarrelling—and when spring came they had to wait again for Eindrid, for whom a new ship was being built. Harald Maddad's son, now seventeen or eighteen, was to stay in Orkney, to rule the Earldom with Thorbjorn Clerk as his councillor; and at last, in the late summer, Rognvald led a fleet of fifteen sail to adventure and the Holy Land.

Down the east cost of England and through the Channel was their course—none opposed their passage, for England was near to anarchy under Stephen's nominal throne—but foul weather met them in the Bay, and the voyage was briefly delayed while they harried some parts of the coast of Spain and skirmished with the Moors. Close-hauled they sailed through the Strait of Gibraltar, and headed north into the Gulf of Lions. For some time they lay in the sheltered waters off Narbonne, and temporarily the purpose of the voyage was driven from Rognvald's mind by the young beauty of the Countess Ermengarde.

This was the age of the great troubadours, and Rognvald himself was a poet. There is no doubt of Ermengarde's charm and beauty, for her memory lived long in Orkney, but Rognvald was a man of fifty or so, and in due course remembered the Holy Land. That Ermengarde wept to see him go is not recorded, but the voyage was resumed and somewhere on the coast there was more fighting, and a castle was captured. But for some reason a quarrel broke out between Orkneymen and Norwegians, and when the fleet put to sea again, Eindrid with five ships set another course and parted from Earl Rognvald.

Near Sardinia, in calm and foggy weather, Rognvald and his men boarded and captured a great ship of the Saracens called a dromond—a vessel that towered like a castle—and foolishly set it on fire before they had found the treasure it held. They landed somewhere in North Africa, they lay for shelter under Crete till a gale blew itself out, and went ashore at Acre. The voyage had been sufficiently eventful, and on idle days Rognvald and two of his fellow-voyagers—Arnod and Oddi the Little—made poems; many of them in praise of Ermengarde.

In Acre a sickness attacked them, and many died; but the survivors rode over the plain of Esdraelon and when they entered Jerusalem Earl Rognvald wore a cross on his breast and carried a palm-branch. There was no one to fight, however—no chance to show their piety in battle—for the Latin kingdom of Palestine was at peace under Baldwin III. So, to continue as a holiday what purported to be a crusade, they returned to Acre and set sail for Constantinople and the court of Manuel Comnenus, Emperor of Byzantium. They cannot have been pleased to find Eindrid and his Norwegians already there.

The Emperor offered to take them into his service, but this they refused, and when winter was over sailed for Italy. Somewhere in Apulia Earl Rognvald, Bishop William, and the noblest of their company went ashore, bought horses, and rode to Rome. Thence, "by the Roman way", to Denmark and Norway; and in the winter of 1153 Earl Rognvald sailed westward and returned to Orkney.

Rognvald had been absent from the islands for nearly two and a half years, and Orkney had had a more troubled time than he and his crusaders. Young Harald Maddad's son had been attacked by a Norwegian army under one of the bastard parti-Kings of Norway—he was on his way to warfare in England—and Harald's cousin Erlend, with the help or approval of the King of Scots, invaded Orkney. A peace was patched up between them, and Erlend went to Norway to look for allies. But Harald also had trouble of a nearer sort to plague him.

His father was dead, and his mother Margaret had come to live in Orkney. The widowed Countess, still a sprightly woman, fell in love with Gunni, a brother of Sweyn Asleifsson, and bore him a child. The young Earl, full of anger, outlawed Gunni, and provoked Sweyn to equal wrath. Sweyn took reprisals, and remembered that he had once promised his allegiance to young Erlend. When Erlend returned from Norway, where the parti-King Eystein had cynically awarded him Harald's share of the Earldom, they attacked Harald and after stiff fighting drove him out of Orkney and into Caithness. Erlend was weak and unreliable, but Sweyn kept him out of trouble, and when Harald in mid-winter returned with four small ships and a hundred men, the raid was unrewarded and Harald returned to Caithness empty-handed.

His mother, the gamesome Dowager of Atholl, now fell in love with a young Shetland chieftain who carried her off to the Broch of Mousa, and provisioned it against a siege. Harald followed them, but admitted his inability to storm the broch. He gave his mother reluctant permission to marry her young Shetlander, and presently all three of them sailed east to Norway.

Sweyn and Erlend took advantage of Harald's absence to enjoy a viking cruise to the coast of Northumberland, and captured a richly laden ship off Berwick. They escaped a fleet that set out in

Kirkwall
(overleaf) *St. Magnus' Cathedral: exterior, Bishop's Palace in foreground, and interior*

search of them, and the saga says—though one may doubt its truth—that Sweyn paid another visit to old David, King of Scots, who gave him "a costly shield and many fine gifts as well".

But now Earl Rognvald was on his way home, and arrived in Orkney before Yule. He had left Harald and Thorbjorn Clerk in charge of the Earldom, and found Erlend and Sweyn of Gairsay in command. Harald was in Norway, trying to recruit new strength, and Thorbjorn Clerk, who had taken no part in the political warfare of the past two years, was sulking in Caithness. Rognvald, with no fleet and only a handful of men, retained his Norse realism and accepted the *fait accompli*.

He made a new alliance with Erlend, and with Sweyn and Erlend prepared to meet Harald's expected invasion. In the spring Sweyn and Erlend went north to Shetland, Rognvald to Caithness where many were still loyal to Harald. Harald, it was thought, would make for one or the other. But when Harald put to sea, with a fleet of seven sail, a gale divided them, and the three that reached Shetland were captured by Erlend. The other four came to Orkney, and Harald quickly made up his mind to see Rognvald before Erlend and Sweyn could join him. And now foul weather came to Harald's assistance, for a great gale scattered Erlend's fleet, and before his ships could re-assemble, Harald was in Thurso.

Rognvald was in Berriedale, at the wedding of his daughter. He rode north, and all about him urged the need of reconciliation with Harald. The boy Harald, they said, had been his foster-son, and that was a relationship which none could break. Rognvald's old counsellors—Kol his father, and Bishop William—were no longer with him, and Rognvald had always been a kindly, pliant man. He met Harald, and they got on well together. They were talking in the castle at Thurso, when their discussion was interrupted by the sound of fighting outside.

Thorbjorn Clerk had arrived with a large following, and immediately attacked Earl Rognvald's men. Rognvald himself was wounded in the face before the fighting stopped, and now Thorbjorn Clerk joined those who pleaded with him to remember his old friendship with Harald. There was no cowardice in Rognvald's mood—no shadow of cowardice ever touched him—but an excess, perhaps, of good temper. And his alliance with Erlend had been made under duress; while Sweyn, most certainly, had broken his treaty with Harald. So Rognvald yielded to

Bishop's Palace, Kirkwall

persuasion, and with his old friend and thirteen ships sailed through Hoy Sound into Scapa Flow, and over to Widewall Bay in South Ronaldsay.

Erlend and Sweyn, having come down from Shetland, lay with their ships to the south of Widewall Bay in Bardswick, where they were at grave disadvantage: Bardswick had been a good place from which to watch the Firth, but now they were cut off from the Mainland of Orkney, and short of provisions as well as out-numbered and out-manœuvred. They had little reason for confidence other than Sweyn's genius for war; and that proved sufficient.

They crossed to Pentland Firth, drove cattle for the harness-cask, and let the tale go round that they were bound for the Western Isles. When winter approached they headed west, and doubled Cape Wrath. Their passage through the Firth was seen and reported, and in Orkney Earl Rognvald brought his fleet into Scapa Bay, and kept his men aboard. Sweyn went as far south as the Point of Stoer in Assynt, and then turned north again, under sail before a favouring wind, and crossed the Firth to Walls, where he heard that the Earls Rognvald and Harald lay under Knarston in Scapa Bay. They now had fourteen ships; Sweyn and Erlend had seven.

It was October 24th, and the night was cold and stormy, promising sleet. Earl Rognvald, with a few companions, rowed ashore to drink with an Icelander, Botolf, who lived at Knarston; but Sweyn decided to attack. Out of the bitter gale came Sweyn's ships, and his storm-lashed men leapt fiercely aboard the sleeping, anchored vessels in the narrow bay. There was some hard fighting, but all fourteen were captured, and when Harald escaped there were, of his crew, only five left living. He and Rognvald met in Orphir, and in two small boats—with three men in one, four in the other—sailed perilously across the Firth to Caithness. For his share of the plunder Sweyn demanded everything that was found in Rognvald's ship; and sent it all to the defeated Earl.

Sweyn made plans for the islands' defence, but Erlend withdrew some of the watching ships and went to spend Yule on the little island of Damsay in the Bay of Firth. There, drunk, he was surprised on a moonlit night by Rognvald and Harald, leading a swift and sudden raid, and killed on the weedy shore of Damsay. The two Earls were clement, and without penalty accepted the submission of the rebellious islanders. Only Sweyn and his immediate followers were not included in that indulgence. Rognvald, indeed, tried to reconcile Sweyn and Harald, but Sweyn was recalcitrant and Harald hard to satisfy. More blood was spilt, there was hot pursuit and hardy evasion before at last peace was made; but the tardy reconciliation of Sweyn and Harald Maddad's son was the beginning of a warm and lasting friendship.

Peace was celebrated, by Sweyn, with another viking cruise that led to the Scillies and a victory at Port St. Mary which yielded a great booty. There was now no dissident element in Orkney but Thorbjorn Clerk, whose persistant ill-nature could not be appeased. He was outlawed, and fled to Scotland, after killing one of Rognvald's bodyguard.

Two or three years later, in the early autumn, the Earls went over to Caithness, as was their custom, to hunt the red deer; and there they heard that Thorbjorn, who had been living with the King of Scots, was now in the north again with a considerable following. Stalking was postponed, and with a hundred men they set off on a man-hunt. Rognvald, riding far in advance, was taken in ambush at the farm of Forsie, and mortally wounded. Thorbjorn and his men stood to defend themselves, and after long parleying he and eight others fought to the death, and died well. But Rognvald was dead—Rognvald the warrior-poet, the kindliest of men and the gayest of pilgrims—and throughout the islands there was lamentation for the loss of his great spirit and ready friendship.

Harald Maddad's son now succeeded to the whole Earldom, for Rognvald's only child was his daughter Ingigerd, married to Eric Staybrails; and from 1158, the year of Rognvald's death, till 1206, Harald ruled the islands with undisputed power, a hard heart, and little wisdom.

9

Decline and Fall

Sweyn of Gairsay and Harald continued to live on friendly terms, and Sweyn acquired what may, by a liberal understanding, be regarded as a settled way of life. That is to say, he divided his time between farming and fighting. He lived on the little island of Gairsay—a hillock of an island six or seven miles due north of Kirkwall—where throughout the winter eighty men-at-arms lay in or about his drinking-hall. In the early months of the year they ploughed the land, in Gairsay and the nearby parish of Rendall, and put to sea on their spring viking. They came home to cut their crops, and went off again on the autumn viking. Then they drank the winter down, till days began to lighten and a new year brought in an old routine.

For some fifteen years this habit endured, and in 1171, or thereabout, Sweyn led a fleet of five ships as far south as Dublin, where he captured two English ships laden with wine and mead and English broadcloth. He took their cargoes, let the sailors go, and sailed north under canvas to which the bright captured webs were sewn. After this, his Broadcloth Cruise, he meant to make only one more voyage—or so he told Earl Harald—before retiring from the sea and his arduous profession.

His last voyage, with a fleet of seven ships, took him to Dublin again, which he stormed and captured. At this time much of Ireland was in a state of anarchy, for in 1169 two Norman-Welsh nobles invaded it; Richard Strongbow, Earl of Pembroke, reinforced them a year later; and in 1171, alarmed by Strongbow's ambition, Henry II of England followed with a considerable army.—The English ships that Sweyn captured in the spring of that year were probably carrying supplies to one or other of the invading armies.—In the autumn Sweyn may have had a fighting force of about 600 men, and perhaps Dublin was held by an

English rearguard. No one knows. All that can be said, with reasonable certainty, is that he trusted his defeated enemy too easily, and his trust was betrayed.

The garrison made terms, and agreed to pay a ransom for the town. Sweyn and his men returned to their ships, and the next morning, coming for their reward, walked into an ambush. They tumbled into pits masked with brushwood, and the town's defenders killed their leaders and drove the rest in angry flight to the harbour. Sweyn was killed, and according to the saga his last words were: "Let all men know that I belong to the bodyguard of Earl Rognvald, and now my trust is in him where he stands with God."

It is hard to believe this, but the sentiment is admirable, so let it stand. The saga continues, in the words of Taylor's translation: "Now is Sweyn's story ended. And it is the judgment of men that he has been the biggest man in every way in the lands of the west, both in days present and days past, among men who were not of higher rank than he."

The story of Orkney in its heroic age was also coming to an end, and he who hastened its conclusion was Harald Maddad's son. In 1184 the kingdom of Norway fell to a man of dubious ancestry, but whose military genius was unquestionable. His name was Sverri, and he claimed descent from the house of Harald Fairhair. Ten years later his rule was challenged by a new party whose leaders were a couple of Norwegian chiefs and a distant cousin of Harald Maddad's son, known as Olaf Earl's-kinsman. They met in Orkney and asked help from the Earl. Harald, most foolishly, gave leave to all who wanted to join them, and a great number of Orkneymen and Shetlanders made ready for a disastrous adventure.

Olaf's invading army consisted almost entirely of islanders—they were nicknamed *Eyskeggs*, or Island Beardies—and at first they overcame all opposition, and their numbers grew. But after a winter in Bergen King Sverri came with a fleet of twenty "rather small" ships, and attacked their fourteen larger vessels in the Sound of Floruvoe. The fighting that ensued was extraordinarily severe, the islanders fought with the utmost bravery but with no one to direct their battle, and in the end were practically annihilated. Earl Harald, summoned to Bergen, was heavily and harshly punished for his folly. The King claimed possession of the estates of all who had fallen in the battle, giving their heirs three years in which to redeem them by purchase; he took Shetland under his own control "for tax and tribute"; he sent his own bailiffs to the islands; and demanded one-half of all the legal fines to which Harald was entitled. The Earldom thus lost both its wealth and the large measure of independence which it had usually, if not always, maintained.

With Harald on this humiliating journey went Bishop Bjarni, a poet more learned and skilful than Earl Rognvald: the greatest, indeed, of Orkney poets till, some 800 years later, another was born on the same little island from which Bjarni came. Bjarni, a son of the chieftain Kolbein Hruga of Wyre—long remembered as "Cubbie Roo"—was the author of the *Jomsviking Drapa*, the heroic lay of the most famous of viking associations; and to him also may be given the major credit for Earl Rognvald's canonization in the year 1192. A son of Sweyn of Gairsay was Bjarni's brother-in-law: the islands of Wyre and Gairsay lie close together, and Bjarni, who was consecrated in 1184, must have known Sweyn and heard from him stories of the Earl's grace and gallantry; though few, perhaps, of any remarkable piety. But with a cathedral and a crusade for evidence, Bjarni had argument enough for his candidate.

In 1198 Harald the Young, a grandson of Rognvald—eldest son of his daughter Ingigerd and Eric Staybrails—who already held half the Earldom of Caithness, claimed also half of Orkney; but was defeated and killed in a battle near Wick. Harald the Young had acquired his share of Caithness by favour of William the Lion, King of Scots; and his quarrel with the elder Harald involved the Orkney Earl in a dispute with King William that apparently followed and aggravated an earlier dissension. Records of the time are confused, but what emerges is another instance of the folly that bedevilled Harald's old age. He invaded Caithness, seized and brutally maimed its Bishop, and offered battle to the King; but then thought better of it and begged for peace. He was allowed to keep his Caithness Earldom for the price of every fourth penny of its rents, and lived another four years. The saga calls him one of the three mightiest of the Earls, but it is impossible to accept this verdict unless one equates length of days with greatness: he had been Earl of Orkney for sixty-seven years, and ruled alone for forty-seven. But Orkney never recovered from his rule.

Harald was succeeded by his sons David and John. David died

in 1214, and for sixteen years John ruled alone, and ruled ingloriously. Adam, Bishop of Caithness, had made himself so unpopular in his diocese, by reason of his greed, that in 1222 a great crowd surrounded his house and burnt him to death. Earl John was in Caithness at the time, but refused to intervene, and for his inaction had to pay a heavy fine to Alexander II of Scotland. Eight years later King Hakon of Norway launched an expedition to the Hebrides and Man, which recruited nearly half its strength in Orkney, sailed south to the Firth of Clyde, and after furious fighting stormed Rothesay Castle. Hardly had the Orkneymen returned before John was involved in a foolish, unnecessary quarrel that provoked his murder, after a drunken brawl, in a cellar in Thurso. And the line of Norse earls came miserably to an end.

10

A Forced Marriage

The Earldom had, indeed, lost much of its ruling Norse blood by the accession of Harald Maddad's son—whose father was a Scot—but he had lived most of his absurdly long life in Orkney, and identified himself with the islands. In favour of the murdered John there is nothing to be said, for even in his death he bequeathed disaster. His murder was followed by what was intended to be a court of adjudication in Norway; but assassination proved easier, nothing was decided, and when the noble witnesses who had been summoned set sail for home, "all went in one ship, the best men of the isles. That ship was lost, and all who were in her." So says Hakon's saga.

In these circumstances the Earldom passed obscurely to Magnus, son of an Earl of Angus; who died in due course and was succeeded by a shadow called Gilbride, of whom nothing is known; who was followed by yet another Magnus. He does appear, for a brightly lit moment in history, but did nothing to deserve the illumination he shared. It was in his time that King Hakon of Norway sailed on his second expedition to the Hebrides, and failed to achieve his purpose of re-mustering the Western Isles among his subject people. He recognized defeat at the so-called Battle of Largs—the year was 1263—and returned to die in Kirkwall. Something more will be said of this melancholy occasion in a later chapter; here it is enough to record that this late and insufficient Magnus of Orkney gave his help neither to the King of Norway nor to the King of Scots.

Of a third Magnus of the Angus line it is known only that he died in 1284; but Magnus the Fourth in that family was one of the nobles of Scotland who in 1320 signed in Arbroath their robust assertion of Scotland's independence for the benefit of Pope John XXII. This fact may be relevant to the belief—so strongly buttressed by circumstantial evidence—that Robert the Bruce, in the winter of 1306, found refuge in Orkney. The school-books say, or used to say, that he lay hidden on the small island of Rathlin: an improbable assertion, as anyone can see who looks at a map. Some English chroniclers say he fled to Norway; but he was in Arran again in February of 1307, so that is unlikely. But let "Norway" include the reduced Norwegian dominions, and Orkney will fit the description of his refuge—"a remote island"—that the Lanercost Chronicle offers. There is, moreover, an Orkney tradition that his winter-host was an odaller called Halcro, who later followed him to Bannockburn. It may, then, be just to give Magnus IV (of the Angus line) credit not only for signing the Declaration of Arbroath, but for an early acknowledgment of his allegiance to the Bruce, when Bruce's kingdom was more of a promise than a reality.

Magnus IV had no heir, and the Earldom passed to Malise the great-grandson of an Earl Malise of Strathearne who had married Matilda, daughter of the shadowy Earl Gilbride of the Angus family. Another Malise followed him; then a Swedish noble who had married his daughter. He fell foul of King Magnus of Norway, who deprived him of his title, and for some twenty years the Earldom had no Earl at all. But in 1379 the gap was filled by Henry Sinclair of Roslin, whose wife was a younger daughter of the last Malise: in that year he was formally invested by King Hakon of Norway, and his rank acknowledged as next to the royal house and above all the Scandinavian nobility.

He is said to have been a notable sailor, an explorer who "discovered" Greenland; which may mean that he re-discovered it. It is also stated, in the lineage of the present Earl of Caithness, that Earl Henry was killed in battle in Orkney in 1404; in that year, according to Holinshed, a marauding English fleet attacked the islands. In Kirkwall Earl Henry had built a castle, of which nothing now remains, so strong that two centuries later it roused a thought that the devil himself must have helped to raise its walls. Unlike his immediate predecessors, Henry I did identify himself with Orkney, and apparently lived there in considerable style.

His son, Henry II, married a grand-daughter of Robert II, King of Scots; and after a long delay, during which the people of Orkney suffered grievously under a rapacious steward, he was succeeded by his son William, who was also created Earl of

Caithness. A strong Earl was badly needed in the islands, for in the fifteenth century the Hebrides were taking a little revenge for the innumerable raids they had suffered in the Norse age. For some years Orkney winced and complained of wild Lewismen and Irish caterans; especially of one John, Earl of Ross and Lord of the Isles. The days of its independence and security were gone for ever, and the islands were about to suffer a total and disastrous change in their condition.

The change had its origin in long dissension between James II of Scotland and Christian I of Norway and Denmark. Some time before 1460 there were conversations designed to make peace between them, and it was proposed that Prince James, later James III, should marry Christian's daughter Margaret. The Scottish delegates asked for Orkney and Shetland as part of Margaret's dowry; but before agreement was reached, James II was dead.

In 1468 the conversations were renewed, and King Christian consented to let Orkney become part of the dowry, provided it was redeemable for 50,000 florins of the Rhine; the whole dowry being a promise of 60,000 florins. The marriage contract was signed, but a year later the 10,000 florins in cash were still unpaid, so Shetland was pledged for 8,000; and the people of the islands were ordered to be obedient and pay rents and dues to their new rulers.

In 1471 the two archipelagos were annexed, and the Earldom of Orkney and the Lordship of Shetland united to the Crown of Scotland, "not to be given away in time to come to no person nor persons except only to one of the King's sons got of lawful bed."—At no time in history has the pledged word of a properly constituted government been worth very much, and the Scottish promise of 1471 can claim no great distinction because it was worth nothing at all. Again and again the Earldom was given away, but never to the sovereign's legitimate son.

Earl William was translated to Fife, and there given a royal estate in exchange for his lost islands. Orkney and Shetland were farmed out to tacksmen who paid a rent and took what profit they thought suitable. The first two tacksmen were Bishops of Orkney, who traditionally were men of considerable power in the islands; and in 1489 Lord Henry Sinclair, grandson of Earl William, got the tack. He seems to have been a sympathetic, generous man; but in 1513, on the dark field of Flodden, he fell with his King.

The old Norse laws still remained in force, but the old Norse families were losing their lands and authority: the Scots were moving in. After Lord Henry's death at Flodden his brother Sir William Sinclair of Warsetter became the King's Justice, and Henry's widow drew the rents. In effect, a new ruling family sat down in Kirkwall, and the high-spirited Sinclairs bred a clutch of unruly sons who shook the peace of the islands. One of them, another William, seized the Bishop's Palace; but his mother, the dowager Lady Sinclair, contrived to get him appointed Justice Depute, and undertook to supply him with food, fire, and candles when he removed to the strong castle of Kirkwall.

From there he was evicted, with great violence, in a surprise attack by his cousins James and Edward; and found refuge in Caithness. The Scottish Crown took note of this irregularity, and in May, 1529, the two cousins were commanded to restore the castle and face certain charges of homicide. But James Sinclair threw the royal messenger into prison.

William Sinclair, who had been expelled, got help from his kinsman the Earl of Caithness and raised a considerable army with which, on June 7th, 1529, they landed on the Orphir coast of the West Mainland; somewhere between Houton and Waukmill Bay. Their objective was Kirkwall and its castle. But the brothers James and Edward Sinclair of Warsetter had popular support in the islands, and in Kirkwall had mustered an army to meet invasion. They marched out, and the two armies met at Summerdale in the moors of Stenness: some two-thirds of the way up the road, past the loch of Kirbister, that now runs from the Orphir road to the main road from Kirkwall to Stromness.

This was an improbable site for the battle. For the invading army Summerdale was not on the road to Kirkwall, and for the defenders it was not on the road to the invaded coast. It may be, however, that the landing was opposed, and the defenders deliberately withdrew into the hills until, at Summerdale, a reinforcement from the northern parts of the West Mainland gave their commander sufficient strength to join battle. The invaders may well have been taken by surprise, for a sudden charge seems to have thrown them into disarray. At the first onslaught the Earl of Caithness and thirty of his men were killed, and the impetus of the virtuous defenders drove their enemy back to the inland sea of Scapa Flow, where many were killed or drowned: 300, says a Sinclair narrative; but 500, says Holinshed. The men of Caithness were clearly out-matched, for St. Magnus himself—or so it was reported—came down from heaven to help his fellow-Orkneymen on the heathery slopes of Stenness.

That was the last battle fought on Orkney soil, and a lively memory of it survived in farmhouse kitchens till the early years of this century. Now the astonishing sequel to the battle was an admission of defeat by the Scottish Crown, and the rewarding—with a knighthood and a large grant of land—of James Sinclair of Warsetter, who had led the Orkney rebels. That happened about four years after James V had granted the whole lands of Orkney and Shetland to the Earl of Moray; but Moray, or so it seems, declined acceptance of so perilous a gift. He may have been wise, for about this time Denmark was apparently making some effort to redeem the islands, and had it been able to shake 58,000 florins from the royal sleeve, the political situation might have been dangerous. But negotiations came to nothing, and in 1539 the valiant Sir James, for no obvious reason, committed suicide.

That year his brother Edward and thirty others who had fought at Summerdale were officially pardoned, and in 1540 King James himself paid a visit to the islands. He appointed one Oliver Sinclair his sheriff and tacksman, and thereafter a succession of sheriffs, nominated by the Crown, represented and exercised its authority. Orkney and Shetland had finally and conclusively become part of Scotland.

That this should happen was, of course, inevitable; for geography made it so. But the marriage enforced by geography brought no immediate happiness to the islands; which, indeed, got no mite or crumb of advantage from their compulsory alliance until long after Scotland had become part of Great Britain.

11

The Years of Misery

The year of Reformation in Scotland was 1560, and one of its immediate consequences was a re-distribution of landed property which gave the more astute and able of the Reformers a rich reward for their piety. In Orkney the old landowners, with the remnant of odal values—both social and material—dwindled into insignificance, and in 1564 their total eclipse became imminent when Mary, Queen of Scots, gave to her half-brother, Lord Robert Stewart, the Crown estates in Orkney and Shetland.

Lord Robert was an illegitimate son of James V and Euphemia Elphinstone. At the age of seven his comfort had been assured by a grant of the Abbey of Holyrood, and twenty years later he was on friendly terms with the worthless Lord Darnley, whom the luckless Mary was soon to marry. Contemporary opinion had nothing good to say of Lord Robert, but Mary—now three years upon her Scottish throne, and trying valiantly to rule a rapacious and divided land—is not to be blamed for her ill-advised generosity to him. On none of her counsellors could she depend for impartial and sound advice, and for the only time in her life she was in love: in love with Lord Robert's friend, the tall, girlish-looking, vicious young Darnley.

A few years earlier Gilbert Balfour, Master of the Queen's Household and scion of an ancient family in Fife, had acquired the bishopric estate of Westray, on which he built that remarkable edifice, Noltland Castle, of which more hereafter; and Adam Bothwell, the last Catholic Bishop of Orkney—one of whose sisters became the mother of John Napier, inventor of logarithms—had retained the tenancy of his Palace by an early demonstration of the tactics that were later made famous by the Vicar of Bray. He accepted the Reformation. "When idolatry and superstition were suppressed, he suppressed the same also in his bounds, preached the Word and ministered the sacraments."—So he himself reported.

His time-serving made it easier for Lord Robert to extend his interests. He presently persuaded Bishop Adam to exchange the whole estate of the Orkney bishopric—or what was left of it—for the Abbey of Holyrood, which his royal father had given him in his childhood; and by 1567 he had also become Sheriff Principal of the islands, an office previously in the hands of Gilbert Balfour. Lord Robert was thus in a position of almost unassailable power, of which he made liberal use to enrich himself and impoverish his subjects.

The old laws of the country, which had been guaranteed by the Scottish parliament, were altered and enlarged by a useful edict that none should leave the islands to make complaint against Lord Robert; though he was free to banish malcontents. Rents were raised, common lands appropriated, and the burgesses of Kirkwall forbidden to trade except under his licence. He used such ingenious devices as accusing dead men of old crimes, and confiscating what property they had left. Living men were burdened with the compulsory entertainment of himself and his numerous household, and by increasing weights and measures he raised all those taxes which were paid in kind. He stopped all traffic by ferry, except at his pleasure, and reduced the law and its sentences to mere expression of his own will.

A very clever and extremely wicked man was Lord Robert Stewart; and though he fell into trouble when he tried to open negotiations with Denmark—for which error in judgment he lay in prison in Linlithgow for a year or two—he got back his freedom and his sheriffdom in 1579, and in 1581 was created Earl of Orkney: his hapless half-sister being by then a prisoner in England.

Earl Robert now took to the simplest form of aggrandisement: the ejection of their owners from properties that he coveted, and the re-granting of feu charters to the old odal lands. It may be said in his favour that he rewarded several of his mistresses and endowed some of his illegitimate children with handsome gifts, but apart from this domestic amiability neither history nor those who knew him can find a word to say in his defence. He died in the ripeness of iniquity in February, 1592 or '93, and was succeeded by his son Patrick.

Earl Robert, who flourished by injustice, has suffered posthumously from injustice; for Earl Patrick lived to be remembered with such obloquy and hatred as never rewarded his father, and Black Pate—so he was called—did not really deserve such high distinction. Scoundrel though he was, we who did not suffer under him have some cause to be grateful to him.

Earl Patrick was sublimely arrogant, and where his father had used some cunning, some show of perverted law, to justify his exactions, Patrick assumed a despot's right to take what he fancied and do as he pleased. Confiscation and a vastly increased taxation were not enough for him; he imposed forced labour, both by sea and land, on "gentlemen tenants as well as the common people, and in particular he compelled them to quarry-work, for he was a great builder." His father had built the great Palace of Birsay, the meagre ruins of which still testify to a rude, original magnificence, and Patrick followed and enlarged this grandiose example by altering the old Bishop's Palace; by building the admirable and elegant Castle of Scalloway in Shetland; and by his commissioning and partial building of his New Place of the Yards—the noble and exquisite ruin of which, now known in Kirkwall as the Earl's Palace, is a sad reminder of the brief glory of a house that has been called the finest structure of the sixteenth century in Scotland. No one can look at the grace and strong beauty of the Earl's Palace without some sympathy for Black Pate's insensate arrogance; for with it he combined a most enlightened taste for masonry, though he had no compassion for people. But perhaps great architecture has always been anti-social, or evidence of a lack of human sympathy. What hovels the common people of Europe lived in, while its great cathedrals were being raised to God's glory

It was Patrick's misfortune that his self-esteem and the scope of his tyranny knew no constraint, and in spite of ruthless exaction he fell deeply into debt. His principal creditor was Sir John Arnot, Lord Provost of Edinburgh and Treasurer Depute of Scotland; and though his behaviour had been such as to rouse suspicion of treason to the Crown, his indebtedness to Arnot may have been a weightier argument in bringing him to his doom. A new bishop of great ability and stern resolution was also, in the earliest years of the seventeenth century, appointed to Orkney; and he, Richard Law, appealed to his Sacred and Most Gracious Majesty King James VI and I to come to the aid of his "poor distressed subjects" in the islands.

In 1609 Black Pate was arrested and imprisoned in Edinburgh

Castle. Many and amply substantiated were the charges against him, and the main part of Patrick's defence was that whatever he had done, he had had the right to do.

In 1611, however, he was released under a penalty of £50,000 and the prohibition of removing himself from Edinburgh. Bishop Law and Arnot were appointed Sheriffs and Commissioners for Orkney and Shetland, but rumour ran that Patrick would soon be allowed to return to his Earldom. This possibility he himself prevented by appointing his bastard son Robert, a boy of twenty, as Sheriff and Justiciar of the islands, and sending him north to collect rents and recover the properties that the Crown had claimed. Young Robert occupied Kirkwall Castle, but surrendered it again, and Patrick, his Earldom forfeited and annexed to the Crown, was imprisoned in Dumbarton Castle.

But Patrick, being now deprived of sanity as well as Orkney, persuaded his gallant though imprudent son to venture again on his behalf, and in Orkney young Robert managed to recruit a couple of hundred men, from the West Mainland, to support his mad enterprise.—Storer Clouston has suggested, with some ingenuity and large probability, that the mother of this brave, foolish, illegitimate boy was a native of Birsay or Sandwick or Harray; and it was her influence that persuaded so many friends to indiscretion.—Whatever their motive, the West Mainlanders, the men in whom the old Norse blood most strongly ran, marched on Kirkwall and took the Cathedral, the Place of the Yards, and the strong Castle. Orkney was now in open rebellion, and in Edinburgh there was cause for some concern.

A useful emissary of government was found in George, Earl of Caithness, who with a small army and several cannon from Edinburgh Castle embarked in two ships and landed in Orkney to suppress the absurd revolt. It took them longer than they had expected. Young Robert had no gift for leadership, and his assembled rebels unobtrusively returned to their farms. But Robert and perhaps sixteen of his more obviously committed supporters held the Castle for five weeks against the great guns that pelted its thick walls. At last, however, when the Castle was almost in ruins, Robert fell victim to treachery and was made prisoner. Then its desperate defenders were hanged before its shattered gate; while Robert and five who were accounted ringleaders were carried to Edinburgh and there hanged at the Market Cross on January 1st, 1615.

Albert Street, Kirkwall

BANK
SWANSON
HAIRDRESSERS

CWTS 6
QRS 2

Five weeks later Black Pate, his father, was fetched from his prison and beheaded at the same place. His execution was delayed for some days to give him the opportunity of learning the Lord's Prayer; of which, until then, he had been ignorant.

By an act of 1612 the Earldom of Orkney and Lordship of Shetland had again been united and annexed to the Crown, and for some years were again farmed out to tacksmen. In 1643, however, the Earldom estate was mortgaged by Charles I to William Douglas, 7th Earl of Morton. He died in 1648 and was succeeded by his son Robert whose nephew, the Earl of Kinnoul, was then in exile, in Holland, with the great Marquis of Montrose. After the execution of King Charles, in 1649, Montrose sent Kinnoul to Orkney to raise troops, but Kinnoul died, and his son, similarly employed in Sweden, had the ill fortune to lose, in a winter voyage, all but 200 of the 1,200 men he had embarked in Gothenburg. These 200 landed in Kirkwall, where Montrose soon joined them. He seems to have been given a kindly welcome by the leading men of the islands, who freely allowed him to recruit or impress their labourers.—There was much unemployment in Orkney at that time, and military service may have been recognized as a useful way of reducing it.—None of the gentry joined Montrose, but with a thousand untaught rustics or able-bodied beggars, and his 200 soldiers from Gothenburg, he crossed the Firth, marched south as far as Carbisdale by the Kyle of Sutherland, and there, at the end of April, 1650, was utterly routed by a charge of horse. None of the simple Orkneymen had ever seen a dragoon before, and fled in terror at so strange a sight. Montrose himself was captured and taken to a shameful death in Edinburgh.

A couple of years later, in consequence of his visit, Kirkwall was occupied by a Cromwellian garrison, which did not behave badly. The soldiers, indeed, are said to have taught the burgesses of Kirkwall how to make locks and keys—of which, until then, they had had no need—and the neighbouring farmers how to plant cabbage. One of the garrison, perhaps more highbrow than Roundhead—a foul-mouthed, discontented fellow—left as a curious memento of the occupation a set of scurrilous, rhyming verses which, though the present inhabitants of Orkney dislike and resent them, may well be evidence of what an unhappy history is likely to have bequeathed.

Of dairies, for example:

In the Cattle Market, Kirkwall
Tankerness House, Kirkwall

"Haue you ever been
Downe in a Tanner's yard, and have you seene
His lime-pits when the filthy muck and haire
Of twenty hides is wafht and fcrapt off there,
'Tis Orknay milke, in colour, thickneffe, fmell,
Every ingredient, and itt eates as well;
Take from the bottome vppe an handfull on't,
And that's good Orknay butter, fie upon't."

Or of general uncleanliness:

"Their fchooles of learning are in every houfe,
And their firft leffon is to hunt the louse.
Att two years old a wee ill favoured bratt
Will make a good proficient att that."

This sluttishness, of course, is what one would expect as a result of the poverty and degradation not merely produced, but enforced, by the evil rule of the gifted Stewarts: the mass of the people pauperized, with an *arriviste* class of well-to-do merchant-lairds who appear to have shown to their less fortunate neighbours the indifference of an alien ascendancy. There were landowners and burgesses who enjoyed respectable wealth—by the standards of the time—but contemporary with them, in the seventeenth and eighteenth centuries, were wandering beggars, the poverty that comes from an exhausted soil, and a belief in witchcraft that betokened a terrible exhaustion of the spirit as well as material destitution.

There is no doubt whatever that for a long time there was great misery in Orkney, and in general a degree of hardship intolerable to a modern mind or body. And yet—and this is what makes it worth while to emphasize the poverty of this unhappy period—the people's capacity for life and their will to live were not ruined as their fields were ruined. A continuing fortitude preserved them, and maintained in them a spirit sufficient to let them take advantage of every possibility to improve their condition when the climate of history began to improve. Even the poverty of the seventeenth century could not banish all geniality from life, nor extinguish a natural robustitude. Against starvation there was the safeguard of natural riches—the island seas and inland waters teemed with fish, the island cliffs were clamorous with bird-life—and though a disgruntled Cromwellian soldier could complain of the people's sluttishness, there were others who found them comely.

James Wallace, a minister in the island of Sanday, and later, for eighteen years till 1688, in Kirkwall, wrote a description of the islands from which, though it has been quoted elsewhere, and more than once, I may quote again his commendation of the good looks and vitality of his parishioners.

"The Women," wrote Wallace, "are Lovely and of a Beautiful countenance, and very broody and apt for generation; one *Marjory Bimbister* in the Parish of *Evie* was in the year 1683, brought to bed of a Male child in the sixty third year of her age. . . . By reason of the temperance of their Dyet and wholesomeness of the Air, the people usually live to a great Age. A Man in the Parish of *Ham* dyed not many Years since, who liv'd upwards of Fourscore Years with one Wife, in a marry'd state. There is also a Gentleman, yet living in *Stronsa*, who was Begotten of his Father when he was an hundred Years old, and did live till he saw this same Man's Children."

In 1688, the year of Wallace's death, died also Murdo Mackenzie, the last resident Bishop of Orkney, of whom an agreeable tale is told. When he first came ashore at Scapa, it is said, he was offered a traditional welcome: a cup, called the cup of St. Magnus, full of strong ale. He was closely watched to see how he would receive the offering, and when he drank the full cup and asked for more, he was accepted as a good man who would wisely rule his diocese. He was a Mackenzie of the old family of Gairloch in Wester Ross, and his wisdom was inherited by his grandson Murdoch, who in 1750 published a *Survey of the Orkney and Lewis Islands*. In it are eight large maps, drawn with great elegance and commendable accuracy, and a preface that includes an analysis of the Orkneymen's character. This, too, has been much quoted, and is still worth a repetition.

Mackenzie wrote: "A Character given of them by Historians many Ages ago, that they were great Drinkers, but not Drunkards, is in some Measure true still; tho' the Practice of excessive Drinking has been much laid aside within these few Years. They are generally Kind without Caressing, Civil without Ceremony, and Respectful without Compliment; their Resentments of Obligations and Injuries are more quick than perceptible: they are obliging and hospitable to Strangers, and, where no party

Differences intervene, social and friendly among themselves. . . . The *Commonalty* are healthy, hardy, well-shaped, subject to few Diseases, and capable of an abstemious and laborious Life at the same Time; but, for want of profitable Employment, slow at Work and many of them inclined to Idleness. In Sagacity and natural Understanding, they are inferior to few of the Commons in *Britain*; sparing of their Words, reserved in their Sentiments, especially of what seems to have a Connexion with their Interest; apt to aggravate or magnify their Losses, and studious to conceal or diminish their Gains; tenacious of old Customs tho' never so inconvenient, averse to new, till recommended by some successful Examples among their own Rank and Acquaintance, and then universally keen to imitate: Honest in their Dealings with one another, but not so scrupulous with respect to the Master of the Ground. . . . Theft and other Crimes are often concealed, even by those who have sustained the Injury, from an opinion, that it is a Degree of Guilt in a private Person, to become the voluntary Instrument of another's Suffering. . . . The Religion is *Presbyterian*, as established in *Scotland*, without Bigotry, Enthusiasm, or Zeal."

By 1750 the titular Earldom of Orkney—the Earldom that fashioned its early history—had lost all connexion with the islands. The Earls of Morton, after losing their grant under the Commonwealth, were later re-confirmed in it by a charter of 1707, and held the Earldom estate till 1766, when it was bought by Sir Lawrence Dundas, contractor to the Army, for 60,000 guineas. Dundas was the ancestor of the present Marquis of Zetland; who, however, has retained none of the bought acres.

In 1696 Lord George Hamilton, a son of William, Duke of Hamilton, was elevated to the peerage as Earl of Orkney. A very gallant and able soldier, he was a Lieutenant-General under Marlborough and distinguished himself at the great battles of Blenheim, Oudenarde, Ramillies and Malplaquet. He, who became the first Field Marshal in the British service, was a worthy successor of Thorfinn the Mighty. But only in name. Except by his title he had no association with the islands, and none of his descendants has established any relationship with them.

12

The Stubborn Recovery

At the beginning of the nineteenth century there was little change from the general acquiescence in a life of meagre subsistence that the misfortunes of the previous two hundred and fifty years had imposed. Agriculture, in our sense of the word, hardly existed: on the better land oats and bere were grown in alternate crops, but under the runrig system of ownership or tenancy a man's property was divided into widely separated strips, unfenced and untended except at seed-time and harvest. Much of the land was undivided commonty, and high turf dykes separated the sown acres from the grazing grounds.

About the middle of the eighteenth century, however, some small industries had been introduced—the manufacture of linen and yarn, kelp-burning, and later straw-plaiting—and some money from the outer world had begun to seep into the islands: the main sources being the great Hudson Bay Company, and the whaling fleets that fished the Davis Straits. For many years the Company annually enlisted between fifty and a hundred men as boatmen, tradesmen, and store-keepers for its vast dominion; and at Stromness the whalers on their way to the far north-west put in to make up the muster of their crews as well as to fill their water-butts. And much of the money thus earned came back to Orkney and was put into the land.

It was in 1840, or thereabout, that real improvement began, and gradually became visible. The wasteful runrig system was abandoned, farms were consolidated, the commonty divided. Road-building was started after the Orkney Road Act in 1857—winter travel had hitherto been arduous at best, and often perilous—and steamships established a regular communication with the south. The Crofter Act of 1886 gave smallholders security of tenure, and fields began to blossom when a proper rotation of crops became the general practice, and the soil was enlivened by wild white clover and an addition of basic slag. But though the nineteenth century, or its latter half, was a time of growth and recovery in Orkney, life was still hard—if no longer precarious—and conditions were what the affluent society of today would certainly call primitive. There is a detailed and excellent description of country life and its mechanics—its work and diet and diversions—in John Firth's *Reminiscences of an Orkney Parish*, published in 1922.

John Firth, then a bright-eyed old man with a white spade-beard, had a tenacious memory that reached back a full half-century, and was probably enlarged by much that he had heard from men and women who were old when he was a boy. He describes the typical farmhouse as a long, low building, between walls three feet thick, that extended from the ben-end through the but or "in-bye" to the "oot-bye", which was common ground for human occupants, calves, and geese; thence to the byre, to which cows went in by the same door as their owners, and the stable which communicated with the barn and the kiln.

Furniture was simple: straw-backed, hooded chairs for the farmer and his wife, stools for the rest of the family, box-beds which, in an earlier age, had been stone closets through the thickness of the wall. There were no windows, to save paying window-tax, but skylights in the roof; round a central hearth the straw-plaited roof shone brightly black with its accumulation of soot from a peat-fire; and before paraffin lamps were known, the only light against the long darkness of winter came from an iron cruizie in which a rush wick, in a pool of oil extracted from sillock livers, dimly burnt.

Food was plain and simple. Potatoes were the staple diet at those times of the year when meal grew scarce: milk and mashed potatoes in the morning; potatoes boiled in their jackets, with melted butter, at midday; and in the evening more potatoes with perhaps a flavouring of sun-dried sillocks. So says John Firth, and as seriously as a gourmet will deplore the fact that Bordeaux wines have never been the same since phylloxera betrayed them, so he declares that potatoes never regained the fine flavour they had before the famine of 1845. After harvest, he admits, there was oat-meal and bere-meal to provide a more solid fare—oat-meal and kail was a goodly diet—and from milk and butter-milk were extracted some simple dainties. Butcher's meat was expensive, and strictly reserved for Sundays, weddings, and feast-days. It may be, however, that Firth has exaggerated the austerity of his parents' table, for surely it was often supplemented by gulls' eggs in their season, by rabbits caught in a snare, by grouse taken on the stooks, by a young hare that the dogs ran down; or by braxy mutton.

He admits, however, that home-brewed ale was always plentiful—when milk was scarce, ale accompanied the porridge—and a great amount of meal was malted that should have gone to the meal-chest to make bannocks. Nor was there any scarcity of whisky. Whisky for the children on a cold morning; whisky in the bride's cog for weddings; whisky, above all, for a funeral. Whisky, too, for a general medicine: tar for an external dressing, whisky the internal remedy—and what they wouldn't cure, nothing could. Doctors prescribed whisky and sulphur for small-pox and typhus, which were of frequent occurrence; but epilepsy had a cure unknown to science, and the favoured treatment was to bury some part of the patient's clothing where three roads met.

John Firth was a lively old man, and too honest to pretend that poverty and austerity had forbidden all fun and games. His pages, indeed, are wonderfully lighted by reminiscence of groom and groomsman riding on beribboned horses to bid their neighbours to a wedding, and at every house taking a cup of ale or a glass of whisky; of barn-dances with fiddlers playing and the two-handed cog going round till morning; of the festive air at a funeral, and of young men and maidens watching the corpse all night and playing cards to while away the hours. Much money was spent on both weddings and funerals, and the one was kept in sight of the other by the bride's custom of preserving her wedding dress that it might serve for her shroud.

There was no radical change in the scene till 1914; though, of course, houses and their furniture had been vastly improved since the youth of John Firth, and the now rapid progress in agriculture had not only populated the fields with well-fed and better bred sheep and cattle and Clydesdale horses, but enriched the kitchen table. In a simple way, Orkney lived very well in the early years of this century, and in fish and game was far richer than it is now: the trout-lochs were full of fish, the moors loud with the challenge of cock-grouse, and snipe flittered over every marsh. But money was still short, and household trade was largely carried on by barter. It was not until the first Great War, and the coming to

Scapa Flow of the Grand Fleet, that money really began to fertilize the life of Orkney.

Then, in the 1930s, when in the rest of Britain farming was in the doldrums, or the tropics of near bankruptcy, Orkney was cried-up as an example of how agriculture could be made to pay. The small family farm, owner-occupied, which by then had become typical of the islands, was unaffected by depression and the money-famine of the outer world. Orkney was prosperous, its black Aberdeen-Angus or cross-bred cattle were the admiration of all who saw them, and Clydesdale horses with silky-feathered feet trod proudly in their well-kept fields. New land was being brought into cultivation, and, above all, Orkney had discovered the rich profit to be got from eggs and poultry. And much, if not most of the money earned, went back into the land.

It was the second Great War that finally took the islands out of the world that John Firth had known, and on to the fringe—if not into the heart—of the modern world where one does not see, and could not find, much local difference in, for example, habits of dress and dietary. Male and female, the people of Orkney now dress like people in the rest of Britain; in Kirkwall the visitor may buy caviare if he can afford it, or the usual cosmetics when she requires them; gin-and-tonic is now more favoured than home-brewed ale; and every fourth or fifth person, including children, appears to own a motor-car.

Yet much of what Murdoch Mackenzie wrote of them is still true: they are a hard-working, practical people, with a native kindliness, an inborn sturdiness, a sober intelligence, and lively minds more open to the world and the many winds of change than is commonly the case in rural areas. They are still devoted to the land, but increasingly ready to alter the habits of their agriculture to meet contemporary fashion or demand. They have begun to explore and exploit the resources of their neighbouring sea, which for many years they had neglected. Their schooling is shrewdly based on the knowledge that good schooling in the recent past has produced a respectable quota of university teachers; and university teachers not only bring credit to their native soil, but may live agreeable lives. In Kirkwall there flourish musical and dramatic societies that offer imaginative entertainment on a high level of achievement; and a weekly newspaper, *The Orcadian*, is edited with a modern verve and skill that very cleverly present the matter of Orkney—its daily life and work—as necessary reading. *The Orcadian* pays scant attention to news from London or foreign parts, but never fails to report, in a very well-informed column, the seasonal activities of the innumerable birds that frequent its cliffs, and the arrival or departure of some rare migrant. A visiting film actress would not escape attention, but a hoopoe or honey-buzzard, a spoonbill or a little stint, would be more assured of a respectful paragraph.

Reading, indeed—the reading of more than newspapers—appears to be recognized as a real necessity, and one of the most remarkable features of Orkney life today is the County Library in Kirkwall and the service it provides throughout the Mainland and in the outer isles.

In 1963 the number of registered readers using the Library service was 8,366, or nearly 45 per cent of the population; the national average being about 30 per cent. Orkney claims, with apparent justification, to be the best-read and most "library-conscious" county in Scotland. This distinction has been achieved by the high intelligence and imaginative energy of the County Librarian, who has created, as the centre of his traffic, a singularly attractive and most enlightened display of books of many kinds: contemporary books, judiciously chosen, and children's books, brightly attractive; an excellent Reference Room and an astonishing collection, in the Orkney Room, of about 5,000 books and pamphlets of local interest; with a Muniment collection that contains more original documents than any other library in Scotland. But the Librarian has also recognized that—as in the whole trade of the world—distribution is all-important; and he has devised means of distribution that serve the whole archipelago.

Small cargoes of books go regularly to the outer isles, and in North Ronaldsay, Rousay, Egilsay and Wyre the numbers of families enrolled as readers, and library customers, is respectively 91 per cent, 84 per cent, 79 per cent, and 83 per cent of all their small population. The Mainland is served by motor-transport: a travelling van—itself a gay advertisement for reading—that either halts in a village to act as a temporary branch library, or in the farther districts goes to the house-door; and in these latter districts 84 per cent of the population are its customers.

Of special importance is the fact that the Librarian has taken great pains to supplement, with a large variety of books, the teaching in country schools, and has persuaded the majority of schoolmasters that a sufficient library-service is essential to their task. Orkney enjoys the popular entertainment of the television screen, but television has not ousted reading; and this is right and proper—but none the less notable—in the islands which saw the first public library in Scotland: the Bibliotheck of Kirkwall, founded by William Baikie of Holland in Stronsay, nearly 300 years ago.

Reference was made to that room in the Library which holds some 5,000 books and pamphlets of local interest; and the bibliography of Orkney is indeed astonishing. The absence of anything that can be called a local culture must be admitted, but history and geography are both to be blamed for that: the old Norse tongue died out under Scottish influence—the Orkney "Norn" survived fragmentarily until the eighteenth century—and in the destitution that followed the Stewart Earls there was no energy surplus to that needed for self-preservation. Bishop Bjarni had no successor until recent times, and then, in the small island of Wyre of which he was a native, a humble house gave birth to Edwin Muir, a poet of austere and lonely genius—and of classical accomplishment—than whom no one in Britain, in the present century, has used with a more consistent familiarity the high thought and native tongue of poetry. Yeats and MacDiarmid may be more brilliant, and usually more astonishing; but the mind of Muir lived always in the purity of his thought, and his expression was calmly competent for the isolation of his thought.

Edwin Muir was born in the late 1880s, and a school-contemporary of his in Kirkwall was Stanley Cursiter, now the Queen's Limner in Scotland. Cursiter is well known as an accomplished portrait-painter, but more properly deserves to be remembered as the man who discovered colour in the Orkney landscape. For some considerable time, of course, Scottish painters have not only revelled in colour, but shown a native mastery in its handling; Cursiter, however, in his paintings of the Orkney scene—especially of its rock-bound coast and adjacent seas—surprised even his fellow-artists by the sun-lit brilliance of his canvases. His depictions were true—true to fact—for the dominating influence of the Orkney landscape is light, and brilliance is characteristic of it. But to reveal that characteristic, in an archipelago commonly regarded as grim, storm-bound, and boreally dark, required courage as well as talent; and to Stanley Cursiter all Orkneymen are infinitely indebted for his bold assertion of an intrinsic truth and a prime cause of native happiness.

Now these two were not alone in what may be called, in minimal type, the Orkney renascence. Older than they, but approximately of the same generation, was Storer Clouston—whom I have quoted once or twice—and he, of another old Orkney family, devoted himself to the history of the Earldom, and in a manner that seems to have preceded a current fashion in history, concentrated his attention on its material background: on land-tenure, on the individual ownership of land and the changes that occurred under changing authority, on law and its application, and the migration of authority. He was a dedicated scholar, a self-taught scholar though he had some apprenticeship at Oxford, and his *History of Orkney*, locally published in 1932, is the most valuable addition to our knowledge of the islands since the writing-down, in Iceland, of the Earls' Saga.

Auxiliary to him is Hugh Marwick, born in 1881, sometime Director of Education in Orkney, but more permanently memorable for his studies of the Orkney Norn, of Orkney place-names, and of the merchant-lairds who dominated island-life in the seventeenth and eighteenth centuries. He is another dedicated scholar whose work has enlarged knowledge and added to that enjoyment of a heritage which knowledge of it bestows.

Muir and Cursiter, Clouston and Marwick—to these four the Orkney renascence owes much, and its literary expression has not died with Muir. A much younger poet, George Mackay Brown, has lately shown a fine capacity for transferring very striking visual images to verse; and Robert Rendall, older than he, has with a charming idiosyncrasy added to a more traditional versification a singular skill in conchology. The production of intellect, however, and much more so the production of creative intellect, is utterly incalculable: a genius may be born tomorrow, or there may be no appreciable talent for another hundred years. What can, to some extent, be assessed, is the agricultural strength of the islands, on which their material revival was founded, and on which their material welfare must depend in the foreseeable future.

What worries the social analyst—or anyone, indeed, who feels a friendly concern for Orkney and its future—is their progressive depopulation and the drift of people from the north isles. Elsewhere I have said that recent depopulation in Orkney is a symptom, not of want, but of prosperity; and at this moment of writing, in June, 1964, I have found confirmation of that in a letter written to *The Orcadian* by the Vice-Convener of the County Council.

He analyses both the changes in population, and the productivity, of the North Isles over ten years from 1951 to 1961; and finds that while their population fell by 22 per cent, the value of their exports per person rose by 43.6 per cent.—Modern methods and machinery create human redundancy, but enrich the necessary residue: that is what emerges. So the question arises: Can Orkney, against the competitive attractions of the more crowded and more animated south, retain the residue necessary to use and exploit its natural wealth, and provide a breeding stock sufficiently varied to beget and bear successors of the sturdiness that endured the centuries of leanness, of the intellectual capacity which—once in every few hundred years—can produce a cathedral-building Kol, a Bishop Bjarni, or an Edwin Muir?

That is the Orcadian problem today.

13

The Orkney Landscape: the South Isles

Something has been said in an earlier chapter of the Pentland face of Hoy—of the great rampart of its cliffs that look like a defensive wall—and of this aspect there is not much to be added except a passing lament for the decay of the little, lonely settlement at Rackwick: a stony, dangerous bay some two or three miles east of Rora Head.

Picturesquely situated on steeply sloping fields, its cottages looked down at the fearsome waters of the Pentland Firth, and its people were skilled and daring seamen. I remember, as a very young man, fishing off Rackwick and watching Atlantic rollers break upon the beach, and in their surf, holding a boat head to sea, stood five men intermittently lost to sight behind the spindrift. Seawise and patient, they were waiting, waist-deep in water, for the little interval of calm that will come between great waves and let a boat be launched. I wanted to see the moment in which they thrust and leapt aboard—but a codling took my hook, and when next I looked at the shore, they were safe and rowing strongly out to sea.

They were the last of the Rackwick fishermen of the old sort; who, as well as being mighty men at sea, had a dashing reputation as dancers, in the country style, to fiddle-music. They had six or seven miles to walk to the nearest dance-hall, to the other side of their end of Hoy, opposite the green isle of Graemsay, but they and their women-folk would pack their good clothes and their dancing shoes in a sack, and with the sack over their shoulders walk the rough pass between Cuilags on the one side, 1,400 feet, and Ward Hill on the other, nearer 1,600 feet, and dance till morning; then put on their boots and walk home again.

Such people breed their own sort of stories, and there is a good Rackwick tale—tragical but comic too, and profoundly realistic—

of a man who lost his wife in a great gale of wind that threatened disaster to his only cow, that was tethered in a field as steeply sloping as the roof of a house. His wife went to save it from the storm—pulled up the stake of the tether—and in a wild gust of wind was carried, she and the cow together, over the cliff.

For some months her husband seemed inconsolable, but with the return of spring he walked over to the other side of the island, and took passage in a boat bound for Stromness, where there was a monthly market. That afternoon his parish minister met him, in the long street of Stromness, and for the first time since the previous autumn saw him looking happy. Not merely happy, but exuberant and gay.

"Davy, Davy," said the minister, "what's come over you? I havena seen you look so blithe since you lost your wife."

"I lost my wife and I lost my coo," said Davy, "and I thought the warld had come to an end. But I came to Stromness, and here in Stromness I've got me a younger wife, and a far, far bonnier coo."

But Rackwick and its brave people did not survive prosperity and rising standards of living. The school closed in 1954 for lack of children, and of the fourteen people who, in 1958, occupied the remaining crofts, nine were over the age of sixty-five.

Of the middle parts of Hoy there is little to be said except that they consist of steeply tumbling hills—Ward Hill the highest—and innumerable burns and little lochans. In the rocky glen of Berriedale, inland from the Old Man, there is a luxuriant growth of dwarf birches, rowans, alders and honeysuckle; and there, it is said—but nowhere else in Orkney—grasshoppers can be heard. Deep, almost impenetrable heather covers some of the hill-slopes, and there are broad, sheltered parts where those fierce predators the Great Black-backed gulls nest in large colonies; whose eggs, if they are taken fresh, are almost as good as the gourmet's pleasure, the eggs of the little Black-headed gull. Within this wilderness of steep and sullen hills, in a valley infested by biting midges, under a ribbon of stony cliffs, lies the island's most famous relic of antiquity: the celebrated Dwarfie Stone.

This is a huge block of sandstone—28 feet long by 14 feet broad, and at one end over 6 feet high—in which a passage and two cells have been cut. In the sixteenth century opinion held it to have been carved by a giant, the larger cell being designed to accommodate his pregnant wife; but she must have been a giantess of the most modest sort, for the cell is no more than 5 feet long by 3 feet broad with a height of less than 3 feet. In the more enlightened view of the nineteenth century it was a heathen altar that had been converted into a hermitage by some wandering and solitary recluse. It has as now been identified as a rock-tomb of the Neolithic or early Bronze Age, and unique in Britain; where no other tomb of this sort is known.

Beyond the Stone is the Trowie Glen that leads up, and southward, to the Knap of Trowieglen, a hill some 1,300 feet high. Both, it may be assumed, owe their names to Norse incomers during saga times, for trolls, or *trows*, those sinister creatures, were denizens of Norway; they were of fearsome aspect, savage in temper and immensely strong, and lived in mountains. When the medieval giant who chiselled the stone turned into the Dwarf who gave it his name, is not known; but it can hardly be doubted that, in one or other of his malignant shapes, the Norsemen thought he took his exercise in the Glen. The word still survives in Orkney speech, but *trowie* now implies a wizened, pallid, sickly look: like the complexion, presumably, of someone who used to live underground.

The only road in Hoy—except for the indifferent path to Rackwick—winds along its eastern shore. On this side, in its northern part opposite Graemsay, the island shows a kindlier aspect. Green fields and a few sycamores about the Old Manse are brighter by contrast with the dark hills behind them; but in all this end of Hoy, where at the beginning of the nineteenth century there was a population of about 500, there are fewer than 70 people, and when the road has passed Sea Geo it skirts, for six or seven miles, an empty land. Below it, however, the little cliffs of the White Breast are tenanted by shags or cormorants, and with surprising tolerance a few wrens nest near these ungainly fowl.

Humanity becomes visible again at Mill Bay, and nearby the ghost-town of Lyness and a row of gigantic cylinders sunk into the hillside—storage chambers that once held oil for the Fleet—are an ugly memorial to a gallant Service. It is a thousand pities that when the Admiralty decided to abandon the Flow, it lacked the courtesy to remove or destroy its discarded buildings: they are a hideous eyesore, a blot on the landscape that ought to be expunged.

Along this shore are several burns, large by an Orkney standard, that used to be well-known and respected for the sea-trout they attracted. They were ruined by fuel-oil, spilled from many ships, but may now have recovered; and if so, are worth fishing. The hotel at Longhope would be a suitable base for a fisherman of a pioneering or experimental temper.

Beyond Lyness the road runs down to the north shore of Longhope—"hope" means a bay—and circumscribes the inlet. There is a sailing-club here, and in high summer a regatta. But Longhope is famous for seafaring of a more arduous sort, and the lifeboat stationed here has a record for life-saving and skill at sea—heroism may be taken for granted—that is probably unsurpassed in the British Isles; though the lifeboat crew in Stromness might challenge that assertion. The sea-parish of the Longhope boat includes the eastern end of the Pentland Firth and the menacing coast-line of Hoy; and a parish reaching from Rora Head to the Pentland Skerries turns on a winter night into a wilderness of elemental fury that would daunt all but the stoutest hearts, and defeat all but seamen taught by blood and native aptitude. The Longhope men have wrought miracles in these waters.

The Hope was much used by sailing-ships in an older time, and the Martello towers that guard its entrance are, unlike Lyness, an agreeable memento of the war for which they were designed. It is a quiet and unfrequented bay now, and the mansion-house of Melsetter, that stands among trees at its head, wears a lonely look. This was once the seat of the Moodies, an old Orkney family, but the present imposing house, in one of the most attractive situations in all Orkney, was built by a rich man from the Midlands of England who fell in love with the islands, had the good sense to engage a good architect, and presumably enjoyed his garden and his view until he died.

The southern extremity of Hoy is almost another island. It is called South Walls—North Walls lies on the other side of the Hope—and is joined to its larger neighbour by a very narrow isthmus known as the Ayre. South Walls is fertile, well-farmed land, in vivid contrast with the dark bulk of Hoy, and its southern cliffs have a curiously tormented look: their red, twisted strata seem to be a relic of creation's fearful agony. Kirk Hope, a lesser bay, intrudes into the eastern end of the peninsula, and it was here that Sigurd the Stout, in 995, was caught by that militant Christian Olaf Tryggvisson, and submitted to baptism under pain of death.

Mainland country scene

The lighthouse at Cantick Head, the southern extremity of the bay, may usefully remind one of the light of revelation that so timely came to Sigurd's help.

Lying east of Hoy and Walls, in the waters of the Flow, are the islands of Cava, Rysa Little, Fara, Flotta and its Calf, and Switha. Flotta has a population of about 140, and three people live—or did till quite recently—on Fara. The others are uninhabited, but Cava is used for grazing. Fara, though so precariously tenanted, was formerly in high repute for the richness of its pasture; but good pasture without easy communication is no longer an acceptable reason for habitation. On Switha, at the entrance to the Sound of Hoxa, there are Standing Stones, and the little storm-petrel nests in burrows in its light soil.

Flotta is a low-lying island—hence its name—and during the last war became an armed camp. In 1939 it had an air of engaging simplicity, emphasized by the fact that a couple of large and placid oxen were still used in harness or at the plough. But that aspect of an older world gradually disappeared under gun-platforms and a searchlight-station at Stanger Head, under a rude suburbia of army huts, and finally vanished beneath a great flaunting of barrage balloons. The first balloons blew away before a south-easterly gale, but they were replaced, and from a distance Flotta wore the look of an island vainly striving to become air-borne.

The island is mostly moorland, but there is grazing and fairly good cultivated land. The wartime occupation left good roads and two concrete piers; there is communication with both Kirkwall and Stromness—equidistant at eleven miles or so—on most days of the week, and there are three shops on the island, a primary school, a doctor, but no resident minister. Most of the farms are very small, but lobster-fishing supplements agriculture, and Flotta—though the proportion of old people is too high—retains an air of vitality.

It looks across Hoxa Sound, the southern entrance to the Flow, at South Ronaldsay and Burray, which are now, by virtue of the Churchill Barrier, a long continuation of the East Mainland.

South Ronaldsay is about eight miles long, and on an average three miles broad: a fertile land that nowhere rises so high as 400 feet, though its Ward Hill, south of the waist between Sand Wick and Newark Bay, offers a view of astonishing extent for so modest a height. Beyond the Firth and its stormy islands to Caithness, Hoy lifting to the west, and the Flow lying bright

Stromness

before the Orphir hills: all the southern parts of Orkney, and their neighbours, are seen like a map in high relief.

The east coast, on which low cliffs give way to two or three good white beaches, looks eastward to the vacancy of the North Sea; but the west side invites a backward look into history. At Bardswick Sweyn Asleifsson and the unreliable young Erlend lay in their ships during their little war against Earl Rognvald and young Harald; and were cut off from the rest of Orkney when Rognvald and his fleet came unexpectedly into the broad shelter of Widewall Bay to the north of them. It was then that Sweyn, with the odds against him, rowed west through the Firth, and round Cape Wrath, and came back in winter darkness to take Rognvald by surprise.

In the north-west of the island, where the land comes round in a stiff hook to Hoxa Head, there are the ruins of a broch on the isthmus. It stands on a conspicuous mound which, it is thought, was later used for the burial of Thorfinn Skull-splitter; he, after dying with unexpected passivity in his bed, was "howe laid" here, or somewhere nearby. To the east is St. Margaret's Hope, opening northward into Water Sound, that is so called after an old chapel dedicated to St. Margaret, Malcolm Canmore's queen, and not—as sometimes thought—after Margaret the Maid of Norway, who died either in Orkney or on the voyage, in 1290.

Nearly thirty years before that, in 1263, King Hakon of Norway's great fleet lay here on its disastrous voyage to the Firth of Clyde. This voyage, that was to mark the end of Norse dominion in the Hebrides, brought into Orkney waters the biggest assembly of warships they had ever carried, or were to carry until, in 1914, the Grand Fleet came to Scapa. Hakon had sailed first to Bressay Sound in Shetland, then to Elwick Bay in Shapinsay, and came to the Hope before August 5th; when there was an eclipse of the sun. His own ship, built of oak, dragon-headed and ornamented with gold, was a great vessel of 37 benches; and when the Norwegian fleet entered Scottish waters he had, with Orkney and Hebridean reinforcement, about 120 ships in all. But by then it was late in the year, he was storm-bound in the Firth of Clyde, and though he may be said to have had the better of a little scrambling battle on the beach near Largs, he lost his campaign and had to turn north again without that acknowledgment from the King of Scots, of his title to the Hebrides, for which he had mustered so large a force and so recklessly set sail.

In Orkney again, Hakon let many of his ships sail home to Norway, but he decided to winter in the islands, and in Kirkwall, in the Bishop's Palace, he fell ill and died. He was buried, before Christmas, near the shrine of St. Magnus in the Cathedral, and in April of the following year his coffin was exhumed and carried aboard his dragon-ship for a last stormy voyage—even in death he was unlucky with weather—and a more lasting burial in Bergen. There followed a period of bargaining, of financial arrangement not meant to be honoured, and the Hebrides, detached from their precarious association with Norway, settled down, though far from happily, as part of Scotland; as geography had intended.

Hakon's last voyage is well documented, for his saga was written, within a couple of years of his death, by the Icelander Sturla Thordsson. We know nothing whatever of some extraordinary voyages that must have been made—in heaven knows what sort of boats—some six centuries before King Hakon's day; or perhaps earlier. Nothing, that is, except their purpose, which was to find a home for Christian hermits or missionaries who came presumably from Iona; or possibly from St. Ninian's earlier settlement on the Solway. Evidence of their purpose, and their arrival, is succinctly noted in the *Inventory of Monuments*, where there is a list of the sites of seven vanished chapels in South Ronaldsay: one dedicated to St. Ola, three to St. Colm, one to St. Margaret, one to St. Ninian, and one to St. Andrew. There are, too, the remains of four churches or churchyards: Rood Chapel in Sandwick, and others dedicated to St. Peter, Our Lady, and St. Mary. That some of these are of Celtic origin seems undeniable, and they may commemorate the anonymous priests for whose safety Columba got pledges from King Brude at Inverness; but perhaps they are older still, and South Ronaldsay may, before history took to keeping records, have been well known as a field for missionary enterprise, or much favoured as a kindly refuge for hermits. It may even have been the resort of pilgrims.

In the church of St. Mary at the south end of the island there is a block of whinstone, approximately boat-shaped, of something less than four feet in length and nearly two feet broad. On one side of it are two hollows that resemble, to a credulous eye, the impression of naked feet. A stone on which penitents were forced to stand? That has been suggested, but there is an older and more imaginative legend that declares a man called Gallus, who was in trouble of some sort, put to sea and was then threatened by shipwreck. To avert imminent danger he vowed to build a church, and dedicate it to the Virgin, if he were permitted to reach land in safety. Whereupon the Virgin despatched a sea-beast of some sort—a porpoise, perhaps?—which carried Gallus ashore. Whereupon the porpoise was turned to stone—permanently engraved with its passenger's footprints—and Gallus built a church on the shore of a little loch. That, surely, is a story good enough to attract pilgrims.

That there was a pre-Christian population is attested by such earlier relics as the ruins of brochs and cairns and earth-houses; and it would be strange indeed if so pleasant an island had not found inhabitants in an age of much wandering. It is possible that deeper exploration would bring to the surface much more than as yet has been made visible.

Before leaving South Ronaldsay one should, perhaps, mention the "gloup" that can be found near Halcro Head at the south end of the island. A gloup is in essence a hole, and as such has a morbid fascination that few, among those who go to inspect it, would deny. But not many do go, for it is some distance from a road, and consideration of it will be deferred to the next chapter. There is another, more accessible gloup in the East Mainland, that is of equal interest, not only to the morbid, but to the etymologist.

The adjacent, much smaller island to the north of South Ronaldsay is Burray, shaped something like a caltrop with one spur buried. Burray has a splendid great sandy beach on its east side—three quarters of a mile of bright sand—and the remains of two brochs to guard its north shore. It is a singularly pleasant little island, with a grim story attached to it.

In the seventeenth and eighteenth centuries the Stewarts of Burray were the landed family, whose behaviour sometimes showed an arrogance that even then was considered a little old-fashioned. In 1725 the laird, Sir James, was compelled to flee the country in consequence of loyalty to his brother and a high-handed action on the Broad Street of Kirkwall.—His brother Alexander (or so the story goes) was enjoying an affair with the young wife of a retired naval officer, Captain Moodie of Melsetter; and being rash or careless was one day surprised, in compromising circumstances, by the irate husband, who gave him a severe thrashing. Sir James's pride was as sorely hurt as his brother's back, and when in Kirkwall the two brothers and some of their followers met the Captain on Broad Street, a quarrel began that ended too loudly with a shot; and the Captain lay dying on the causeway. The brothers escaped and fled from Orkney; Alexander is said to have died in exile, but Sir James was pardoned a few years later, and came home again.

In the 1740s there was, in Orkney, a good deal of Jacobite sentiment among the gentry, but most of them were content to express their feelings by drinking to the King over the Water. When, in 1745, the Prince raised his standard at Glenfinnan, and presently stood to battle on the grim field of Culloden, it seems that only one of his Orkney sympathizers had joined him; who was Sir James. Again he escaped, came home to Orkney, and on Burray—though now the story seems too good to be true—was captured by a son of the Captain Moodie whom he had murdered on Broad Street. Sir James died in a London prison, and the people of Burray may have lived more easily thereafter; though perhaps some regretted him. An energetic Victorian traveller in Orkney, J. R. Tudor, who published an admirable account of both archipelagos in 1883, solemnly declares that under these island Stewarts the *droit de seigneur* survived "till a very late date".

Tudor also quotes from two earlier travellers—Wallace and Brand—a curious tale of the occasional appearance of "Finn Men" in Orkney waters. From a description of these Finn Men and their little boats, they must have been Eskimos in their unsinkable kayaks. Wallace reports one as having been seen at the south end of Eday in 1682, another near Westray in 1684; and Brand, who was in Orkney in 1700, says that a year before that two more had been observed by natives of Westray and Stronsay. Wallace adds that "one of their boats which was catched in Orkney was sent from there to Edinburgh and is to be seen in the Physicians Hall", and "there is another of their boats in the Church of Burray". But of the latter boat Tudor could find no trace or record.

Between Burray and the parish of Holm, on the southern side of the East Mainland, are the two islets of Glims Holm and Lamb Holm, now straddled by the Churchill Barrier. It was after the sinking of the *Royal Oak* that Winston Churchill issued his imperative command that the sounds between these islets, and Water Sound between Burray and South Ronaldsay—all the eastern entrances to the Flow—must be permanently closed; and that belated ukase had an unexpected result.

The tide ran swiftly through some of these passages, and the task of blocking an ocean stream of five or six knots was immense. But the order was not to be evaded, and great ingenuity as well as vast industry was put into its execution. Ponderous cubes of concrete were cast and thrown into the seas—such a tonnage of concrete as would have built new pyramids and dwarfed the work of Cheops—and to expedite this labour Italian prisoners of war, of whom there was a ready supply, were imported. They were housed in such comfort as our own soldiers enjoyed, and fed on the same or equivalent rations. But many were devout Catholics, and no provision was made for worship. So they asked and were given permission to make a chapel in a Nissen Hut, and this they did with simple good taste and such agreeable craftsmanship that when the war was over, and the Italian exiles had returned to their own land, their abandoned chapel became—not indeed a place of pilgrimage—but a new attraction that probably drew more visitors than Skarabrae or Maeshowe.

With the years, however, their workmanship began to fade and crumble; and in Orkney, that sober, Presbyterian country, its decay was much deplored. So much deplored that an effort was made to re-discover the prisoners who had decorated the chapel; who were then invited to return and renew their work. They accepted the invitation, and the chapel was restored, with more lasting material, to the bright, ingenuous charm of its first dedication. It stands now, a little monument to piety in exile, that both touches the heart and pleases the eye.

History indeed is full of irony, for of all the many tourists in Orkney who now cross Sir Winston's barrier, the majority use it to go in search of an Italian shrine.

14

The Orkney Landscape: the East Mainland

As the East Mainland is contiguous with the islands of Burray and South Ronaldsay, it is convenient to begin a survey of the whole Mainland from its eastern extremity; which is an irregular quadrilateral of land called Deerness.

Like the parish of South Walls, almost enislanded from the greater bulk of Hoy, the parish of Deerness is very nearly cut off from its neighbours to the west. Its eastern front runs from the Mull Head to the Point of Ayre, a rough exposure of low cliffs about five miles long, broken in the middle by a beach. The Point of Ayre looks south-east to the steep green island of Copinsay, dominated by a lighthouse, and a cluster of holms and skerries on its shoreward side.

The cliff of Copinsay, some 200 feet high, is populous in summer with kittiwakes and common gulls, guillemots, razorbills, and shags; but the farmhouse at the foot of its sloping fields is now empty. It was tenanted till a few years ago, and the farm was accounted a good one, though difficult to work; but isolation was a handicap not to be countered by profit, and the island was abandoned. In the distant years when isolation was valued, there was a chapel on the small, adjacent scrap of land called Corn Holm; and the Horse of Copinsay—a tall, grass-topped, seemingly unapproachable stack north-east of the island—was apparently grazed when grazing was scarce; for there used to be a saying that it would fatten one sheep, feed two, and starve three.

Somewhere off this coast—"under Deerness" or "east of Deerness" says the saga—Thorfinn the Mighty fought a stern battle with the mysterious "King Karl", who may have been King Duncan or his lieutenant. It was a proper Norse sea-fight, with ship laid against ship and the Earl himself leading the attack: "then Earl Thorfinn leaps off his poop forward into the King's ship and lays about him boldly." Karl had eleven ships to Thorfinn's five, but the Orkneymen's onslaught was irresistible, and Karl fled south into the Moray Firth. The circumstances of the battle are so clearly told—how Thorfinn's ships, as he came north over the Pentland Firth, were seen by Karl, though Karl followed unseen—that one regrets again the saga's failure to tell us who King Karl was.

Off the Mull Head, or between the Mull and Tankerness on the other side of Deer Sound, was fought that other battle between Earl Paul and Olvir Rosta—Roaring Oliver of Helmsdale—the issue of which was settled when the Earl's champion, Sweyn Breastrope, hurled a great stone that hit Olvir and knocked him overboard. A mile or two inland from the Mull there is a monument that marks the scene of a very different calamity: the dark conclusion to the miserable battle of Bothwell Brig in 1679. The Government forces under the Duke of Monmouth defeated the rebels—Covenanters, Whigs, or Recusants: call them what you will, they deserve pity, for their own ministers were praying against each other instead of looking to their front—and for five months about a thousand of them were imprisoned in the kirkyard of Greyfriars in Edinburgh; where many died and others signed an undertaking that they would not again resort to arms. But 250 stubborn ones refused to accept terms, and at Leith, in November, were put aboard the ship *Crown* to be shipped either to the Barbados, Jamaica, or Virginia; for accounts vary.

In early December the *Crown* was wrecked at Scarva Taing, on the north shore of Deerness, and most of her complement, of crew and captives, were drowned. In the *Diary of Thomas Brown*, a lawyer in Kirkwall, there is this brief account of the disaster:

"The 10th of Decr. 79, being Wedinsday, at 9 in ye evening or yrabout, the vessell or ship callit ye Croun, qrin was 250 or yrby of ye Quhiggs takin at Bothwall Brigs to have bein sent to Verginy, paroched at or neirby ye Moull Head of Deirnes."—This is sandwiched between a note that on December 1st: "Rot. Richan depairted this lyfe"; and another that on the 23rd a son of Murdoch Mackenzie, Bishop of Orkney, married Margaret, eldest sister of Robert Stewart of Newark. There is no further mention of the wreck, nor of survivors, though it is clear from his pages that Thomas Brown had little news to record.

When the story came to be written by Robert Wodrow, "the faithful and glorious author of the History of the Sufferings of the

Church of Scotland"—who was born in the year of the wreck—it acquired a more sinister look. Compelled by rough weather to seek shelter, says the pious Wodrow, "they came pretty near the shore, and cast anchor: the prisoners, fearing what came to pass, intreated to be set ashore and sent to what prison the master pleased: but that could not be granted. Instead of this, the captain, who, by the way, I am told was a papist, caused chain and lock on all the hatches."—When the anchor-cable parted, the vessel struck, whereupon the crew cut down the mast, which gave them a bridge to the shore, and despite the efforts of the crew to prevent their escape, some forty or fifty of the prisoners saved themselves on pieces of board. Such is Wodrow's story, and little conviction does it carry. The Covenanters and their apologists were early experts in propaganda. But the monument which now at Scarva Taing commemorates the wreck, does commemorate the death of some unhappy creatures, though it proves neither the villainy of the captain nor the malignancy of those who chartered the *Crown*: a genial addition to the story suggests that she was never meant to reach her destination in the Barbados, Jamaica, or Virginia.

Of ancient buildings in Deerness the most famous—though little now remains of it—was a chapel not far from the Mull: a place of pilgrimage until the end of the seventeenth century. A mysterious sixteenth-century writer, known only as "Jo. Ben", says that in his time it was a famous resort for male pilgrims of all ages, who would walk barefoot round the chapel, throwing stones and water behind them and uttering invocations. In this curious exercise there may be Christian symbolism, or the degenerate memory of some pagan ritual. It is to Jo. Ben that we owe preservation of the South Ronaldsay legend of Gallus and the stone porpoise.

Elsewhere in the parish are the remains of a couple of brochs, but the "gloup" that I mentioned in the previous chapter has a larger attraction. It is to be found about a mile north of the old parish church at the beach of Sandwick. The cliffs beyond the beach are some 70 feet high, and running inland from them is a fault, a narrow cavern about 150 yards long. Over its inner half the roof has fallen in, to expose a chasm into which the sea comes surging with foam and fury, and with a reverberating growl—or so it sounds—of wrath and indignation at being so confined. A very pretty scene, and as nicely calculated as its fellow-gloup in South Ronaldsay to stir a morbid fancy. But how did it get its strange name? The etymologist cannot tell us, but an attentive ear will give the answer that its origin is pure onomatopoeia, the forming of a name from the sound that the thing makes. For every now and then, as the surge of the sea returns, it sucks from an emptied hollow in the rock a sort of cavernous and reverberating sigh or protest. "Gloup," says the sea, and echo answers "Gloup!"

A pleasing, well-tended, well-cropped corner of Orkney is the parish of Deerness, and the road by which one approaches it—or, in this narrative, leaves it behind—traverses a narrow isthmus marked by a great mound which is the overgrown broch of Dingieshowe. North of the road is a round, almost enclosed, shallow incursion of the sea called St. Peter's Pool, which, when the tide is ebbing, exposes a great stretch of sand that in the proper seasons attracts a multitude of wading birds. Ring-plover and dunlin, oyster-catchers and redshank are common; as, on the enclosing shores, may be curlew and whimbrel. Waders are notoriously difficult to distinguish, but a good pair of field-glasses may be able to show, at the proper time of year, knots, godwits, turnstones, and perhaps a greenshank. To Deer Sound, opening to the sea, come many duck in the back-end of the year.

The bulk of the East Mainland—to which Deerness is an appendage—is traversed by two divergent roads from Kirkwall, the one leading through Dingieshowe to the appendage, the other to the pleasant village of St. Mary's in the parish of Holm; which, despite its spelling, has the homely pronunciation of *Ham*, and signifies a haven. During the second Great War the parish was dominated by a complex structure of tall, cloud-reaching, steel masts and wiry filaments that rose from Nether Button to create—a mysterious and closely guarded novelty in those days—a radar station that transmitted news of military urgency; and Nether Button today is still a site of prime importance, for from it rise a pair of masts that transmit the television programme of the British Broadcasting Corporation. All the inanities, the glimpse of far-off tragedy and glance at occasional profundities, which make up modern entertainment, are here captured and purveyed to Orkney; and as though to insist on the irony of history, the mast is also a landmark for the wreck of the battleship *Royal Oak*, that lies under the low cliffs of Deepdale, not far away.

Some years ago there was a proposal to raise the old ship, presumably with the intention of selling it for scrap metal.—The

German High Seas Fleet, scuttled in 1919, was raised with great ingenuity and sold with profit before 1939.—But Orcadian sentiment was aroused, and so loud was the indignant protest against the impiety of disturbing the graveyard of 800 sailors, that the proposal was dropped or withdrawn, and the *Royal Oak* remains. There are many in the islands who remember the horror with which news of her loss was received, and the strange, unnerving vacancy of the anchorage where she had lain. Most of those who escaped owe their lives to a drifter that was alongside the battleship when she was struck. Hurriedly awakened sailors clambered down or tumbled into her, and the drifter did not pull away till she was in danger of sinking too. A few men managed to swim ashore through the oil-thickened sea, but the majority of her crew went down with the doomed ship.

The seaward side of Holm wears a gentle look, and most of its land is kindly. The state and nature of its agriculture are fairly typical of conditions elsewhere on the Mainland, though the land, on the whole, is a little better than the average. There are—or were till quite recently—a few small holdings of less than 10 acres, and one large farm of more than 1,000 acres. The great majority of farms vary between 20 and 100 acres, and the pattern of agriculture is dominated by a family's capacity for work and a six-year rotation. With modern machinery to help them, a man and his wife and an able son can work a 40-acre farm, and their land will produce oats, turnips, hay, potatoes, grazing grass and perhaps some of the coarse sort of barley called bere. Bere was formerly a crop of major importance, but little is grown now, and the acreage under turnips has also decreased as more silage has been made.

The principal purpose of farming is the rearing of black cattle—either Aberdeen-Angus or Aberdeen-Angus crossed with Shorthorn—and the crops produced are used to feed the cattle; very little crop is sold. The over-all quality of the beef cattle reared is hardly so good as it used to be, because some years ago it was discovered that dairy farming had become profitable, and on the Mainland there are now more than 100 dairy-farms whose stalls are filled with Ayrshire cows. The dairy cows are served by Aberdeen-Angus bulls, the calves they drop are black and not easily distinguished from the pure-bred Aberdeen-Angus—but their beef is inferior.*

The numbers of livestock that the ground carries have shown

*There is now a great variety of cattle breeds in Orkney.

greater changes than the human population, and in general, of course, have increased. In 1939 there were, in the East Mainland, some 7,500 cattle and about 14,500 sheep; twenty years later the numbers were more than 10,000 cattle but only 12,000 sheep. The number of horses had fallen from 1,150 to 160—such was the victory of mechanization—but pigs had increased from 370 to 1,600. And over the whole Mainland the census of poultry had risen from 343,000 to 431,000; poultry-farming has brought a very large income into Orkney, but its profits fluctuate. In general, agricultural figures have shown that fewer people are growing better crops and rearing more beasts; but in that process the countryside has lost much that used to please the eye. The picture of a pair of good Clydesdale horses straining at the plough, and gulls white against a wintry sky gathering on the opened furrows, was a nobler sight than even the most efficient tractor can offer; and the old autumn scene, when half the country was coloured by golden stooks standing on a golden stubble, has vanished quite. A modern harvest goes at factory speed, and the year has lost a season.

The northern part of the East Mainland pushes out two peninsulas divided by Inganess Bay, which opens into the Sound of Shapinsay. On the right of the bay are the lands of Tankerness, diversified by a loch and much agreeable coastwise scenery, and at the head of the bay is Orkney's new port, the Grimsetter aerodrome. British European Airways serve it with their customary efficiency, and have removed from island life the last disability of isolation—except, unhappily, the additional costs of freight and travel. But in aeronautical history a farm called Wideford, a few miles nearer Kirkwall, is of more interest; for there, in 1932, on a field of modest size, was inaugurated Orkney's first air service, and the first regular internal air service in Britain.

It was started by a remarkable man called Captain Fresson; lately dead. He flew, in those early days, without any of the modern aids to safety and navigation, but maintained his service without accident or failure, and introduced an inter-island service which BEA has not continued. Fresson was a true pioneer, gifted with hardihood and genius, and the revolution in locomotion that he introduced was the more dramatic because, in his time, many of the Orkney people had never travelled by train: they stepped down from a horse-and-trap and climbed straight into one of Fresson's little aeroplanes. He employed several pilots as the business grew and prospered, but it was always rewarding to be flown by Fresson himself; once, I remember, when with several hundredweights of mail I was his only passenger, he flew at cliff-top height along the rugged coast of Caithness in order to count the nesting fulmars. The excellent service provided by BEA* never offers such incidental interest.

Before leaving the East Mainland it is seemly to record that it contains one of the few small wooded areas in Orkney. This is situated at Berstane House above the west side of Inganess Bay, and is only a little copse of rather tenuous, wind-shaped trees; but trees in Orkney have the distinction of rarity, and the bright blue bay, closed on one side by the Head of Holland, on the other by Yinstay Head, is all the better for its unusual decoration.

*Now British Airways.

15

The Orkney Landscape: Kirkwall

In an early chapter I wrote that one of Orkney's characteristic and distinguishing features was its architecture, and the variety of its architecture ranges from the late Stone Age—with Maeshowe for its masterpiece and Skarabrae for its most engaging exhibit—to that surprising Romanesque creation of the heroic or saga age, St. Magnus Cathedral. On another line of country it reaches from the Dwarfie Stone, which is unique if not commodious, to a pair of truly astonishing buildings of the sixteenth century—stark and warlike Noltland Castle on the island of Westray, and the utterly different, wholly charming ruin of the Earl's Palace in Kirkwall. And a third line is possible, from such a simple dwelling as Nether Benzieclett in Sandwick—such a house as John Firth describes in his *Reminiscences of an Orkney Parish*—to the massive domestic dignity of Tankerness House, and the Victorian extravagance, so typical of its time but so unexpected in Orkney, of Balfour Castle in Shapinsay. As is right and proper, the major pieces of this wide assortment of differing styles stand in Kirkwall, the islands' capital

Now Kirkwall is a modern town. That is to say, its people enjoy all the usual facilities of modern life, and its shops offer them and their visitors all the customary goods, clothing, furnishing and furbishing, confectionery, natural produce and commercial products of other modern towns. Its governing purpose is commerce, its common hope is of profit. But its several busy streets and all its domestic parts are dominated by a trio of buildings, of no economic value, that were built, or re-built, in bygone ages when life, on the whole, was very poorly furnished, but the minds of men—or of a dominant few—were naturally at home with grandiose imaginings and innocent of the calculations of profit.

Chief of these buildings is the Cathedral, founded in 1137 by the grace, genius, and imagination of Earl Rognvald's father Kol, and built by the Earl's bounty and Durham masons. A cruciform church, about 230 feet long by approximately 100 feet across the transepts, it is small in comparison with other and better-known cathedrals, but from the inside appears to be much bigger than it is; and this impression of magnitude is the consequence of the comparatively great height of the nave and choir, and the admirable proportions of the whole. From the west door one enters, as it seems, a tall magnificence of great strength—the seven columns on each side of the nave are round and massive—and a severity that is curiously tempered by the rose-red colour of the stone, for the walls and the columns recede in a rose-tawny gloom, and soar to lighter hues and the sky's illumination of the clerestory.

The arches of the arcade are semi-circular, as are the arches of the triforium, but above them the arches of the clerestory are pointed; and if, from midway in the nave, you look up, that ponderous elevation of stone takes on, or is seen to possess, a quality of spiritual elevation that is strangely congruous with the earth-bound solidity of the round sandstone piers on which it is based. For this happiness of design one must be grateful to the art of English masons; and yet it is a very *native* church, for the old rock of Orkney has been shaped with an extraordinary strength and grace to proclaim the glory of God and yet not lose its persistent kinship with the island cliffs.

That the cathedral is a repository of history as well as a place of worship was demonstrated in 1919 when human bones, including a skull, found in a wooden case in the broad pier of the south arcade of the choir, were identified by Professor Robert Reid of Aberdeen University as those of the martyred St. Magnus; and bones previously found in an oak case in the corresponding broad pier in the north arcade were accepted as those of St. Rognvald. The cathedral is a family tomb, a mausoleum for a man of eccentric holiness—but a man whose holiness was strong enough to grasp, as if in his hand, the imagination of his people—and for another man who invited wild adventure on his pilgrimage to Jerusalem, and lived his whole life with courtesy and kindliness and generosity. It is this close association with the two Earls, as well as its manifest origin in the intrinsical geology of Orkney, that makes the cathedral such a genetic assertion of the islands' soil and spirit: of their spirit when, for a very little while, their spirit soared beyond the common mean of life, but of their soil throughout history that has never failed to sustain a hardihood of bone.

When the foundations of the whole church had been laid, the work of building walls and piers began at the east end, and by about the middle of the twelfth century the choir and transepts were complete. It is my guess that some day, when repair or reconstruction is necessary, there will be found in these ancient parts a third entombment, and the coffin of Kol Kali's son—Kol who begat Rognvald and fathered a vision—will be disclosed; for surely Kol said to his son, "Let me be buried in my masterpiece"—and quite surely Rognvald was not the man to refuse so just a request.

However that may be, the Romanesque style of building presently yielded to Transitional, the masons worked westward till about 1180, when the walls had risen as far as the window-tops in the sixth bay west of the transepts. But it was more than 300 years after its foundation when the whole building was finished, with a choir extending beyond the original plan and a west front which, though eminently agreeable to look at, has not the splendour common to the façade of a cathedral: the splendour, it may be, that was envisaged in Kol's spacious mind. The west front, indeed, has been called parochial.

The cathedral was completed only a few years before the islands were pledged to Scotland in lieu of a dowry, and Earl William Sinclair, in 1471, resigned his Earldom to the Crown. It is the second of these transactions which explains the subsequent and highly improbable history of the church.

Pending payment of the dowry, the marriage treaty of 1468 transferred to James III of Scotland the sovereign rights over Orkney previously enjoyed by King Christian of Denmark; the rights of the Earl, which included the tax called skatt, remained with the Earl. From the Scottish point of view the situation was unsatisfactory, for Scotland wanted the islands, and only the Danish lack of 60,000 floorns held them to her. But James III saw how to strengthen his position, and persuaded William Sinclair to exchange the Earldom for a royal property in Fife. The Scottish King thus acquired the Earldom of Orkney with its rights and revenue, and a title that Danish money could not dislodge. He also succeeded in arranging the transfer of the

Site of the old well at Stromness
Grimsetter airport
(overleaf) *Lobster fishing and seaweed drying*

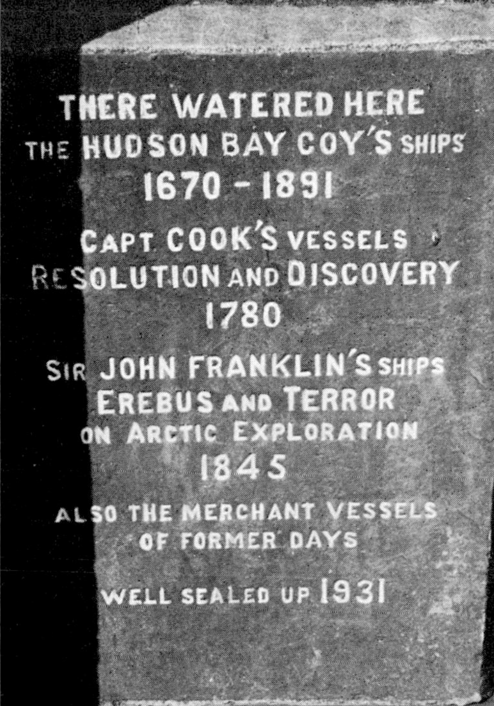
THERE WATERED HERE
THE HUDSON BAY COY'S SHIPS
1670 - 1891
CAPT COOK'S VESSELS
RESOLUTION AND DISCOVERY
1780
SIR JOHN FRANKLIN'S SHIPS
EREBUS AND TERROR
ON ARCTIC EXPLORATION
1845
ALSO THE MERCHANT VESSELS
OF FORMER DAYS
WELL SEALED UP 1931

bishoprics of Orkney, and Sodor and Man, from the metropolitan See of Trondhjem in Norway to St. Andrews in Scotland.

In 1486 James granted the charter of a royal burgh to Kirkwall, with full administrative and judicial privileges, to which he added a considerable gift of land, and—a most astonishing gift to the Magistrates, Council and Community of Kirkwall—the heritable possession of St. Magnus Cathedral, with the schools and lands pertaining to it, in perpetuity. Half a century later a charter of confirmation was signed by James V; and another, in 1661, by Charles II. The Magistrates, Council, and Community of Kirkwall were securely in possession of a unique gift.

What was the King's purpose in so enriching the youngest of his royal burghs? Perhaps, in a recently and insecurely established dominion, still subject in spirit to a foreign power, he hoped to win by bribery the allegiance of his urban subjects. Or he may have distrusted the Bishop of Orkney. From the time of William the Old, the Bishopric had been held—not always indeed, but recurrently—by men of some strength of character and with temporal interests that occasionally rivalled the Earl's. King James may have thought a burghal administration safer than episcopal domination; and he had the power and the right to do what he pleased with the cathedral for the simple reason that it was part of his property as Earl of Orkney, as it had been the private property of Earl Rognvald Kol's son.

In 1560, some seventy years after the town's acquisition of the cathedral, came the Reformation. The last Catholic Bishop of Orkney was Adam Bothwell, who succeeded Robert Reid, a man of outstanding ability. Bothwell preferred discretion to zeal. He let the clergy then in office dispose of their church lands as profitably as they could, and accepted the new dispensation without protest, and the Reformation created no stir in Orkney. When the wicked Lord Robert Stewart came to Orkney, Bothwell exchanged the temporalities of his bishopric for the abbacy of Holyrood; and in 1567 it was he who married Mary, Queen of Scots, to James Hepburn, Earl of Bothwell.

Side by side with the Cathedral—separated only by a climbing road—is the ruin of the Bishop's Palace that once housed the last days of King Hakon Hakonsson of Norway. What the Palace looked like then is unknown, though its principal part may have been a square tower of which the dilapidated remains stood till a

(previous page) *Marwick Head and Kitchener Memorial*
Harvest in West Mainland

century and a half ago. Nothing now visible is certainly older than the latter years of the fifteenth century, though the main block—an oblong measuring some 90 feet by 30—may to some wear the rough aspect of greater antiquity. Its most conspicuous feature is a round tower whose gaping walls still rise through five storeys to a garret; this is a sturdy memorial to good Bishop Reid who built it. Bishop Reid, in the mid-sixteenth century, rebuilt the whole Palace, raising the main block to a height of three storeys with a garret above; but in Edinburgh he left a larger monument, for it was he who, by its initial endowment, founded in the capital the fourth of Scotland's universities.

The ruin of Bishop Reid's Palace looks old and rude and powerful. Its neighbour, a little way uphill from it, is elegant and graceful and would wear—if only it were whole—that timeless look which is the inheritance of true art. This is the creation of the reprehensible Earl Patrick Stewart—"Black Pate" of evil memory—and most signally it stands as evidence to the ability of the worst of men to leave memorials of enduring delight. Black Pate was a monster of iniquity, but a man of taste; and though no one has done more harm to Orkney, no one has endowed it with a more enchanting ruin. Though he had no respect for people, he had an artist's reverence for stone.

The *Inventory of Monuments* describes his Kirkwall Palace as "not only the finest secular building in Orkney, but possibly the most mature and accomplished piece of Renaissance architecture left in Scotland." Its principal glory is the great hall, roofless now, that was warmed by an enormous fireplace whose noble arch is straddled by a cross-bar of keyed stones fourteen feet long; and lighted by great windows—of three tall pointed lights to the south—with broad bays on the east. This is a room of real splendour, that lifts the mind from ordinary levels to the superb and ruthless elevation of an autocrat whose royal blood was quickened by an artist's purpose; and ancillary to that splendour are the graceful turrets propped-out over airy corbelling, while the economy of the great building, and the security its occupants required, can be traced in the huge kitchen with its gigantic fireplace of a domestic sort, and storerooms, guard-rooms, and a somewhat perfunctory system of loopholes for a potential though never seriously considered system of defence.

It is a ruin of quite extraordinary beauty, and our ability to look at it in comfort we owe entirely to the Office of Works, for until forty-odd years ago the precincts of both these ruined palaces were choked with weeds, nettles, rubbish-dumps and debris. We who grumble at Government interference and the ineptitude of Government—often with good reason—must give Government praise when its officials do well for us; and in the last half-century the Office of Works has served us admirably.

What else should be said of Kirkwall? It has, among its ancient buildings, the tallest trees in Orkney, and Tankerness House on Broad Street, facing the west front of the Cathedral, is a domestic building of great charm and interest—its oldest parts dating from the sixteenth century—that may well provoke search for other parts of the old town that modern prosperity has enveloped or destroyed. With its square courtyard and arched gateway, with its armorial panel on the little balcony above, Tankerness House is easily the most impressive remaining testimony to a limited, urban well-being that continued to exist at the centre of the islands' general penury; but elsewhere are other houses, built in the seventeenth and eighteenth centuries, that are proof of a persistent commerce which somehow thrived on rural poverty and maintained a minority of citizens in conditions of some comfort when the substance of Orkney, its agriculture, was in tattered decay. These houses may be found in the Strynd, in Shore Street, in Palace Street, in Bridge Street, and Watergate Street; and are memorials to Scotch enterprise. In the most obstinately rural parts of Orkney, in the north isles and the West Mainland, there lingered till the early years of this century a suspicion of townsfolk and shopkeepers—of their superior cleverness and unfair advantages—that had outlived and was stronger than the distrust, still common in Shetland, of landowners.

Kirkwall has a pleasant little harbour, an enclosed basin at the butt-end of a long pier that points into the expanse of a broad bay, all of which are overlooked by the Kirkwall Hotel; but its waterfront to the east was spoiled, a good many years ago, by the demolition of some houses that, in a northern European fashion, pointed their gable-ends to the sea. Its outward road to the West Mainland passes a land-locked water called the Peerie Sea, which used to be fully tidal and of much greater extent; the Peerie Sea might have been so cherished and managed, by an imaginative town council, as to create a boating-pool and a *piccola marina*, but with base expediency it has been degraded and diminished by the use of its shore as a rubbish-dump.*

*The Peerie Sea has now been rehabilitated for boating and canoeing.

But Kirkwall is an attractive town, and the small domestic charm of some of its old closes and gardens—overshadowed though they are by the grandeur of the Cathedral—should not be ignored. Nor should the view which the Cathedral tower affords, for from its height can be seen much of the lands and islands for which Kirkwall is the metropolis. Due north, at a distance of some few miles, is the little dark hill of Gairsay, where old Sweyn Asleifsson wintered with his eighty men-at-arms; the booty that he brought home was a token of Orkney's earliest industry, other than agriculture, and Kirkwall, in its youngest days, must have owed to him some of the prosperity on which it was built. The recent recurrence and growth of prosperity are brightly demonstrated by Kirkwall's shops; fifty years ago they were very small and modest—they offered for sale little but the necessities of wear and diet and household furnishings—but today they cater, and cater well, for pleasure as well as need.

A mile or two south of the town is the distillery that a Grant from Speyside founded in 1798, and Highland Park produces one of those great malt whiskies that are among Scotland's major contributions to the art and knowledge of life. These unblended, so-called "single" whiskies show great differences, one from another, and Highland Park has an individual essence quite unlike that, for example, of Talisker or Glenlivet. There are some who find in it a slight affinity with Irish whiskey, and certainly it combines, with fine effect, an innate sturdiness with a quality that must be called ethereal; when suitably aged it has a remarkable bouquet.

The great barrels herded together in the vast store-room, or bonded warehouse, of the distillery provoke a sensation of awe that is not altogether remote from the lingering, half-superstitious recognition of power, both spiritual and temporal, that the bold tower of Bishop Reid's Palace re-creates; and if one pauses to think of monetary values—and realizes that only a mile or two away, on the shore of Scapa Bay, there is another distillery—why, there may occur the striking thought that if the total revenue earned by these two distilleries were all enjoyed by Orkney, Orkney could endow, not only its own islands but the neighbouring archipelago of Shetland and the nearest Highlands, with such an income as would give everyone living between the Great Glen and Muckle Flugga a handsome income and generous privilege.

The distilleries of the Scottish islands and Highlands contribute a prodigious sum to the Exchequer, and the old argument that the remoter parts of Scotland do not pay their way is blatant nonsense.

16

The Orkney Landscape: Orphir and Stenness

Between Kirkwall and Stromness lies that part of the West Mainland, roughly quadrilateral in shape, in which are the parishes of Orphir and Stenness, a fraction of the parish of Firth, another fraction of Kirkwall and St. Ola. On the north it is approximately bounded by the main road between the two towns; on the south-east by the waters of Scapa Flow; and on the west by the Bay of Ireland and that rather indeterminate waterway called Clestran Sound, that faces Hoy Sound. Here is the tallest of the Mainland hills, the Ward Hill of Orphir, nearly 900 feet high; east of that a long range of high moorland, the Keely Lang, part of it over 700 feet; and nearer Kirkwall, Wideford Hill of about the same height. The Orphir hills look down to the Flow, the Keely Lang to the Bay of Firth, and the moorland masses are divided by a valley in which are the Kirbister road and the site of the battle of Summerdale in 1529. A glance at the map and inspection of the ground should be enough to persuade anyone that the invading Sinclairs did not choose their battlefield, but by a tactical withdrawal were induced to fight there.

From Kirkwall the road to Orphir leads first to the sands of Scapa Bay, and at this date of writing—the summer of 1964—it seems appropriate to recall the strange appearance of the beach at the beginning of August, 1914: just fifty years ago. On the bright sands lay a great huddle of rather battered furniture: chairs and tables, pianos that looked as if they had suffered hard usage, rolls of carpet, pictures and bookcases—the surplus furniture of the wardrooms and gunrooms of Jellicoe's great fleet that had put to sea—the lesser ships through Hoy Sound, the greater ones by Hoxa—stripped for action. It is often said that in time of war the first casualty is truth; but in the Kaiser's war pianos took precedence.

Beside the Flow the Orphir road marches roughly westward to the pleasant, sandy inlet of Waulkmill Bay on the one side, the loch of Kirbister on the other; and beyond the bay, on a small peninsula, is Smoogro House where the late Storer Clouston lived: a monument to scholarship and local piety. Two or three miles away, beyond the Bay of Swanbister and close to the shore above the little Bay of Orphir, is a more ancient monument to Christian piety and the rude behaviour that, in saga times, co-existed with Christian faith.

This is the sturdy little apse at the east end of the parish church: all that visibly remains of a building, or an association of buildings, that are spoken of, with some detail, in the Orkney saga under the date 1135: "There was at Orphir a large drinking-hall, and there was a door in the south side wall under the east gable, and a magnificent church stood facing the hall door; and one went down steps from the hall to the church."

The apse survives because, apparently, it was too stoutly built to be demolished when the rest of the old church was quarried for stone for a new building; but of the drinking-hall nothing remains other than part of its foundations, including the base of a south wall more than 100 feet long and 4 feet thick. The old church was dedicated to St. Nicholas, and who played host in the drinking-hall, during an eventful Christmas season, was that Earl Paul whom Sweyn Asleifsson later kidnapped on the Rousay shore.—Young Sweyn was his guest, whose father had lately been killed in Caithness, his brother drowned in the Stronsay Firth. Young Sweyn was in no mood for Christmas merriment; and Sweyn Breastrope, the Earl's champion, had neither respect for the season nor any taste for jollity. Sweyn Breastrope sat drinking while the others went to church, and muttered in his cups that "Sweyn must be the death of Sweyn." But young Sweyn was warned of his danger, and when the Earl had gone to evensong he stood near the door of the hall, in a corner where ale-casks were kept, and waited, axe in hand, till Sweyn Breastrope, with a ready sword, came out. But young Sweyn struck first, and killed his man. He fled across the Orphir hills to the Bay of Firth, and later found refuge with Bishop William; but the Earl declared him an outlaw.

The road—the main Orphir road—follows the shore, above the little, almost enclosed Bay of Houton, and turns north to meet the Kirkwall road at the Bridge of Waithe. It is more rewarding, however, to go by way of Scorra Dale, between the Hill of Dale and the Hill of Midland, for this lesser road commands a very fine view over Scapa Flow, to the south, and on the other side of Scorra Dale to the noble, many-coloured prospect of Hoy and its White Breast, and the green island of Graemsay in the throat of Hoy Sound. The Scorra Dale road rejoins the main road to the Bridge of Waithe, and a mile or so short of the bridge another minor road, branching right, can be recommended for the view it offers of the Loch of Stenness.

Stenness is one of the two largest lochs in Orkney—the other is Harray—and is nearly four miles long with a greatest breadth of something less than a mile and a half. As a fishing loch it can be very good; and it can be heart-breaking. It always looks good, its waters seem to promise an unfailing harvest, and its fish, when they yield themselves, are of admirable quality: coral-pink and firm of flesh, golden bellied, and stubborn, lively fighters. The largest brown trout on record, a monster of 29 pounds, was caught here, many years ago, on a night-line. But the loch empties into the sea at the Bridge of Waithe, and with the help of high tides the sea can pour into the loch. There is, I believe, no difference but of habitat between the sea-trout and brown trout, and that old favourite on the menu-card, the "salmon trout", is any fish whose flesh is a perceptible pink. But habitat has a profound influence on some fish, and though the sea-trout makes itself immediately at home in fresh water—appears, indeed, to become blissfully intoxicated in fresh water—the brown trout is sickened or bedazed by salt water, and lies sulking or inert. For this reason the loch of Stenness, or much of it, may be dumbly unresponsive; but because it is so big, its recurrent sullenness need not affect its whole area. At its far end, at Voy, there may be rising fish though nothing shows near Waithe; and at Voy, where the loch narrows, it is possible to wade and cover good water. A fisherman, indeed, should always take thigh-boots to Orkney, for often there is so much wind as to make boating uncomfortable, if not impossible, but a booted fisherman can usually find a shore sufficiently sheltered to let him wade and cast.

To complete the circuit of Stenness and Orphir one rejoins the Kirkwall road near the Standing Stones Hotel, and a mile or two farther on, by the mill of Tormiston, the upturned green pudding-basin of Maeshowe shows itself at a little distance north of the road. There is a description of Maeshowe in an earlier chapter, and now, when the tumulus and its environment are both visible, something of its recorded history may be added. Much of its known history lies in some two dozen runes inscribed on its walls, and what they tell is of no importance whatever; but they throw a little light on the habits and nature of those viking folk who, in a general apprehension, lived lives so starkly different from ours. They were not, however, entirely different. They liked to write their names on walls.

One of the inscriptions reads: "The pilgrims to Jerusalem broke into Orkahowe"—Orkahowe was the Norse name for Maeshowe: the howe of the Orc, of the People of the Boar, of whom Pytheas spoke in 330 B.C.—and Earl Rognvald and some of his cheerful pilgrims returned to Orkney near the end of 1153. But howe-breaking was a popular adventure, and one cannot believe that Maeshowe was undisturbed till then. From other inscriptions, indeed, it appears that Maeshowe was used for more purposes than burial. There is one that reads: "Thorny was bedded; Helgi says so." And another: "Ingigerd is the best of them all." While a passing philosopher wrote: "Many a woman, for all her airs and dignity, has had to stoop to get in here."

A few years ago that most distinguished of Icelandic scholars, Professor Sigurdur Nordal, came here with Hermann Palsson, of Edinburgh University, and the brilliant young journalist Magnus Magnusson; they deciphered the longest of the inscriptions, a four-line stanza, and produced, as Magnusson reports it, the translation: "These runes were incised by the best runester in the west, using the axe that Gauk Thrandilsson once owned in the south of Iceland." But their scholarship went farther than that, for Palsson remembered that Gauk had been killed by a man called Asgrim—the story is told in Njal's Saga—whose son, Thorhall Asgrimsson, lived at Byskupstunga in Iceland; and, moreover, that Earl Rognvald sailed home from Norway to Orkney in a ship owned by an Icelander, another Thorhall Asgrimsson, who lived where his great-grandfather had lived: at Byskupstunga. Gauk Thrandilsson's axe had been kept in the same family for 150 years, and then left its mark in Maeshowe.

At the beginning of 1153—the year of Earl Rognvald's return—the little civil war between Earl Harald Maddad's son on the one side, Sweyn Asleifsson and the unreliable young Erlend on the other, was still unresolved, and it is related that on January 3rd Sweyn was drinking with his men on Gairsay when suddenly a thought struck him, and rubbing his nose he said, "I have a notion that Earl Harald is now on his way to the Isles." The others thought that unlikely, in so rough a season of the year, but Sweyn was right, and Earl Harald with a hundred men in five small ships already lay off Stromness. Some twenty of them landed, and on the 13th set out for the Bay of Firth, hoping to kill or capture young Erlend; but being overtaken by a snowstorm sought shelter in Maeshowe. There two of Harald's men went mad; and that, as the saga says, "caused them much delay." It was near daybreak before they reached Firth, and Erlend, though he had been drinking ashore all the previous day, had gone aboard ship, and so escaped them.

It is curious that two of Harald's men should have been tormented by supernatural fear when Helgi who bedded Thorny there—and Ingigerd with him who so deeply admired her—were untroubled and unperturbed. Can one suppose that the ghosts of Maeshowe were well disposed to lovers, but hostile to men at war?

One continues on the Kirkwall road—ignoring, on the left, two roads that leads to the northern parishes of Birsay and Harray—and presently one sees, and is gratified by the rarity of the view, the wood of Binscarth. This is much the largest plantation in Orkney, and is now recovering from the great damage done to it by that ferocious gale which, at the end of January, 1952, devastated so many woodlands in Scotland. The house of Binscarth, standing boldly on the hill above, is the home of Robert Scarth*, Orkney's Lord-Lieutenant, who in a happy demonstration of the consanguinity of the two archipelagos is a cousin of Robert Bruce, Lord-Lieutenant of Shetland. Binscarth owes its situation to the foresight of Robert Scarth's grandfather who, before building it, planted flagstaffs in a dozen different places, and having left them exposed to the winds of winter, inspected them in the spring, and found one whose flag was much less tattered than the others. And there, on a site comparatively sheltered, he built his house.

The road now dips downhill through the village of Finstown, where the houses are all trim and well-tended, and whose name is improbably derived from an itinerant Irish soldier called Phin, who settled there in 1822. He built a cottage and established a public-house, the Toddy Hole, where the Pomona Inn now stands. The village grew, and the Post Office new-christened it,

* Died on 18th May 1966

with a simpler spelling. That Phin was a benefactor can hardly be doubted, and from the days of his Toddy Hole comes a pleasant story of the charity and tolerance he fostered.—Two Orkneymen, who lived nearby, had fought in the American Civil War and survived it. One had served on the Northern side, the other with the South. He who had fought in the victorious army received a monthly pension; the other got nothing for his pains. But once a month they met, to drink the Federal pension between them, and always they toasted the name of another man of Orkney descent, that General Cursiter—or Custer, in the simplified, American spelling—who had won fame both in the Civil War and on the frontier, and died in a celebrated "last stand" while fighting the Sioux.

Beyond Finstown the road to Kirkwall becomes two: the older road takes to the moor, the new one clings to the shore, and in their division they embrace Wideford Hill, 740 feet high, on the western and northern slopes of which are good chambered cairns, with an earth-house at Grainbank on the east.

In the Bay of Firth there used to be prolific oyster-beds, and early in this century an attempt was made to enlarge them and increase the bay's fecundity. Experts recommended the introduction of foreign oysters, but the foreigners brought disease to which they and the Orkney natives all succumbed. Oyster-stew was once a local dish—a favoured meal for Saturday night, I have been told—but Sam Weller might have had Orkney in mind when he said that "poverty and oysters go together". It was in 1914 that poverty was banished, and the oysters went with it.

Two small islands decorate the bay: the Holm of Grimbister close to the shore, and Damsay beyond it. The Holm is snugly farmed but has no recorded history, while Damsay is untenanted but in the saga's time was the scene of young Erlend's death during the war that he and Sweyn fought against Earl Rognvald and young Harald. Sweyn had warned him to be on his guard and sleep always aboard ship; but it was Christmas-time and Erlend had little control over his men. They chose to lie ashore in the hall that stood then on Damsay, and Erlend, though he went aboard his ship, that lay nearby, was dead-drunk. He and his following were taken by surprise, though a full moon shone in a cloudless sky, and Erlend was killed. Two nights before Yule his body was found on the Damsay shore: "A spear-shaft was seen sticking out of a heap of sea-weed, and when a search was made, the spear was stuck through the Earl."

It is said that neither rats nor mice can live on Damsay; that there was once a nunnery there, and a chapel dedicated to the Virgin; and that it owes its name to Adamnan, the biographer of St. Columba. But of none of these assertions can I guarantee the truth.

17

The Orkney Landscape: Stromness and its Hinterland

For a survey of the remaining parts of the West Mainland—all that lies north and west of the road from Finstown to the Bridge of Waithe—it seems convenient to make an arbitrary division, and consider first the town of Stromness and the rocky side of the island that lies behind it.

Less than a mile west of the Bridge of Waithe there is a secondary road, leading away from the Loch of Stenness, that rises to a height of some 200 feet and provides a fairly comprehensive view of Stromness and its immediate environment: of the sharply rising ground behind the town, of the two little holms that guard its harbour, of Graemsay grass-green in the sea, and the dark bulk of Hoy beyond.

Stromness has the advantage of a more attractive situation than Kirkwall—of more varied and picturesque surroundings—but whereas Kirkwall is manifestly at the economic centre of the archipelago, Stromness, as clearly, is eccentric; and it is much younger. Stromness appears to have come into being, about the middle of the seventeenth century, as a market town for the West Mainland. "It owes its beginning to the enterprise of younger sons," said Storer Clouston; and as might have been expected, the younger sons quickly earned the hostility of their elders and betters in the royal burgh of Kirkwall. Until 1693 only the freemen and burgesses of a royal burgh were allowed to engage in foreign trade, but in that year the parliament of Scotland—in its last period of life more active than it had previously been—extended the right to lesser burghs on their payment of an agreed tax, and from 1719 to 1743 Stromness shared the privilege of its elder neighbour in return for relieving Kirkwall of a third of the duties paid there. Then it protested, saying that such a proportion was excessive and more than its trade was worth. The dispute was referred to the Convention of Royal Burghs, and from there to the Court of Session, which in 1754 decided that Kirkwall had no right to mulct the village of Stromness of its legitimate profits, and Stromness should be freed of that imposition. The decision was confirmed by the House of Lords in 1758, and the victory won by Stromness ensured a like freedom to all other minor burghs. Near the head of the pier is a drinking-fountain that commemorates the name of Alexander Graham, who led the village in its high-spirited and decisive revolt.

In the eighteenth century Stromness grew not only in consequence of the freedom that Graham had won for it, but because of its geographical situation; and simultaneously opened a drain for the young manhood of Orkney. The town became a last port-of-call for many west-bound ships, especially for whalers on their way to the Davis Straits and ships engaged by the Hudson Bay Company. They put in to Stromness to water and fill their fo'c'sles or the indifferent accommodation reserved for apprentices to the Hudson Bay trade. Eventually these services brought a lot of useful money to the West Mainland, but they resulted in a temporary disproportion of the sexes, and Stromness was often left with an embarrassing superfluity of females.

Near the sound end of the town there is an inscription over a well, where many a good ship watered, that reads: "Site of Login's Well. There watered here the Hudson Bay Company's ships 1670–1891; Capt. Cook's vessels *Resolution* and *Discovery*, 1780; Sir John Franklin's ships *Erebus* and *Terror* on Arctic exploration, 1845; also the Merchant Vessels of Former Days."

The well was sealed in 1931, but its water had sustained much enterprise of an essential sort—especially, perhaps, in the latter years of the Napoleonic War—and brought a great deal of beneficial trade to the town. The revolutionary change, upon the sea, from sail to steam diminished its revenue, but for some years about the turn of the century, and till shortly before 1914, Orkney was a centre of the migrant herring-fishing industry, and Stromness and Whitehall in Stronsay were its two main ports. Stromness flourished, in a rather rowdy way, but in the 1920s, when the herring had gone and motor-cars were coming in, it lost its seafaring customers and much of its landward trade, which was attracted to the larger town. The second war redressed the balance when Stromness became the headquarters of Orkney and

Shetland Defences, and a General's staff occupied the main hotel. Against the infinite harm done to most of Europe by that unnecessary and abominable war must be set—in the smallest of type—a little profit, much needed, that it brought to Stromness and most of the deserving islands of Orkney. But since the war Stromness has again found it difficult to meet the competition of Kirkwall.

What the younger sons who founded it did, for enduring pleasure, was to establish a little town of singular charm. It meanders, it straggles, in a single narrow street under the steep shelter of Brinkie's Brae, that guards it against westerly gales, and on its seaward side many of its houses thrust their gables into the bay and instead of domestic gardens have the privilege of a small pier or jetty. It has one foot in the sea, and all the traffic of its harbour enlivens the windows of its favoured half.

Its street is paved, and in several parts of its mile-long extent it is too narrow for vehicles to pass—so patience and good manners are made compulsory for all who use it—and on its landward or upper side it is broken by neat, engaging, narrow lanes, one of which must commemorate some military adventure and is called the Khyber Pass; while beyond it is a steep road called Hellihole. In recent years there has been some building, at either extremity of the street and on the hill above—where there is a good and commodious school—and for a town whose economy is said to be precarious there appears to be a superfluity of banks.

The head of the pier is a social rendezvous, and the visitor may watch a boat-builder at work without moving more than a yard or two from the main avenue. There is a little museum with a comprehensive collection of Orkney birds, some of the fossils that Hugh Miller found, and pleasant ship-models; throughout the length of the street there are intermittent views of the harbour and boats in movement or bobbing at their buoys. To those who know the mainland of Scotland—especially in its northern half—it may be useful to add that Stromness has, in the most agreeable way, a general atmosphere of the west coast, whereas Kirkwall, by reason of its situation and long association with Fife and Aberdeen, has closer affiliations with the east.

The street, in its southward course, leads to golf links and a terminus called the Point of Ness. There are other links near Kirkwall which are larger and perhaps will give the good golfer a better game; but the Stromness course is scenically preferable and may yield more unpredictable consequences. Once, I remember, I hit a great, emphatic drive there, which in a half-gale of wind went veering away to the right and hit in the ribs a plump sheep; one of several grazing on the adjacent fairway. The sheep was a pregnant ewe and when my ball hit her, she went down on her knees, grunted loudly, and promptly gave birth to a very frisky lamb. So dramatic a conclusion to a mis-hit drive cannot be guaranteed, but, on the whole, the Stromness links are likely to produce more unexpected results than the conservative course at Kirkwall.

From the Point of Ness is visible something of the swirling, circling, Hoy Sound tide—the ponderous great slopes of Hoy magnificent behind it—and past the Ness there is a very attractive shore-side walk past an old cemetery and the Kirk Rocks to the Black Craig. The walker, indeed, may go farther along the cliffs, for some six or seven miles, to Yesnaby and beyond that to the Bay of Skaill. But before essaying so brisk a journey it should be said that the nearer hinterland of Stromness, from Innertown to Outertown, or from Brinkie's Brae to The Loons and high ground overlooking the Loch of Stenness, offers shorter and attractive excursions; and from somewhere above the little town it may be profitable—before turning north—to recall for a moment three good sailors with whom it is associated, and one bad one.

When Captain Cook's ships watered at Login's Well they were on their way home from the Pacific, where their great leader had been murdered. Franklin was on his way to the Arctic, and did not return. It was an Orkneyman, John Rae—himself an explorer—who was the first to bring home news of that disaster. There are three good men—one of them a very great man—and to balance the account is a bad and maladroit person called John Gow, whose father was born in Caithness but settled in Orkney. John Gow became a pirate.

His life of crime apparently began somewhere on the Barbary coast of North Africa, when Gow was second mate in a ship called the *George*, then loading beeswax for Genoa. The captain and three others were murdered, Gow took command, and the *George* was renamed *Revenge*. That was in early November, 1724. Several ships were taken, but brought no great reward, as most were loaded with dried cod from Newfoundland. The coastal

Standing Stones of Stenness
Noltland Castle, Westray

seas of Spain and Portugal had become dangerous, however, and Gow sailed north into home waters. The *Revenge* anchored in Cairston Roads, behind the Holms of Stromness, and a party under the boatswain tried to rob Clestrain House, the home of Sheriff Honeyman on the opposite shore. They were disappointed, but compelled the Sheriff's piper to play them back to their boat. Some unseemly adventures followed, about which accounts differ: according to one story two girls were kidnapped on Cava, and after a few days were sent home again, so loaded with presents that both speedily found husbands; but another story declares that three women were so badly treated that all were disabled and one of them died.

The *Revenge* then sailed north-about to Eday, and got into trouble in the fast tides of Calf Sound. The owner of Carrick House on Eday was an energetic young man called James Fea, who is said to have been a schoolfellow of Gow's. He was cleverer than the pirate, and when an armed party landed, Fea captured them all, and later took Gow prisoner. That was in mid-February, 1725, so Gow's career in piracy was short. He and seven others were hanged at Execution Dock; Gow, indeed, was hanged twice, for at the first attempt the rope broke. He was given time to recover, and forced to mount the ladder again.

In 1814 Walter Scott—not yet Sir Walter—came to Orkney in the Lighthouse yacht, and in Stromness met Bessie Millie, the witch who lived at the top of one of the lanes and sold favouring winds to credulous sailors. It may have been from Bessie herself that he heard the story of Gow, and the conjunction of pirate and witch had an irresistible effect on that fertile mind. The ensuing novel, however, was not one of Scott's happier creations, and one may leave *The Pirate* without further comment, and return to the cliffs.

Beyond Outertown the Black Craig rises to some 360 feet, but north of that the cliffs are of modest height yet constantly agreeable to the eye by reason of their sea-sculptured, ever-changing aspect and the romantic isolation of the lonely stacks that occasionally rise from a foothold lost in foam. A mile or two inland are farmhouses and comfortable fields, but the walker by the cliffs will see, for several miles, no human habitation—no living thing but gulls and perhaps some basking sharks—and the sense of remoteness is pleasantly enhanced by a distant view of Scottish hills. The stack called Yesnaby Castle is very fine, in a

Orkney fishing boat off St. John's Head, Hoy

steeply walled small bay, and hereabout grows—if one can find it—the rare and dainty little plant called *Primula Scottica*. The Broch of Borwick, north of Yesnaby, dominates a sheer-sided promontory, some 90 feet high, under which, to the south, is a little, sandy, reef-bound beach. The seaward part of the broch has fallen away, and outbuildings that once existed have disappeared. But the remains can still be seen of a wall that ran from cliff to cliff; behind which the broch must have stood like a very formidable keep. But what it guarded—what its purpose was—is hard to imagine.

The Bay of Skaill is a great white sandy breach in the west wall. At its southern corner, where the cliffs rise to about 200 feet, there is a natural arch called the Hole of Rowe, and on the nearby edge of the bay is the Stone Age village of Skarabrae. Skaill House stands above it, in a green and comely landscape; its oldest part dates from the first half of the seventeenth century when it was the home of Bishop Graham, one of Orkney's many redoubtable prelates. But much has been added to the original building, and within the last few years the present proprietor has again enlarged his house. This spirited decision to reverse the modern preference for cutting down and reducing big, old houses has had a very happy result, and Skaill House has now an admirably *finished* look, as if the latest addition to it had completed a design long since intended.

Perhaps the best place from which to appreciate this achievement is somewhere on the south side of the Loch of Skaill; or from the loch itself. The loch, however, is one of the very few private waters in Orkney, and though it holds big fish—up to five or six pounds—the fact must be accepted that the angler will have plenty of time to admire the view; for the Skaill trout are reluctant to rise to even the most delicately presented fly.

The long beach of Skaill is one of the most attractive places in the West Mainland, and a consciousness of ancient history deepens the charm of the view. Skarabrae brings the late Stone Age to life, and to the north of the bay, near the parish church, a great treasure was found that lightened the grim stories of the saga times with a glimpse of the splendour that occasionally decorated the more fortunate vikings and their women. It was in 1858 that the Skaill Hoard was found: great silver brooches, neck-rings and arm-rings, and ingots of silver. The treasure weighed 16 pounds, and Anglo-Saxon coins and coins minted in Baghdad—the latest struck in 945—revealed something of the far traffic of those days. Most of the treasure is now in the National Museum of Antiquities.

Northward again, for three or four miles, the cliff leads to Marwick Head, a noble habitation for gulls and guillemots and razorbills, that nest in great numbers and long rows on the ledges of the headland, which here rises to nearly 300 feet. It was here that the cruiser *Hampshire* struck a mine on the evening of the 5th June, 1916, and sank with the loss of nearly all on board. This disaster was regarded as a national calamity—news of it ran like a wave of dismay over Britain—and provoked wild rumour that echoed and re-echoed long after the war was over. Among those drowned was Field-Marshal the Earl Kitchener of Khartoum, Secretary of State for War: a man of whom it could truly be said that he had become a legend in his own lifetime.

Kitchener was on his way to Russia. The Czar had invited him, and his intention was to visit the Russian fronts and give some sorely needed advice. On 4th June he took the night train from London to Thurso, and on the morning of the 5th crossed the Firth in a destroyer. In Scapa Flow he lunched with Jellicoe aboard the *Iron Duke*, and shortly after 4 o'clock boarded the *Hampshire*. The weather was very bad, and Jellicoe suggested that sailing be deferred. But Kitchener preferred to sail at once.

Escorted by two destroyers, the *Hampshire* sailed about 5 o'clock, and took the westward route. About 7 o'clock the destroyers were ordered to return because of the heavy seas, and some forty minutes later, approximately a mile and a half off Marwick Head, the cruiser struck a mine that had been laid on the night of May 28th by the German submarine U. 75. The cruiser sank within fifteen minutes, and there were very few survivors: the exact number is uncertain, but it was commonly said that there were only seven or eight. In Orkney it was strenuously maintained that there might have been many more if local people, who knew the shore, had been allowed to help in the search for survivors. But some perverted regard for "security" forbade all local assistance, and some of the naval rescue teams were late in arriving because they had lost their way or been misdirected.

Many foolish tales were propagated—there were those who said that Kitchener had been deliberately sent to his death, there were others who believed that he was still alive—and the curious reticence of the Admiralty certainly deepened what appeared to be a mystery. The few survivors who had reached the cliffs, a little way south of Marwick, were not allowed to be interrogated by the press, and it was commonly believed that they had been posted, severally and apart, to remote stations to prevent interrogation. A further difficulty was created by the official report of the sinking; which, if my memory is correct, was not published till long after the disaster. It was stated there that the gale which was blowing when the *Hampshire* sailed was north-easterly; but in Orkney it was confidently said to have been north-westerly, and this seems to be substantiated by the fact that the escorting destroyers had to be sent home because of heavy seas. In a north-easterly gale the ships would have been under the lee of the land from the south end of Hoy to the Brough of Birsay. It is, moreover, hard to believe that any survivors would have reached the cliffs if a violent, off-shore wind had been blowing. Admittedly the tides in that vicinity are strange in their behaviour, but I remember seeing a Carley float—a kind of raft—jammed in the rocks a little way south of the Head; and could the tide have carried so light and buoyant a craft against a gale-force wind?

The monument on Marwick Head commemorates the loss of a good ship and a very remarkable man who, though less able than was generally supposed, had captured the imagination and commanded the confidence of the vast majority of people in Britain. If it also commemorates a popular mystery, that is due to official reticence and a misguided respect for security.

18

The Orkney Landscape: the North-West Mainland

To make a circuit of the West Mainland one must leave the Marwick cliffs, rejoin the road, and continue sharply downhill to Birsay: a pleasant little village with a running stream, a great forecourt of sandy links, and the ruins of the palace built by Earl Robert Stewart. A noble building in its time, perhaps 170 feet long by 120 feet broad, it filled three sides of a great courtyard, and had projecting towers at three corners; but now it is so fallen away—much has been removed to build elsewhere—that it is very difficult to reconstruct, in imagination, the splendid rooms that a visiting clergyman called Brand, writing about the year 1700, described as "prettily decored, the Ceiling being all Painted, and that for the most part with Schems holding forth Scripture Histories, as *Noah's Floud*, *Christ's Riding to Jerusalem*, &. And the Scripture is set down beside the Figure: It was inhabited within these 20 years, but is now fast decaying."

Above the main entrance, on the south side, are the initials of Robert, Earl of Orkney, and the date 1574 is inscribed on a window. Above the gate, according to Brand, could be seen the inscription that made Robert suspect of treason: ROBERTUS STEUARTUS FILIUS JACOBI 5ti REX SCOTORUM HOC AEDIFICIUM INSTRUXIT.—A bad Latinist, but not necessarily a traitor: he should have written the genitive *regis* to agree with *Jacobi*, and not the nominative *rex* which agrees with *Robertus*. And his palace was assuredly meant for use, not ornament. There were gun-loops in its walls, and the precincts included a rabbit-warren, a kail-yard, a herb garden and a flower garden, peat-stacks and cornfields, barns and stables, as well as archery butts and a bowling green.

Beyond the Palace one must walk along the shore—above a weedy beach where commonly a pair of shelduck may be seen—to reach the Brough of Birsay: a tidal island, of about 50 acres, to which there is a narrow and partial causeway which disappears before high water. The cliffs and the high sides of the Brough face the sea, and it slopes steeply down to its junction with the Mainland; where there has clearly been a lot of erosion. On it are the ruin of an early medieval chapel, and the extensive remains of a viking settlement.

The chapel, now known as St. Peter's—though its earlier name may have been St. Colm's—dates from about the middle of the twelfth century. The nave, some 30 feet by 15 feet broad, has stone benches along its walls; on either side of the chancel arch is a round cell for an altar; and at the east end—but only approximately pointing to the east—is a tiny, horseshoe-shaped apse. This charming little building stands upon the foundations of a much older Celtic church; and to the north are the remaining walls, or foundations, of a small cloister and the buildings of what was evidently a monastery. The monastic buildings may be of the fourteenth or fifteenth centuries.

By the south wall of the precinct the fragments of a large memorial slab of red sandstone were discovered in 1935; and when pieced together they showed the incised figures of three bare-headed warriors, each carrying a square shield and a spear, and girt with a sword. Above them, on the stone, are the so-called Pictish symbols of the mirror, a V-shaped rod and crescent, an elephant, and an eagle. The stone, now in the National Museum in Edinburgh, is conclusive proof that the earlier chapel dates from the sixth or seventh century.

Between its foundation, and its supersession by the twelfth century chapel, the vikings came and built what seems to have been a village of appreciable size. Below the church and above the eroded shore are the remnant walls of a dozen or more living-rooms—with long, narrow, central hearths and rounded corners—and of store-houses or stables. Higher up the slope are the foundations of yet other houses, and the Brough may at one time have been a strong and well-garrisoned fortress with ramparts along that shoreward edge of the island which the sea has torn down.

Before leaving the island it is well worth while to climb to the height of its slope for the long views that it commands: on the one side all the West Mainland cliffs, with Hoy beyond, on the other the long pale shape of Westray, beautifully graven—if the weather is good—on a pale blue sea; and the cliffs rising to Costa Head. On the east side, in a small geo, there are usually some puffins, gravely absurd and comically pompous behind their painted beaks. But it is advisable to keep an eye on the returning tide.

Of "the splendid minster" that Earl Thorfinn built at the village of Birsay—the church in which he was buried—nothing visible remains, but it seems to have stood near the present parish church. Till the end of the eighteenth century the foundations of what are described as "vast buildings" could be seen in the minister's garden and other nearby gardens. It was here that the body of St. Magnus lay, for some years after his murder, and drew to his grave the sick, the halt, and the blind to seek a cure in his sanctity.

A mile or two inland from the village is the north end of the Loch of Boardhouse: one of the more notable fishing-lochs in Orkney. It is some two miles long with a greatest breadth of rather more than half a mile, and can be very good indeed. Fish of well over a pound in weight are by no means uncommon, and they are stiff and stubborn fighters. All parts of the loch are fishable moreover, and this is a useful provision against the strong breeze that often blows: a sheltered shore is usually to be found, or a boat can be manœuvred into a long drift over open water that is almost as likely to yield a fish as some more favoured position, near a rocky point, that becomes uncomfortable in rough weather. It must be said, however, that Boardhouse has its sullen seasons when no fly in the book will raise a trout; but against this there is the chance—admittedly not much more probable than drawing a winning ticket in the Irish Sweep—of an occasional grilse or salmon.

From Birsay the main road, round the corner of the island, runs roughly parallel with the great cliffs that rise to Costa Head; then dips to meet the north end of the Loch of Swanney, and marches south-east to the village of Evie.

Costa Head can only been seen properly from a boat, or from the island of Rousay; and at sea-level it looms prodigiously dark and severe. It is possible, however—and some may think it rewarding—to walk to the shore, south-east of the hill of Costa, to where a small burn tumbles into the sea and a good rough corner of ledgy rock gives perfect shelter from a south-westerly wind, and a fine view to seaward.

The Loch of Swanney is another good loch, with plenty of

fish weighing better than a pound. There are local fishermen who prefer it above all others. It is dark water, and the fish are darker in hue than those of Boardhouse. The best part of the loch is near its southern end, or about an islet called the Muckle Holm. With a westerly or south-westerly wind blowing, it is possible, in this part of the loch, to wade far out on long rocky fingers, and stormy weather is no deterrent to fishing from this shore; though in a really strong wind the loch can be rough enough to make boating very uncomfortable.

Between Boardhouse and Swanney there is another loch, called Hundland, shallower than the others, and now, I believe, fishing fairly well. Some years ago its fish were poor and dark, and many diseased; but I was told, not long ago, that they have completely recovered.

On its way to Evie the road looks north-eastward over a view of great charm and some magnificence. In Eynhallow Sound, in a roost of the tide—over a large area pointed waves may be dancing in furious abandon—lies the little island of Eynhallow: *Eyin helga*, or holy isle, the Norsemen called it. Its holiness became confused with magical qualities, and it used to be said that neither rats nor mice could live there, and its soil rejected steel. Even more remarkable was its habit—long since cured—of defying geography and vanishing on some inexplicable journey.

Beyond Eynhallow rise the rough brown heights of Rousay above its sea-splashed cliffs; and farther away is the splendid profile of Westray, with its steep Noup Head pointing to the north. The dark parts of Rousay slope down to green fields, and beyond them, shadowy in the distance, are Eday, Stronsay, and a corner of Shapinsay. The sands of Evie are white and smooth, and the tide comes in a pale green flood to cover them. The little bay curves out to the point of Aikerness, on which is the very notable Broch of Gurness, which has been described elsewhere.

This good road continues through the parish of Rendall, into Firth and Finstown again, with distant views of the lesser islands for most of the way; but a coastwise circuit of the West Mainland, rewarding though it is to the eye, ignores much of importance that lies in its inner parts. Most significantly, the parish of Harray.

This is the only inland parish in Orkney, and traditionally the most conservative. It used to be known as the parish of a hundred lairds, and though they were very small lairds they represented something of real importance. It was here that the old odal system of land-tenure endured longer than elsewhere, and the now prevailing pattern of family ownership, on which Orkney's agricultural prosperity was founded, probably owes much to the envied example of the Harray farmers. Eccentric some of them were, and their coastwise neighbours made fun of their supposed simplicity, their apparent ignorance. On a rare visit to the seaside, it is said, a Harray man was surprised and hurt by a crab that seized hold of his big toe. "Let be for let be!" he cried, proclaiming both innocence and benevolent neutrality.

The parish church of Harray stands conspicuously on a hill overlooking the district of Russland, and for nearly thirty years, until the very end of the nineteenth century, the parish minister was a redoubtable Dr. Johnston, who established a very high standard of eccentric behaviour. In his youth he had ministered in Unst, in Shetland; but spent much of the year in Oxford. When he came to Orkney he laboured prodigiously in his parish, was a fluent and powerful preacher, a strict disciplinarian, but yet had time to write interminable letters to the public press and engage in arguments in which he never admitted defeat. He was a scholar, and in 1893 was appointed to the Chair of Divinity and Biblical Criticism in the University of Aberdeen. He proposed to teach there in winter, and minister to his parish in summer. At the General Assembly in 1894 he refused to resign his charge, and at the university his classes erupted in strident pandemonium. But he refused to resign his Chair, and fought against expulsion till he died. His memory was long preserved in ribald anecdote.

But Harray has outlived its old reputation for conservatism and peculiarity, and its farmers are now as progressive as any in Orkney. In the last forty years the hills that rise to the east—hills with such resounding names as the Kame of Corrigall, Hindera Fiold, and the Knowes of Trotty—have, in common with much of the high ground in Orkney, changed astonishingly in appearance as hill-ground has been ploughed and seeded, or brought under crop. Orkney, that used to be a prevailing brown, has grown greener with every decade, and there is a truly impressive demonstration of its husbandry at the annual West Mainland Cattle Show in Dounby: a village that lies at the crossing of the two main roads that traverse the West Mainland. Dounby wears no architectural distinction, but its Show day in August presents every self-respecting farmer with an obligation that he dare not deny. To all who take husbandry and agriculture seriously—and I know of no one who does not—it is a holiday that is still very near to being a holy day.

For the visitor, however—the visitor who carries a fishing-rod—the main importance of Harray lies in its loch. The Harray Loch, largest in the island, is about four and a half miles long, and near its upper part over two miles broad. Except in the middle, where it is fairly deep, navigation is a little difficult, for there are many shoals and small islets: these, and the quality of its trout, make it so good a fishing loch. The average weight of Harray trout is rather less than that of Boardhouse or Swanney, but Harray is less temperamental: there are very few days on which a reasonably active fisherman will not have something to put in his basket.

In the latter years of the last century it was monstrously overfished—by net and night-line and that ingenious contrivance called an otter—and yet never failed to refill its plundered waters. It was fed by many good streams that provided spawning-ground and sheltered nurseries for infant fish. With the advance of agriculture these streams became part of an extensive land-drainage system, and lost their old utility as spawning-grounds. But now the Orkney Trout-fishing Association accepts the responsibility of re-stocking, and this admirable service it has maintained for a good many years without recompense or, indeed, much gratitude from visitors who often know nothing about it; for the Association does not advertise itself.

It could well be less modest, and might even introduce a little discipline. In the Loch of Harray there is no excuse for using thread-line and spinning-reel, and that pernicious little whirlygig should be forbidden. In Stenness, or parts of Stenness, it may be permissible, but Harray is manifestly made for the fly-fisher—though no sensible person will complain of the worm-fisher, who needs real skill to manage his bait.

Harray is such a splendid loch—so attractive to the eye as well as to the fisherman's greed—that it deserves all the care that can be given it. Nowhere else in Orkney is one guided to a hatch of fly, and rising fish, by so gay a hovering and hawking of terns and black-headed gulls as decorate its island-studded waters. Nowhere else does the fisherman row his boat past such a shining fleet of milk-white swans, or pause to listen to the wild call of a red-throated diver. There are thieves as well—sharp-faced mergansers and their too numerous young, sometimes an invading shag from the sea-shore—but they cannot well be prohibited. The spinner and his mechanical toy, however, should be excluded. No one pays anything to fish on Harray—except to hire a boat—but some respect is due to water that yields the prettiest fish imaginable, wild fighters with brilliant sides and golden bellies, whose pink flesh—if decently boiled or baked—is a gourmet's delight.

19

The Orkney Landscape: the North Isles

On a map the North Isles lie like the scattered pieces of a jigsaw puzzle that no one could reassemble: pieces cut by the altogether freakish forces of geology and the pounding sea. Sanday looks like a fossilized, gigantic bat; Westray is a leg and a boot depending from a partial trunk; Stronsay is a dismembered dragon; and North Ronaldsay an inverted question-mark. In their manner of life, in their economy and their disabilities, there is, of course, a general likeness, but the dissimilarity of their appearance does indicate a real difference—sometimes of history, sometimes of circumstance—that gives them, both severally and together, a curious fascination.

Nearest to the Mainland—or to its capital city of Kirkwall—is Shapinsay, a highly cultivated island which, by reason of its proximity and genial quality, has a suburban character: it is part of the Kirkwall neighbourhood, separated only by the lighthouse island of Helliar Holm and a waterway curiously called The String, and related to the royal burgh as Bressay in Shetland is to Lerwick. Elwick Bay, that is almost closed by Helliar Holm, is where King Hakon's unhappy fleet lay for a few days before the old King sailed southward; and Shapinsay has a shallow toe-hold in literary history as the birthplace of the father of Washington Irving. The elder Irving emigrated to America, where he set up as a hardware merchant in New York. His son, born in 1783 and patriotically christened, became famous as the creator of Father Knickerbocker and Rip Van Winkle, and the writer of much else which made him in his time the leading man of American letters, but most of which is now forgotten.

The Shapinsay landscape is dominated by Balfour Castle, that handsome but incongruous piece of Victorian Baronial which has been mentioned elsewhere; and it is agreeable to record that the present owner*—and the owner of land both in Shapinsay and on the Mainland—was formerly an officer in a regiment of Polish Lancers. He came to Orkney soon after the last war, became a farmer in a modest way, and to the pleasure of all who know him prospered. It is a tribute to Orkney's eclecticism that one of its major landowners should be a Polish Lancer.

Between Shapinsay and Rousay, or clinging to the skirts of Rousay, are four smaller islands: Gairsay and Wyre, Eynhallow and Egilsay. Gairsay, that was once the noisy winter-home of Sweyn Asleifsson, now pastures sheep; but the deserted house of Langskaill is still interesting. Towards the end of the seventeenth century the island was bought by Sir William Craigie, sometime tacksman of the Earldom and a wealthy merchant-laird. On a site near the opposite shore of Rendall he rebuilt or enlarged an older house to make a small but imposing mansion that covered three sides of a courtyard, the front of which was closed by a curtain wall topped by a parapet walk and decorated with an armorial shield above the arched doorway. Craigie was a man of power in his time, but after his death his house was neglected and fell into decay, and was in part used as a farm steading. It was repaired and renovated, it had occupants who came and went, and now it stands empty above the short but massive pier which curves into the sea before a dilapidated bowling green.**

The island is a pleasant place with a green forefoot, a sheltered harbour in Millburn Bay, a dependent islet called Sweyn Holm, and a lively population of seals and sea-birds; but it has no easy means of access.

A little way to the north is the island of Wyre, with a population—that has remained fairly constant—of about forty people who appear fairly prosperous and remarkably contented with their lot. All the eight farms have a telephone, all but one are lighted by electricity from their own generators. That one, and the school, use calor gas. The island also now has a good pier.

In a graveyard near the middle of the island is a ruined chapel of the twelfth century, Romanesque and rectangular, and a hundred yards west of it the scanty remains of Cubbie Roo's Castle. Cubbie Roo, or Kolbein Hruga, was a mighty man who came from Norway in the same century as the church was founded, and built, says the saga, "a good stone castle that was a safe stronghold". He built his stronghold on a fair-sized hillock, and

*Tadeus Zawadski died in 1979

**Gairsay now privately owned and house renovated.

what remains, within a still existent defensive ditch, is a square keep, on the native rock, with an interior side of little more than 16 feet and walls that are still some 8 feet high. This, apparently, was the basement or dungeon storey, and the main entrance was by a doorway in the vanished first floor.

The farm buildings of the Bu of Wyre may stand on the site of Cubbie Roo's farmhouse, the boyhood home of Bishop Bjarni. That the island was also the birthplace—several hundred years later—of Edwin Muir, has already been noted. His *Autobiography*, that was first published as *The Story and the Fable*, has a brilliant and very moving description of the almost idyllic life that he remembered there: wholly idyllic, indeed, from the distance of some miserable, later years in a wretchedly poor part of Glasgow.—Cubbie Roo, the learned and lively Bishop, and Edwin Muir: a strangely gifted trio for so small a piece of land.

West and north of Wyre, in the sound between Rousay and the Mainland, is Eynhallow with its legend of magic and a very old roofless church with outbuildings that are probably the remains of a monastery.

"With a roaring roost on every side
Eynhallow stands in the middle of the tide"—

but it is well worth persuading a boatman in Evie to make the little voyage there, for there is a kind of enchantment in the green island that got a name for its holiness, and is now a bird sanctuary. A bird sanctuary, alas, that is undefended against those villainous pirates the Great Black-backed gulls. There used to be a confident little colony of Eider Duck that nested here, and kept their eggs under warm coverlets of eiderdown; but I doubt if any have survived the Black-backs.

The church became a two-storeyed dwelling-house at some time in the sixteenth century, but when the true nature of the building was discovered, there were revealed porch, nave, and chancel; and the *Inventory* gives it a date of about 1200. The adjacent monastery may have been Cistercian—though this is by no means certain—and there is some suggestion in the saga that the sons of the well-to-do went there for education.

Egilsay, on the east of Rousay, is a larger island about three miles long and nearly a mile and a half broad, though it narrows to a point at its south end. It was here that Earl Magnus was murdered, and visible from a great distance is the tall, chimney-like tower of a twelfth-century church that bears his name and stands on nearly the highest ground of the island. It is a very curious church, roofless now, though its walls are almost entire and ventilated by what are called "put-log holes"; which may have been used for scaffolding. Above the chancel there used to be a second storey, and the tower is said to have had originally three storeys above the ground floor. Its diameter at the base is 10 feet within walls 3½ feet thick, it rises to a height of 50 feet—narrowing to a bottle-neck—and may originally have been taller by 15 feet. Church towers of this sort are a feature of early Irish ecclesiastical architecture, and St. Magnus in Egilsay appears to have strayed from its proper context.

It is not the church where the Earl kept his last vigil, though it probably stands on the site of that earlier building. The place where murder was done, now marked by a stone pillar, is a few hundred yards away.

There are not more than 15 occupied houses on the island, with a population of about 50. At the end of the eighteenth century it was 210. Of the 14 farms on Egilsay, 8 are between 50 and 100 acres, 2 between 200 and 300 acres. There is a pier at the west side of the island, from which a metalled road runs to an axial road a mile and a half long. There is a school at the cross-roads. There is no public supply of electricity or water.

In comparison with much of Orkney, Rousay has something of a Highland aspect. Much of it is moorland—only about a fifth of its soil is arable—and the two hill masses that give it bulk rise to the Ward Hill and Kierfea Hill, both about 700 feet, in the north; and to Blotchnie Fiold, over 800 feet, in the south. These high moors are divided by the valley of the Burn of Sourin, running eastward from two lochs, Muckle Water and Peerie Water, to the shore above the sound that separates Rousay from Egilsay.

The ruggedly handsome west coast, exposed to the Atlantic, is uninhabited. The population is grouped on the coastal ground on the south and south-west; on the east shore as far north as Scockness; and to a lesser extent about Wasbister on the north shore. In 1830 the population numbered nearly 1,000; today, a quarter of that. The disability—the discouragement to island life—is twofold: the available acreage of land that can be profitably worked, by present standards, is limited; and though Rousay lies near the Mainland, communication with it is unsatisfactory and the additional freightage of cattle being sent to market in

Aberdeen, for example, is in effect another tax on the farmer. Beef-cattle, sheep, and lobster-fishing give the island its income.

There is a steamer pier at Trumland, facing Wyre, but the use of it is severely restricted by a tidal rise and fall of 10 feet, and though Trumland is only eleven miles from Kirkwall it appears almost impossible to make a return journey in the course of a day. A motor-boat service supplements the island steamer, but cannot carry stock. Within recent years, however, the sailing time-table has been altered more than once, and by now there may be some happier arrangement.

Though Rousay has not yet adapted itself to the demands of tourism, the intending visitor should not be deterred by the difficulty of making his own arrangements, for there is much to repay him for his trouble. The great broch and the splendid chambered cairn at Midhowe on the south-west coast, the cairns at Rowiegar and Taiversö Tuick, the Stone Age village on the Braes of Rinyo under Faraclett Head—these and other relics of antiquity are of superlative interest. But the island is not wholly dependent, for attraction, on its abundant prehistoric remains. There is a ring-road that offers many fine views, and the north-western cliffs, on the way to Sacquoy Head, are very impressive. On the south-west side, overlooking Eynhallow Sound from its sheltered position in a little copse of wind-blown trees, is the old mansion house of Westness, and the shore below it—or somewhere not far from here—is the scene of that dramatic kidnapping at which Sweyn Asleifsson simplified a political scene of some complexity by removing the ruling Earl, Paul the Silent.

Westness was for long the home of a branch of a family called Traill that first came into Orkney with Earl Patrick Stewart, and lived to proliferate, prosper, and dominate much of the islands' life and commerce till fairly recent times. There were Traills of Holland in Papa Westray, of Elsness and Hobbister in Sanday, of Woodwick on the Mainland—as well as those of Westness, and perhaps elsewhere—and their virtual disappearance, after three hundred years of wealth and influence, is a curiosity either of social evolution or genetic failure.

He who succeeded, by marriage, to the house and estate of Westness was a General Burroughs, whose distinguished military career did not help him to become a popular landlord. He found Westness too small for his needs, and in the latter half of the last century built Trumland House in a fine sheltered valley above the

Old Man of Hoy

pier. This tall, imposing building, that commands a superb southward view, later became the property of that gifted distiller, Walter Grant, to whom we are indebted for so much archaeological discovery. He was a generous landlord.

Beyond this anciently populous and now diminishing island lie Stronsay, Eday, and Westray in a roughly diagonal line pointing from the south-east to north-west. Stronsay, the most fertile of the North Isles, consists of three peninsulas divided by three broad bays; St. Catherine's, Mill Bay, and the Bay of Holland. Its several dependent islets include Papa Stronsay to the north-east and Auskerry with its lighthouse to the south.

From the early seventeenth century until the peace which ended in 1914, Stronsay was a fishing centre of constant importance. Dutchmen were the first to exploit it, and in the early years of this century it had become one of the capitals of the industry built on herring. On Papa Stronsay, the isle of early Christian *Papae*, there were five fish-curing stations, and fifteen more at Whitehall, the opposite village. Every year some 1,500 girls and women came to gut herring caught by 300 boats. Merchants and tradesmen set up their shops, and ships were chartered to export the cured and salted herring to Baltic markets. Between the wars the industry revived and flourished again, but there was no significant revival after the second war.

About the end of the eighteenth century agriculture in Stronsay was considered progressive, and the island had some of the largest farms in Orkney. The population was then just 1,000; it is now under 500. But the change in the numbers of livestock is perhaps even more interesting. In 1795 there were—in round numbers—500 horses, 900 cattle, and 3,000 sheep. Numbered again in 1958, horses had dwindled to 40, but cattle had increased to 3,000 and sheep to over 6,000. There were, at that date, 16 farms of more than 100 acres, of which five were larger than 400 acres, and one over 1,000 acres. Here, most certainly, loss of population has been due to prosperity and mechanization, not to poverty; though there is much complaint about freight charges and an indifferent steamer service: a farmer must spend the better part of two days going to market in Kirkwall, and if he has a long memory he can compare the present price of a ticket, which is 16*s*., with the 3*s*. charged in 1914.

Before proceeding to a description, however brief, of the island of Eday, it may be opportune to say something of the nature of

Village of Birsay with Palace ruins on right
Egilsay Church

inter-island voyaging; for Eday lies approximately in the middle of the northern part of the archipelago, and a few hours aboard one or other of the two ships that serve local needs can be illuminating even on a fine summer day. That is to say, the traveller will see something of the tides and intricacies of navigation that characterize the island waters and require a proper degree of seamanship to use them; and with a little imagination he may be able to envisage the difficulties that come with winter gales and the long darkness of winter.

The steamer, or the newer motor-vessel, that leaves Kirkwall for Eday will go close to the east shore of Shapinsay, and through a narrow passage called the Sound of Vasa between the Skerry of Vasa and the land; here, on occasion, may be seen a pretty tidal dance. The ship then turns east round the long, narrow point of The Galt, to cross the Stronsay Firth. She passes the uninhabited Green Holms, and between them and Warness, the southerly point of Eday, there can be great turbulence if the south-going tide through the Fall of Warness should be opposed by a strong southerly wind. The pier of Eday lies on the east side, in the Bay of Backaland; and from there the ship may proceed between the Holms of Spurness—which, says the North Sea Pilot, "should not be approached within a distance of 2 cables"—and the Holm of Huip on her way to Papa Sound—"from the outer extreme of Jacks reef there is a depth of only 13 feet in the fairway"—and the shelter of Whitehall pier in Stronsay.

Between Whitehall and Kettletoft in Sanday there is no difficulty, though in the entrance to Kettletoft Bay "a shoal with a depth of one fathom over its western end lies near the middle"; but from Kettletoft to Papa Westray is a passage in which the sea may show something of its alarming strength and temper: in Calf Sound and Lashy Sound the tide at springs runs like a river at the rate of 6 knots, and by one or other the ship must go to get into the North Sound, which is open to the north. Pierowall in Westray is an excellent safe harbour, but from there the homeward voyage is through the Sound of Fara—a 4-knot tide and Red Holm with its shoals in the middle of the entrance—and so into the Westray Firth, which is regrettably and widely open to the Atlantic.

In summer the island voyager will probably suffer no discomfort; but, on the contrary, will be rewarded with the sight of narrow passages, great cliffs, the changing geography of the archipelago, and its varied landscapes.—Twice a week there is a "round trip" from Kirkwall that, if the glass is high, I warmly recommend.—But he will remember that those who live in Orkney live there throughout the year, and the ships must serve them in January as well as June.

So much for the voyage, and Eday still waits attention.—It is long and narrow, eight miles long and pinched at the waist, a dark and hilly island overladen with peat. A mile or two south-west of its southern tip are the Green Holms where large colonies of shags and cormorants nest in reptilian squalor; and to the north, neighbourly with its imposing Red Head, is the Calf of Eday, closing the fast tides of Calf Sound where the ineffectual pirate Gow came to grief. There are on Eday some 50 farms of less than 100 acres, and 7 large ones; most of them owner-occupied. The population fell from about 300 in 1950 to about 200 in 1960.

In the southern half there are Standing Stones and the remains of several chambered cairns, but the north end is the more attractive. The northern entrance to Calf Sound is flanked, on the west, by the splendidly coloured sandstone rock of the Red Head of Eday, 200 feet high, and on the east by the Grey Head of the Calf. In the sheltered Bay of Carrick, snug beneath the western hills, is Carrick House, where a gateway to a courtyard is inscribed with the date 1633. John Stewart, created Earl of Carrick in 1628, was the second son of Robert Stewart, Earl of Orkney, and received a grant of the island in 1632; in his youth he had been accused of associating with Alysoun Balfour, a witch, for the purpose of poisoning his brother Patrick, who became the architectural Earl. Poor Alysoun was tortured, and John was acquitted.

Half a mile south-west of Carrick House is the chambered cairn of Huntersquoy—or what remains of it—which is unusual in having two contemporary chambers, one above the other, and each with its own entrance. There is another cairn to the east, on Vinquoy Hill, and the very scanty remains of a stalled cairn, north-east of Vinquoy, on the sonorously named Muckle Hill of Linkertaing.

Westray—that island like a leg and a boot and a severed trunk—is in appearance exceptionally attractive, and its inhabitants, who now number about 900, have a distinctive and very hardy sense of humour. Tudor records a story, that he was told, of a much-respected native whose wife died suddenly on the same day as a school of caain' whales came into the bay. With great presence of mind he summoned the undertaker and ordered him, and his two assistants, to begin work at once on a suitable coffin. Having disposed of three who would otherwise have joined the hunt, and shared its profits, he put out to sea and assisted his neighbours in the excitement of driving the whales ashore and their bloody slaughter in the shallows. When in the evening the parish minister reproved him for his callous behaviour, he replied with dignity that he could not afford to lose both whales and a wife on the same day.

A year or two ago, in Pierowall, I was told two stories, better than that, I think, but of the same sort of temper.—The first described a small boy running breathlessly from the barn into the farm-kitchen, where the family are assembled, and exclaiming, "Feyther, feyther! Uncle Cherlie's hanging by a rope frae a cupple i' the barn!"—Cupples are the cross-beams in an open roof.—"Did thoo no' cut him down, boy?" asks the father.

"God, no," says the boy. "I think he's still alive."

The second is shorter, and more drastic; and for its understanding the word *nile* means the plug for the draining-hole in the floor of an open boat.

The scene is the wild coast of the west side. Under the cliffs there are two small boats fishing in a heavy sea, and as the outer one heaves into sight on the crest of a great wave, a voice comes from it down the wind: "Can thoo lend me a nile, boy?"

If, in Westray, a visitor hires a motor-car, he will do well to drive with care, for the native drivers, with aristocratic simplicity, appear to believe their roads are private. They do not behave like General Burroughs in Rousay, who, whether walking or driving a pair of horses, compelled his humble neighbours to get off the road; but they seem to think that strangers should make room for those who have the better claim to it.

These admirable people—hearty, intelligent, hard-working and generous—live in an island which taxes their ingenuity—once again, freights are a curse upon their economy—but which must give much pleasure to their eyes. Great cliffs, white sands, and the strange pattern of their land afford them a natural variety of scenery, and the population is large enough to provide a variety of interests within a prevailing sense of community.

To the usual relics of antiquity can be added viking graves at Pierowall, and others that have again been forgotten. There are the remains of the two old churches of Lady Kirk and Cross Kirk, and in the northern cliffs there is the Gentlemen's Cave where some local lairds, with Jacobitish sympathies, are said to have gone into hiding after the '45. But the historical monument which dwarfs all others, and endows the island, not only with a grandiose and formidable building of exceptional character, but with a mystery that no one as yet has completely solved, is Noltland Castle.

It stands, superbly alone, under the slope of a hill above the pleasant village of Pierowall, and its walls are pierced with so many gun-loops that from one aspect it looks—this has been said before—more like an old ship-of-the-line than a castle. More realistically, perhaps, it looks as if "it was built for a man with a bad conscience—for a man with fear in his heart". That is the judgment of Dr. Douglas Simpson, than whom no one has a larger knowledge of Scottish castles. It was Dr. Simpson who finally resolved a major architectural puzzle in Noltland; but before discussing that, a brief description is necessary.

The main portion is a rectangle, measuring 87 feet by 36 feet, with large square towers projecting from two of the diagonally opposite angles. The gun-loops which pierce its walls are in three or four tiers, and number 61; in the interior are five or six others commanding the entrance. The entrance, at the angle of the south-west tower, leads directly to the main staircase, which is contained in the tower. The ground floor, vaulted throughout, contains store-rooms, a huge kitchen, and a fireplace measuring 17 feet by 9 feet. Two service stairs used to lead to the great hall, which measures 42 feet by 23 feet; and here, on the first floor, there is a small service-room at the west end, opposite one of the minor stairs, and a private room, with a bedroom beyond it, at the other end; the hall and the two rooms all have fireplaces. The walls of the castle are about 7 feet thick, and at the west end rise only a little above the first floor windows; but in the remaining third they are almost intact. The north-eastern tower contains a chamber on each of its five floors. Windows are few and small. The courtyard, on the south side of the castle, is rectangular, with an entrance from the east, and there is a parapet walk on its south wall. Subsidiary buildings, of a later date, may have provided additional accommodation.

Now this great structure is essentially warlike. It was built for defence, in a position well chosen for defence. The large kitchen and store-rooms, under their vaulted roof, are uninterrupted by partition walls; they could serve as a barrack-room or a fighting deck. But the great stair, though it could be defended, is built with splendour and was made for elegance; it is a palace staircase, not a military ladder. Incongruous in appearance with the grim strength of the building, it is also—to the eye of the scholar of such things—a little clumsily fitted-in to what is certainly an earlier structure. He who built the castle was not he who added the great stair.

It used to be thought that Noltland was built by or for James Hepburn, Earl of Bothwell, who by force married Mary, Queen of Scots, and was by her created Duke of Orkney. Confusion may have arisen from the fact that another Bothwell was the Bishop of Orkney, and in 1560, the year of the Reformation, Bishop Adam Bothwell granted to Gilbert Balfour and Margaret his wife—who was the Bishop's sister—a charter of various church lands in Westray which included the Bu of Noltland. In 1567 Gilbert Balfour—Master of the Queen's Household, Sheriff of Orkney, and Captain of Kirkwall Castle—received a grant of all Westray and Papa Westray.

On the evidence of the building itself—of the style and manner of the main part of the building—the date of its construction is the second half of the sixteenth century; and it is now generally accepted that he who built it was indeed Gilbert Balfour. And what is known of him, other than his offices of state?

In February, 1567, Darnley was murdered in the great explosion that demolished the house at Kirk o' Field, in Edinburgh, where he was sleeping. A few days after the murder a placard was nailed to the door of the Tolbooth: it denounced Bothwell, Sir James Balfour, and two others, and added, "If this be not true, speir at Gilbert Balfour." Gilbert and James were brothers; and a third brother, Robert, was Canon of Holyrood and owned the house at Kirk o' Field.

All three brothers had been implicated in the murder of Cardinal Beaton in 1546. Gilbert, for his share in that crime, was condemned to the galleys, and rowed a neighbouring oar with John Knox. After Bothwell's downfall he prudently withdrew to Orkney, where he quarrelled with the Bishop his brother-in-law; and when Bothwell, in flight, appeared in Kirkwall Bay, refused him entry to the Castle—for James his brother had broken with Bothwell.

In a parliament of 1571 Gilbert was found guilty of treason; and Lord Robert Stewart, the Queen's half-brother, took possession of Noltland. Gilbert fled abroad and took service in Sweden. There he joined another set of conspirators in a plot against the King; and was executed in 1576.

That was the man who built Noltland, and though one may agree with Douglas Simpson that it was manifestly made for a man with a bad conscience, his purpose in building it is still not wholly clear. Did he and his brother-in-law, with two strong castles at their command, contemplate positive treason and the assertion of their independence in Orkney? One would dearly like to have overheard some conversation between those three bad Balfours and the time-serving Bishop.

As to the mystery of the splendid stairway, Douglas Simpson has solved that: it was Earl Patrick, Black Pate, who built it. He, with his passion for architecture, added that proud ornament to Gilbert's fortress.

Side by side with the northern peninsula of Westray is its smaller neighbour, Papa Westray: a fertile, attractive island, conspicuously remote, with a population of about 130. The house of Holland, in the middle of the island, was formerly the home of the Traills of Holland, who owned the whole island. At the beginning of the nineteenth century a pair of Great Auks nested here; the female died or was killed, and the male—almost the last of its kind—was shot in 1813. Off the Mull Head, the island's northern extremity, there is a dangerous tide-race called The Bore, and in gale weather the sea breaks even at a depth of 20 fathoms. Between Papa and the Bow Head of Westray there is another race called The Roost.

Something has been said, in another chapter, of the great cairn on the Holm of Papa, and Papa itself houses an equally beguiling puzzle. The little, pre-Reformation church, on the site of an earlier building, is dedicated to St. Boniface; and beside a small loch are the ruins of a chapel dedicated to St. Tredwell. Now Boniface is known as "the apostle of Germany", and Tredwell is said to have been an abbess who, on a mission to Pictland, aroused the passion of Nechtan, King of the Picts, in the early years of the eighth century. The susceptible King was moved especially by the beauty of her eyes; so the virtuous abbess, escaping his clutches, plucked them out, skewered them on a twig of thorn, and sent them to Nechtan to rebuke him for the folly of admiring her physical endowments. She then retired to Midlothian, and acquired her saintly reputation. How her fame, and that of Boniface, were carried to Orkney is not known; but for several hundred years people with failing sight or inflammation of the eyes used to make hopeful pilgrimages to St. Tredwell's Loch.

Sanday is a large island with a population of about 700. Most of it is low-lying, and in dark or misty weather hardly visible from the deck of a ship. In the days of sail there were many wrecks, which were warmly welcomed by the inhabitants. There is no peat on the island, and a wooden ship provided much-needed fuel. Sanday is one of several places in Britain where a legendary parson is reputed to have prayed in some such words as these: "And if it be Thy inscrutable will, O Lord, in this present season of inclement weather, to inflict the doom of total loss upon some poor hapless ship, let Thy mercy direct her to the grateful shores of this kindly and deserving island."

There is, however, nothing dark or sinister in the appearance of Sanday, or in the temper of its people. Its light, sandy soil has always been easily cultivated, and from comparatively early times its rentals were high. It has many miles of long, bright beaches, and if it were more accessible, and the temperature of its surrounding sea some 15 degrees warmer, it might be one of the great holiday resorts of Britain. As it is, its vast foreshore attracts a multitude of wading birds, and its strange configuration—long peninsulas, and several smaller ones, divided by considerable stretches of water—make it a natural sanctuary. I remember once, many years ago, going out with the local doctor to try and shoot golden plover, of which two great flocks were alternately feeding and flitting, with bright wings and melodious piping, from crisp sands to sheep-nibbled grass and back again. We would approach with care, but always some watchful bird would flute a nervous warning, and the flock would rise and fly, in a leisurely fashion, across the nearest bay. We would walk round—a mile, two miles perhaps—and the flock would return to its original beach. We got a lot of exercise, but no plover.

In the eighteenth century the production of kelp was a major industry in Sanday, and in the early nineteenth century its agriculture was the most progressive in Orkney. The collection of seaweed—to be dried and milled—has again become a profitable activity, and not long ago it was calculated that lobster-fishing brought the island an annual income of about £10,000. But farming is, of course, the main occupation, and the majority of farmers are owners of their land. Practically the whole area of the island is under cultivation, and the six-year rotation—a year of oats, a year of turnips and potatoes, a year of oats or barley with a grass undercrop, and three years of grass—means that every year half the arable land is in crop and half in grass. There is a good pier at the village of Kettletoft, and a small hotel in the village. Rainfall is not high, and in summer the island often suffers from a shortage of water.

Of prehistoric activity there are many sites but few remnants. Both brochs and chapels seem to have been numerous, but domestic building and the demands of agriculture have reduced most of them to invisibility. Apart from its thriving farmlands, the natural charm of its immense foreshore is Sanday's most distinctive asset, and it is a little surprising that the Orkney Mainlanders do not make more use of it as holiday-ground.

Two and a half miles north of Tofts Ness in Sanday is the ultimate fragment of Orkney, the island of North Ronaldsay; the Norse name of which was Rinansey, which is Ringan's isle—and Ringan was St. Ninian, whose Candida Casa at Whithorn in Wigtown was founded in the year 400, or thereabout. Columba's missionaries were not the first to carry news of Christianity into the north.

The interval between Sanday and North Ronaldsay is inclined to be unfriendly water. "During the south-east going stream," says the North Sea Pilot, "there is a race between Strom Ness (the southern tip of North Ronaldsay) and Tofts Ness. . . . During westerly gales, and after, breakers will sometimes extend across the firth in depths of from 8 to 12 fathoms."

Across this firth—from Black Rock in Otters Wick in Sanday—the island's mail, and passengers, are carried in an open motor-boat. There is a newly extended pier at the west end of South Bay, at which the inter-island steamer calls once a week unless prevented by bad weather. The truth as well as the sensation of isolation can be fully experienced in North Ronaldsay, and as if to emphasize or proclaim its hardy independence, the island is surrounded by a wall about 6 feet high. The wall serves to keep the island sheep from the cultivated land, and the native sheep are of great interest. They are small, of a rather goat-like shape, variously coloured, with very fine wool, and except at lambing time—when the ewes are allowed in to grassland—they live mainly on seaweed; their flesh is delicious, and they are, quite certainly, the true-bred descendants of the primitive sheep of the northern islands.

The inhabitants of North Ronaldsay number about 160 and, as has been noted in an earlier chapter, they are the County Library's best customers. They are voracious readers. Unlike the majority of Orkney farmers, they are tenants and crofters; their land is light and fertile and easily worked. They use a pronounced and distinctive dialect, and retain, as from a golden age, the fabled virtues of open hospitality and ease of converse. They have a resident doctor and school-teacher, but no minister. Their island, which is some three miles in length by a mile or a mile and a half wide, nowhere rises more than 50 feet above sea-level. It has been continuously occupied since prehistoric times.

At the southern end of the island is Burrian Broch, with a remnant of walls as thick as 15 feet, and on the landward side four concentric ramparts. Many relics were found in the broch—bone pins and needles, combs and weaving-combs and pottery—of which the most interesting were an oblong sandstone pebble and the phalangeal bone of an ox, both inscribed with the Pictish symbols of the crescent and V-shaped rod, and the mirror.

At Stennabreck, near the south end of Linklet Bay, there is a very odd, irregular ruin, which appears to have been a primitive house of a sort otherwise unknown; and at Kirbist on South Bay there are the remains of what may have been a village of the Skarabrae kind. Near Holland House there is a Standing Stone over 13 feet high, pierced by a hole, and the author of the Old Statistical Account, published in 1793, records having seen "50 of the inhabitants assembled there on the first day of the year, and dancing with moon light, with no other music than their own singing."

There is a curious difference between this, the northernmost part of Orkney, and the northern extremity of Shetland. North Ronaldsay, in the midst of its burly tides, is a quiet and seemly place, girdled by a wall and genial in its isolation; but Muckle Flugga at the farthest tip of Shetland is fierce of aspect, almost unpeopled, and dramatic—theatrical, indeed—in its assertion of loneliness. But despite this and other differences there is a social and economic likeness—a common problem that is social and economic—which unites the two island groups.

It has become apparent, in this discussion of Orkney—and the topic will reappear in the chapters about Shetland—that depopulation, whatever its cause, is a matter of concern to all who are interested in the remoter parts of Scotland and who, for one reason or another, believe it would be a calamity if the process of depopulation in the lesser islands were to continue so far as to cripple or undo their necessary services. But the process may not continue. It may be reversed, and in the course of the next twenty or thirty years some of the farther islands, both in Orkney and Shetland, may receive a small influx of new settlers from the monstrously overcrowded parts of South Britain.

What, says the sceptic, have they got to offer? And to that the answer is: "In the first place, awareness of the realities of the changing year."—Live in Orkney or Shetland, and you know the meaning of summer, the meaning of winter. The year is a living thing, and you live with it. As the months lighten, you pass from the extravagant roughness of a limitless ocean to—on occasional days—the idyllic beauty of life in the midst of a sleeping sea. You are intimately concerned with nature and the procreant forces of the earth. You may have been heroic under the pressure of winter; you will now be happy in the benison of summer. Your imagination, dulled by the meaningless repetitions of city life, is revived by contact with the immediacies of autumn and the spring.

At this time of writing I know of two young people, gifted and well educated, who are leaving the Mainland of Orkney to settle in the more remote and less formalized community of Fair Isle. Their reason? They want to live a fuller, more individual life than the ordered and closely functional existence of people employed by a public authority.

In all the over-populated, southern parts of Britain there are going to be, within the next twenty or thirty years, many people who feel themselves imprisoned by the inordinate pressure of too many neighbours, or unduly regimented by the demands of an increasingly impersonal industry; and some of them, seeking a return to more reasonable habits of life, will look to the unpeopled places of the north. A few may copy the example of older migrants, and go to find new homes: a few—but sufficient, perhaps, to replenish empty lands and half-vacant islands.

PART TWO

SHETLAND

I

Comparison and Contrast

Orkney and Shetland—commonly spoken of in the same breath—are often confused, the one with the other, and sometimes thought to be so alike that confusion makes no matter. But in point of fact they are different in almost every particular. Each archipelago is, indeed, a group of islands with the Atlantic on one side, and on the other the North Sea; and both owe their first solid appearance in history to their discovery by Norse seamen and the imposition on them, or the emergence in them, of a Norse ruler in the time of Harald Fairhair, King of Norway. In other respects, however, there is contrast rather than resemblance.

In appearance Shetland enjoys the compensation often accorded to poor soils, and is far more picturesque than its affluent neighbour. Its tortuous coastline and steep contours require an axial road that constantly rewards the traveller with the unexpected view of yet another small white beach, enclosed by rocky elbows, that lies like a bright doorstep beneath a variously coloured, neatly ordered pattern of growing fields. To the economist, to the agrarian reformer, these minute strips of corn and potatoes—a crofter's heritage, an insufficient livelihood—may be matter for regret; but they make a charming picture, and the crofters' cottages are often more trimly kept, more gaily painted, than farmhouses in Orkney. For this there are reasons which will be examined and considered.

On its Atlantic coast, from Hoy to Westray, Orkney has a majestic, boldly patterned cliff-wall, and from the sea one may admire the large and splendid views that Rousay offers in every direction. But in Shetland the sea-cliffs are part of the whole landscape, which they invade and decorate from either side. A tall, aggressive foreland—Noss, for example—may point above the horizon, and in the foreground there will be lesser cliffs and a domestic intrusion of the sea; while on the west the great bay of St. Magnus sweeps far inland to present from both horns—from Eshaness in the north and Sandness in the south—a tremendous, Gothic spectacle of fantastic, wave-splashed pinnacles of rock and isolated stacks grotesquely sculptured.

There are, too, significant differences in the history of Orkney and Shetland. In the darkness of pre-history Shetland seems to have been invaded by people of a culture unlike any that affected Orkney; and under the Norse Earldom it played a much less important part. That rascally and gifted pair of Stewart earls, who made havoc of Orkney's economy and built so handsomely, appear to have behaved more leniently in Shetland; perhaps because there was less to ruin and less to plunder. For several centuries Shetland was exposed to foreign influence, mainly Dutch; great fishing fleets, as many as 2,000 vessels at a time, gathered every summer in its sheltered waters to fill their holds with a harvest of herring; but Orkney was not much visited except by acquisitive Scots.

It is dangerous to generalize, for any generalization is as full of holes as a colander, but it may be said, with an approximation to the truth, that the Orkneymen have been farmers who, happening to be born close to the sea, have used it with some familiarity; while the Shetlanders have been seafarers who took the sea for their livelihood and regarded their islands as convenient harbours. This historical difference may account for some diversities in character and manner which, despite the levelling effect of all modern influence, can still be observed.

In neither archipelago is there any dislike or suspicion of strangers, but the Shetlander is easier, more open, and more loquacious than the Orkneyman. The bane of shyness is more apparent in Orkney, and the habit of work seems more deeply ingrained; though the industry of Shetland women is remarkable. The Orkneyman is so devoted to his farm—to his land and his animals—that he is often negligent about the comfort and visible amenities of his own house; while the Shetlander, whose croft occupies less of his time and whose income may largely be the product of seafaring or sea-fishing, is likely to pay more attention to his domestic well-being, and with a habit of tidiness learnt at sea, to maintain with more care the appearance of his property.

North Lighthouse, Fair Isle

In both archipelagos the people have a lively awareness of their Norse background, and a staunch belief, not merely in their inheritance of Norse blood, but of its dominance in their constitution. There is no enmity to Scotland, but no inclination to accept more than a political relation with it, and no sense whatever of any kinship with the Hebrides, their neighbours to the south. For this state of mind history is fully as responsible as heredity, for no benefit of any sort accrued to the islands from their association with Scotland until long after Scotland became part of Great Britain. Scotch landowners, indeed, created an "ascendancy" like a miniature of the English ascendancy in Ireland, and though in Orkney there is now no memory of their oppression or ill-will against them—for they have vanished from the scene—there is in Shetland a persistent sentiment of opposition, a sort of ground-swell of antagonism, to its remnant lairds; manifestly unjust though it is known to be.

The sense of Norse relationship is much stronger and more vocal in Shetland than in Orkney, and Scots landowners—most of them came originally from Fife—may well have nurtured it by creating the image, as well as the reality, of an alien and overbearing ruling class. In recent years Norse sentiment has undoubtedly been strengthened by the very impressive annual ceremony of Up-Helly-Aa, an old fire-festival refashioned, with great dramatic effect, as a viking ship-burial illumined by the flames of a burning galley. But there is also a prevailing discontent in Shetland—a vague but persistent feeling of disappointment; of a scarcely definable injustice, perhaps; or more simply, it may be, of ill fortune—that inclines its people to a distant and romantic loyalty.

Shetland, quite certainly, does not enjoy the self-satisfaction which allows many people in Orkney to find in the compass of island life an absorbing mental occupation as well as a sufficient livelihood. A wholesome insularity still characterizes Orkney, and is fortified, not weakened, by its broad and catholic habit of reading, by its new addiction to television; but Shetland is open to the winds of anxiety and discontent.

In neither archipelago is there any trace of religious intolerance, or much memory of religious enthusiasm. Church-attendance, if not general in practice, is widespread and generally accepted as the norm of behaviour. There seem to be more churches, or more denominations of religion, in Shetland than in Orkney; and

Bird Observatory, Fair Isle, and Sheep Crag
Puffins on Fair Isle

perhaps closer observance of Sunday, without, however, the harsh and melancholy prohibitions that in the Hebrides make it a day of gloom. In the old dark ages of poverty witches may have been more prevalent in Orkney, but nowadays superstition, except of a genial sort, has no apparent effect in either group of islands. Both are charitable, and generously subscribe to such causes as famine relief and the comfort of political refugees.

The basic cause of the most important of these differences—economic and historical differences—is, of course, geological. The Old Red Sandstone of Orkney is a kindly rock, and Shetland has too little of it. The long peninsula reaching down to Sumburgh Head, and the isle of Bressay, are Old Red; but the middle parts of the Mainland are solid gneiss, as, under its thick blanket of peat, is Yell. About Scalloway, the old capital, a benign intrusion of limestone promotes a superior fertility, while Unst and Fetlar are largely serpentine. Geology has given Shetland a more various pavement than Orkney, but a much poorer soil.

The climate, however, is unexpectedly kind. Though the long string of islands, nearly seventy miles from south to north, lies mostly beyond the 60th Parallel—that is to say, north of Cape Farewell, the southerly point of Greenland—the weather is never excessively cold. Winter, indeed, is mild but stormy. The islands are plagued by great gales, but the air is warmed by that off-shoot or prolongation of the Gulf Stream which is known as the North Atlantic Drift. In January or March a benighted traveller may be felled by the wind, but he will not be frozen.

2

Fair Isle

Fair Isle lies midway between North Ronaldsay and Sumburgh Head in Shetland, its cliffs rising from stacks and skerries and dancing tides to a height of 700 feet. At its south end the land is low-lying, and there its remnant inhabitants live in what now seems a viable and assured community. A few years ago it was one of a trio of islands—Stroma and Foula were the others—that appeared certain to lose their population. Stroma, only a mile and a half from the Caithness shore, is now deserted, and Foula, an old folks' home remote in the pitiless Atlantic, will not survive much longer as a human habitation.* But since Fair Isle was acquired by the National Trust, from the well-known ornithologist George Waterston, its houses have been repaired, its amenities improved, and its importance widely recognized: it is a haven and a meeting-place, not only for migrant birds of many sorts, but nowadays for bird-watchers who catch, ring, and measure wheatears and fieldfares, pipits and puffins, crossbills, redwings, siskins and bramblings, and occasionally such rarities as pied woodpeckers, barred warblers, and Lapland buntings. For its revival Fair Isle is primarily indebted to Waterston, who bought it from a Shetland proprietor and in 1948 established the observatory at which birds of eighty different species have been ringed.

Fair Isle is famous also for a traditional skill in knitting, and the bright, geometrical patterns of the caps and jerseys which its women-folk still fashion with uncanny skill on flickering long needles. It is said, and widely believed, that the patterns were first brought to the island by Spanish sailors saved from a lost ship of the Great Armada; but though more intricate than Norwegian or Faeroese designs, they are similar to them, and a basic Norse pattern, elaborated in isolation, is a more probable origin than Spanish sailormen.

*This prediction has not been fulfilled. With a population of over forty the decline has been halted and several new houses are now being built on Foula.

It is true, however, that in 1588 a Spanish ship was wrecked there. She was *El Gran Grifon* of 650 tons and 38 guns, the flagship of the *urcas* or fleet auxiliaries. She had been savagely attacked in the English Channel by Francis Drake in *Revenge*, and when the defeated Armada was in the North Sea, somewhere between Shetland and Norway, the *Grifon* was reported missing after a heavy squall on the night of the 17th August. She ran ashore at Sivars Geo, in the south-eastern corner of the island, and of her complement 200 men are said to have been saved. They were hungry already—mouldy biscuits, stinking beef, and slimy water had been their rations for some days—and soon they threatened all Fair Isle with starvation. They devoured cattle, sheep, fish and fowl, ponies too, before their worried hosts relieved the situation—or so it is said—by throwing some of them over the cliffs. The remainder were taken to Quendale on the Mainland of Shetland, where they were hospitably treated till a ship was found to carry them to Dunkirk.

Many ships followed *El Gran Grifon* to destruction on the sudden stacks and channelled cliffs of Fair Isle. In a list compiled by Jeremiah Eunson, a native of the island, fifty wrecks are named, between 1702 and 1937, including the barque *Lessing* of Bremen in 1868, whose 465 passengers—emigrants to America—were all rescued by the islanders; and in the following year the barque *Gazelle*, from the same port, with 310 emigrants aboard, which the islanders saved from total loss after she had gone ashore at Klingersgeo.

Traditionally the men of Fair Isle were magnificent seamen, and in wretchedly small boats they hauled from the savage, surrounding sea a rich harvest of cod and ling, skate and halibut, saithe and mackerel. To their catch they added hens and mutton, the stockings and jerseys their wives had knitted, and rowed far out to trade with passing ships. Sometimes they met a scoundrelly master who robbed them of all they had, but in spite of rough weather and occasional misfortune the islanders fed themselves so well that the population grew far too numerous. About the middle of the nineteenth century, in an island only three and a half miles long, and much of it barren, there were 360 people; of whom 137 presently emigrated to Nova Scotia. Then the remnant population began to dwindle, and fell to some 50 before decline was halted.

It is an island, on a fine day, of great beauty—a wild, sea-sculptured beauty—but in foul weather it wears a forbidding aspect. For communication with the Mainland of Shetland the islanders depend on their boat, of about 50 feet long, the *Good Shepherd*, which is often storm-stayed in North Haven on the east side: a haven into which the sea may run with a forbidding height. With a lighthouse at either end Fair Isle is no longer the menace to passing ships that it used to be, but it still must be reckoned almost as inaccessible as it was eighty years ago when John Tudor, a tireless but prudent traveller, warned all who thought of going there to include in their luggage a pocket enema; because, in the probable event of being storm-stayed, the inevitable alteration in diet was "apt to bring on violent constipation, which purgatives seem at times to increase instead of dispersing."

3

Shetland: the Southern Landfall

The best approach to Shetland is by air. From Kirkwall the flight is very short, no more than twenty-five minutes, and the traveller's introduction to the islands is the abrupt and splendid sight of Sumburgh Head, with a savage tideway called The Roost dancing white at its foot, and beyond it, to the west, the formidable, brooding mass of Fitful Head. This majestic promontory, rising to over 900 feet, is said to afford a superlative view in reward of a short, rough walk, and no doubt it does. *White-fowl* is the apparent meaning of its name, but a reputed denizen at one time more celebrated than sea-birds was Sir Walter Scott's preposterous witch Norna: "Mother doubtful, mother dread, dweller on the Fitful Head."

Should there be a strong north-westerly wind when the tide is at springs and the stream is running to the north-west, Sumburgh Roost will be a rage of white water, a scene of elemental fury; and the dramatic landscape will be enhanced by the melodramatic behaviour of its neighbour the sea. The airfield lies a mile or two north of the Head, on a little area of low ground whose level surface is a rarity in Shetland, and before going further the traveller should visit the extraordinary complex of ruined buildings, called Jarlshof, which is just south of the airfield and contiguous with the gardens of what was once a mansion house, and is now a very agreeable hotel. Jarlshof, which owes its name to Sir Walter and his novel *The Pirate*—one of his less rewarding works—is an architectural curiosity of the highest interest, an impaction of history in which are concentrated the life and labour of three thousand years or more.

Some eighty years ago the ruin of a medieval house stood on a grassy mound beside a small and shallow bay. Great gales eroded the mound, and revealed stone walls. The proprietor,

John Bruce of Sumburgh, began to excavate, and excavation was continued, at intervals, until quite recently. Oldest of the buildings uncovered was the remains of a Stone Age hut like those at Skarabrae. Sand-storms had covered that before the Stone Age was out of date; and people of the Bronze Age built a village above the ruins. They grew corn, kept sheep and cattle, and employed a smith. Then newcomers arrived who had some knowledge of iron, and built circular huts round a central fire. They also dug earth-houses: *souterrains* or weems. Sand obliterated these dwellings too, and later Iron Age people built a massive broch and a courtyard on the growing pile. Next came the builders of what are called "wheel-houses", perhaps in the second and third centuries A.D., and these people may still have occupied the site when the Norsemen arrived at some time in the eighth century; if so, they were presumably the people whom the Norse called Picts.

The viking settlement grew and became extensive on the landward side of the mound. The village may have enjoyed a relatively peaceful existence for several centuries; it was peaceful enough for fond parents to make, out of soapstone, little toy querns for their children's amusement. In the Middle Ages a farmstead was built, and in the sixteenth century a hall that may, for some time, have been the seat of the Stewart Earls. The hall was enlarged by Earl Patrick, changed hands, and was sacked by Earl Patrick. Like all its predecessors it became a ruin, and as such attracted the romantic interest of Sir Walter Scott; but Sir Walter had no notion of the long history that time and forgotten men had written beneath it.

In much that is still inexplicable in this great human quarry, two mysteries stand out enquiringly above the rest. One is the wheel-houses, whose radial walls may be ten feet high or more; and what sort of people, one asks, were the builders who required for their comfort or their luxury so extravagant a height?—The other is the *souterrains* or weems, which are small, dark, damp, and low. Places of refuge, or store-houses? But they are too small for refuge, and must have been too damp to store corn. Were they, perhaps, initiation chambers where adolescent boys submitted to strange rites which inaugurated manhood? And if so, were the huts in which they are found the residence of tribal priests in an unknown faith of the Iron Age?

Before leaving Sumburgh it may be of interest to recall that

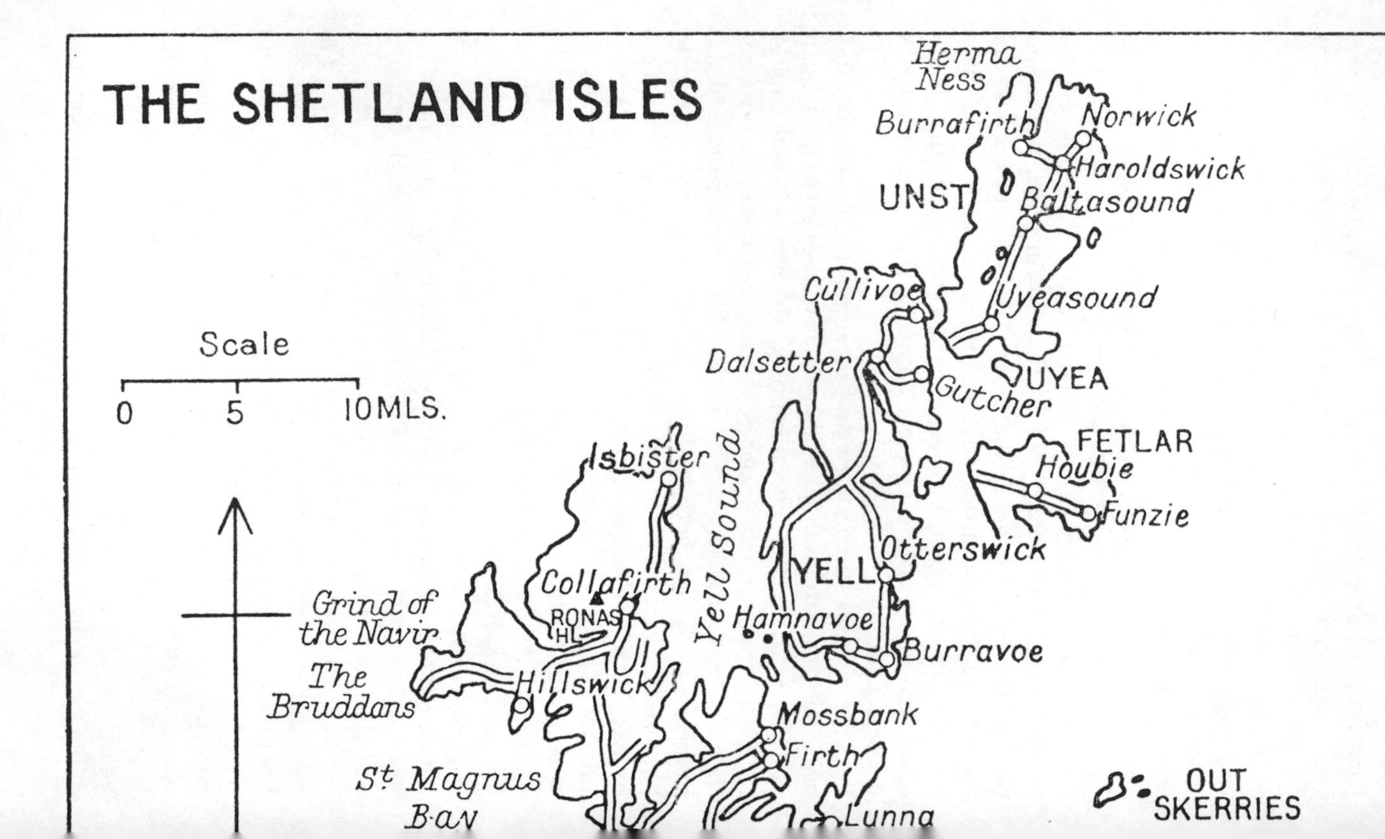
THE SHETLAND ISLES
Scale
0
5
10MLS.
Herma Ness
Burrafirth
Norwick
Haroldswick
UNST
Baltasound
Cullivoe
Uyeasound
Dalsetter
Gutcher
UYEA
FETLAR
Houbie
Funzie
Isbister
Yell Sound
Otterswick
YELL
Collafirth
RONAS HL
Grind of the Navir
Hamnavoe
Burravoe
The Bruddans
Hillswick
Mossbank
Firth
St Magnus Bay
Lunna
OUT SKERRIES

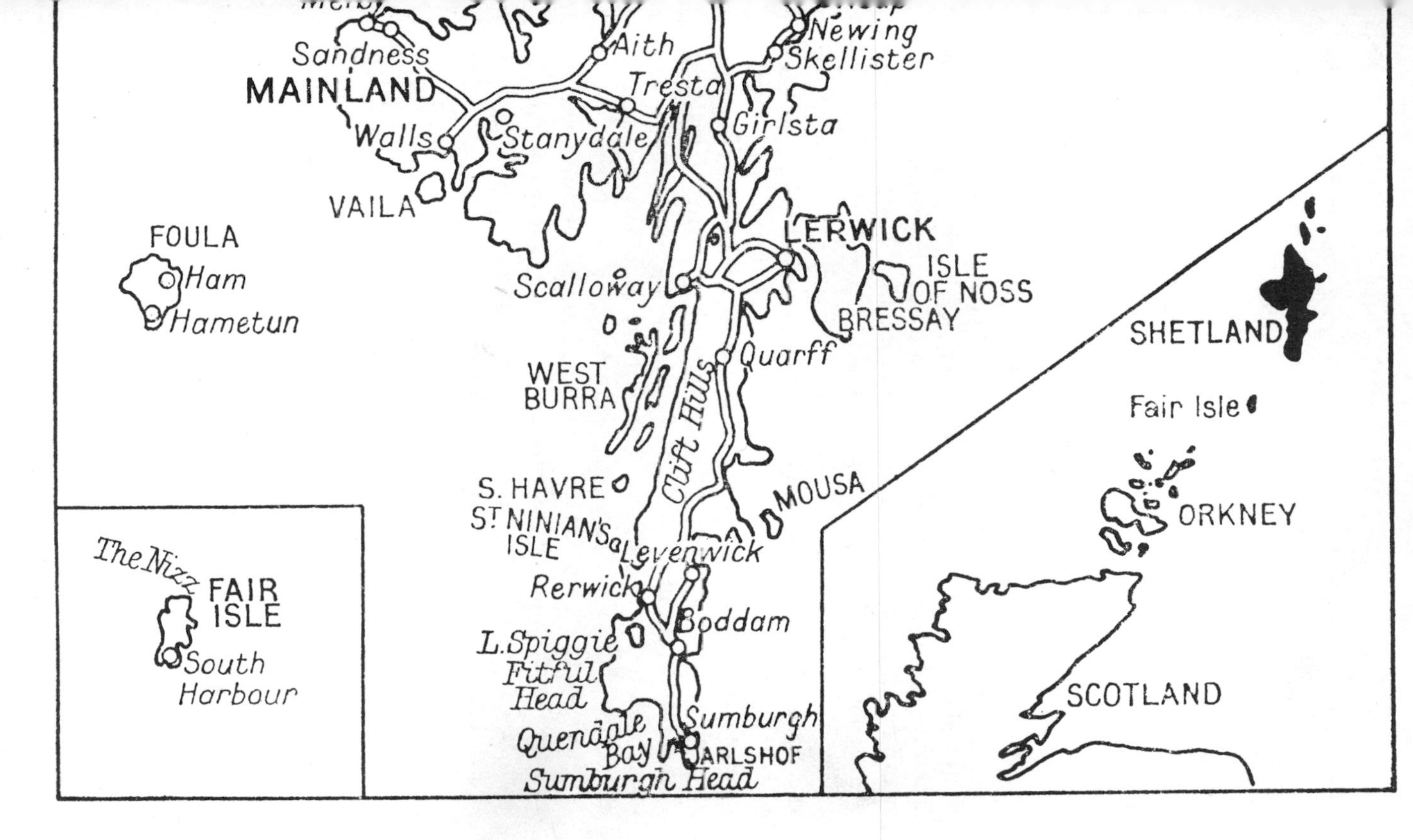
Sandness
MAINLAND
Walls
Stanydale
Aith
Tresta
Girlsta
Newing
Skellister
VAILA
FOULA
Ham
Hametun
LERWICK
ISLE
OF NOSS
BRESSAY
Scalloway
Quarff
WEST
BURRA
Clift Hills
S. HAVRE
MOUSA
ST NINIAN'S
ISLE
Levenwick
Rerwick
Boddam
L. Spiggie
Fitful
Head
Sumburgh
Quendale
Bay
JARLSHOF
Sumburgh Head
The Nizz
FAIR
ISLE
South
Harbour
SHETLAND
Fair Isle
ORKNEY
SCOTLAND

the beach of West Voe is the scene of the only episode in the Earls' Saga in which mention is made of the common people of the country: the poor people who lived, unnoticed, on the fringe of proud events.—The year was 1148, and Earl Rognvald, before setting out on his crusade, went to Norway. On the homeward voyage his two ships were overtaken by a following gale. They could do nothing but run before the wind, and reached a rough landing in Gulberwick, a few miles south of Lerwick.

The Earl and his company were made welcome, and a little while later Rognvald went down to Sumburgh, where the local fishermen were going out in small boats to fish on the edge of the Roost. There was one old man who waited, disconsolate, for his mate; and when his mate failed to come, Rognvald, who was unknown by sight, offered to take his place. He rowed the old man into the Roost, and frightened him badly, but brought him ashore again with a good catch. The fish were divided in the traditional way—a third for each, and a third for the owner of the boat—and a crowd of people came down to the beach to watch: both men and women, "and many poor folk". Rognvald gave all his share to the poor, his identity was discovered, and after that, says the saga, people "learned of many of his feats that were helpful in the sight of God and pleasant in the eyes of men." But the poor folk would never have been noticed but for a chance to show the Earl's good-natured, careless charity.

There are twenty-seven miles between Sumburgh and Lerwick, and the road winds and climbs up that long, narrow peninsula with the repeated invitation of some new and sparkling view ahead. But there is much to persuade one to turn aside, and at the church of Dunrossness the opportunity should be taken of glancing to the west. A secondary road skirts the loch of Spiggie, and with some turning and twisting leads to a hillside from which one looks down to the Atlantic and the arc of a fine beach. Spiggie is a loch with an old reputation for its good trout, but I have found it unresponsive, and I was about to mark it off as one of those many waters which have lost their virtue when I happened to see a reference to it in John Tudor's admirable handbook: the Spiggie trout, he says, are almost as silvery as salmon, as game as you can wish, but "very dour risers". That was written between 1878 and 1880, and the conclusion is that the fishing has neither changed nor deteriorated, but that patience—as well as the proper fly—is and always has been necessary.

North of Spiggie the road marches above the Atlantic to one of the most engagingly fertile parts of Shetland, and approaches an island—which is not quite an island—with a history, almost unknown, that may go back to the very earliest days of Christianity in the north. The farmland of Bigton is rich, and nearby are crofts so well tended and in a good summer so richly burgeoning that one is almost persuaded to dispute the now accepted fact that crofting is a dying occupation. These little fields, all carefully gardened, make a richer and far more varied scene than the large and profitable acres of big farms; but without other employment a man cannot bring up a family on a small holding, and unless small holdings can be joined together to make small farms, there is no future for them—except, perhaps, to fill the leisure of a man in retirement.

The island that is not quite an island is St. Ninian's Isle. It juts out from Bigton on a stalk of land that is bordered on either side by slightly curving, marvellously fine beaches—scimitars of white sand, 600 yards long—and till a few years ago it had little more than its name to substantiate an association with the heroic missionary who, a hundred years before Columba came to Iona, dared to preach the gospel to the island Picts. Till the beginning of the eighteenth century the scanty ruins of a chapel were indeed a place of pilgrimage, and in 1878 some pieces of stone inscribed with Ogham characters were found there. But in 1955 even the ruins had vanished—the stones had been used to build a wall—and when a party of young archaeologists from Aberdeen University began to dig there, their confidence in discovering what intuition bade them look for cannot have been high. But four years later their search was fantastically rewarded.

They opened up the foundations of the church, exposing its twelfth-century apse, altar, and nave. Nearby were a burial ground of the late Bronze Age, and the remains of a pre-Norse church. Stones inscribed with Pictish symbols were found, and the skeleton of a man six feet tall. Then, under a thin slab of stone in the nave of the twelfth-century church, in a box of rotted larch—but the larch was not planted in Britain till the eighteenth century—the treasure was discovered: a hoard of silver bowls and great penannular brooches; a sword-pommel, a Communion spoon thought to have been used in the Pictish church; and ornate conical mounts that may have been silver caps for ceremonial staves. It is a superb collection that illustrates both the splendour of antique piety and the opulence of barbaric costume. Those strongly fashioned, intricately decorated brooches pinned cloaks of scarlet and blue, and the piety of reckless, dedicated missionaries had engraved and hammered their patterns into silver vessels as splendid as the silver ornaments that marauding vikings stole for their savage-hearted, pagan women. How these relics, of an ancient church and the Norsemen who later bowed to its teaching, were brought together—who packed them roughly in a box of Norwegian larch, and buried them so hurriedly—and what was the new danger from which they were hidden, will never be known; and the treasure found by Professor O'Dell and his Aberdeen students is a challenge to imagination as well as a delight to the wondering eye.

The secondary road from Spiggie to Bigton rejoins the main north-going road on the eastern side of the long leg from Sumburgh, and the traveller looks down at a broad indented bay and another scene of tidy cottages and brightly growing strips of crofting land. The nearest indentation is Levenwick, where in the smuggling days—and that is more than a hundred years ago—the Dutchmen used to come with tobacco and illicit brandy; and in Levenwick a story was long remembered of a woman and a naval officer in the preventive service. He was an able, determined, energetic officer, but not without pity—not without courtesy—and when, while searching busily for a lately landed cargo, he came to a cottage where the poor woman lay in the pains of childbed, he not only called off the search, but from his own ship sent her soup and wine. In due course she was safely delivered—not of a child, indeed, but of a great roll of black tobacco that she had hidden under the blankets.

North of Levenwick is Channerwick, and east of that the other indentations: Hoswick and Sandwick, the former of which is associated with whales and the irony of justice. Until fairly recently the appearance off shore of a school of caain' whales (or blackfish) was not only an occasion for local excitement and communal sport, but an opportunity—rare in poverty-stricken times—to get enough oil to keep lamps burning through a long winter. In the Faeroes, those prosperous and heroic islands that lie 200 miles north-west of the Shetlands, caain' whales are still hunted with a formalized enthusiasm, and their slaughter—the *grindadrap*—provides meat and blubber which are said to be palatable when cooked together; and formerly the heads were rendered down for oil. In Shetland there was less ritual about a whale-hunt, and except in emergency the meat was not eaten; but the value of the catch was jealously calculated, and the exactions of landed proprietors had long been resented. The landowner claimed a third of the catch, and the Church a tenth.

At Hoswick, in 1888, a great school of more than 300 whales was driven ashore and killed; and to resist, by legal action, the landlord's claim, a fighting-fund was raised. Money was collected, not only in Shetland itself, but from Shetlanders living abroad; and by the decision of the courts the complainants won their case. The whales were the property of the crofters and fishermen who had killed them, and no one else had any title to the oil that could be extracted or the money for which they could be sold. But from that day to this the caain' whales have avoided Shetland, except for small, inconsiderable schools of possibly immature creatures.

Sandwick, the outermost indentation, runs deep into a parish which is notable for an extinct copper-mine, the ruins of a broch of unusual size, and its proximity to the remarkable island of Mousa. The copper-mine was opened in 1798 and worked for a few years; then worked again, but not for long, in the 1870s. It lay near the house of Sand Lodge, the home of Robert Bruce, the present Lord-Lieutenant of Shetland, who owns the island of Mousa and the adjacent shore. The ruined broch of Burraland is rather more than a mile south-east of Sand Lodge, and was obviously built to reinforce a position of great natural strength. It stands at the inner end of a dramatically rough, steep promontory called Hoga—a fortress in itself, deeply carpeted with grass—and the broch, whose thick wall is still in places a dozen feet high, has an internal diameter not less than 40 feet. Originally it must have been a formidable structure, and possibly the keep or dominating tower of a system of small, domestic outbuildings; but these are now so ruinous that their design or pattern is quite obscure.

What adds greatly to the interest of Burraland is the neighbouring broch of Mousa, on the edge of the opposite cliff. The island of Mousa, a mile and a half long, is separated from the Mainland by a channel little more than half a mile broad, and the two brochs overlook the channel at its narrowest part. As decisively as the comparable pair in Orkney—the broch of Gurness in Evie, and the almost vanished broch of Burrian in Rousay—they could be said to command the channel between them if their occupants had had the use of any form of artillery. I have already admitted the natural tendency to doubt the possession of a weapon so sophisticated as a catapult by a people so primitive in their habit of life as the Iron Age dwellers on these coasts two thousand years ago—though it has to be said that their architecture was not unsophisticated—but no one who stands in the ruined fortress of Burraland, and looks across a narrow seaway at the round tower of Mousa, can fail to suspect a relation between them and some reason for their having been sited with such tactical advantage.

The island of Mousa is now inhabited only by a flock of native sheep and a herd of plump and lively ponies—dark-coated, with shaggy manes and large, melting eyes—which run loose and look after themselves, without apparent difficulty, through the winter months in which they are often isolated by storm. It was farmed, by a resident farmer, in the nineteenth century, and in the long lapse of time between him and the Iron Age builders the broch, on two occasions, gave romantic shelter to people of some fame or notoriety in the heroic age of the north.

In Egil's Saga—one of the great Icelandic sagas—there is the story of a young man called Bjorn who, in Norway, loved a girl called Thora Jewel-hand, and abducted her from her father's house. For a winter she lived, her virtue untarnished, under the care of Bjorn's mother, somewhere on the Sogne fjord; and when spring came Bjorn's father gave him a trading-ship and the sound advice to make for Dublin, where there was good business to be done.—This was about the year 900.—But Bjorn insisted on taking Thora with him; they ran into foul weather, and after a wild voyage in tumultuous seas they went ashore on Mousa. They saved the ship, however, and while the sailors repaired her, Bjorn and Thora got married and set up house in the broch. There they stayed till another spring, when word came that Norway's King Harald had pronounced sentence of death on Bjorn, and there was no safety for him in Scotland or Ireland. His ship was ready for sea again, and this time they sailed north—again in bad weather—and found a friendly welcome in Iceland; where, to make a happy ending to a long honeymoon and rough voyaging, Thora gave birth to a daughter who was prettily called Asgerd.

The other visitors of a romantic nature—or impelled by a romantic impulse—came in 1152, when the crusading Earl

Rognvald of Orkney was in Constantinople. As described in one of the Orkney chapters, the islands had been left in charge of the young Earl Harald, whose mother Margaret—daughter of Earl Hakon who murdered St. Magnus—had married the Scots Earl Maddad of Atholl. Young Harald, who was nineteen or twenty, had a troublesome time: he was challenged in his Earldom, and had to fight for it; and he was much embarrassed by his mother's behaviour. Her husband having died, she returned to Orkney, and presently enjoyed an intrigue with Sweyn Asleifsson's brother, to whom she bore a child. Then she attracted the attention of a Shetland chieftain, Erlend Ungi, who carried her off to Mousa, and having provisioned the broch prepared to stand a siege. Indignant at this insult to his authority, Harald followed the impetuous runaways, and prepared to take the broch by storm. But, as the saga tells, he found it "an unhandy place to get at", so after due reconnaissance, and perhaps an abortive attempt, he made the best of a bad business, and having given his mother permission to marry, got Erlend as an ally in his still continuing contest for the Earldom.

Almost on the verge of the low sea-cliff, the broch rises to a height of over 40 feet, and because the batter of its outer wall gives it what is called an ogee curve, it has something of elegance in its simple outline. Its diameter, on the ground, is about 50 feet, and 40 feet at the top. The inner wall appears to be perpendicular, and some 10 feet above ground level the internal diameter is no more than 20 feet; or about half that of Burraland on the opposite shore. It is built of curiously small stones—a locally quarried schistose slate—and one's feeling of astonishment before so large a building on so small an island is doubled, and doubled again, by wonder at the skill with which its walls were raised, and its enormous weight supported on layer upon layer of building stone that is not much heavier than suburban bricks.

The walls, between 7 and 12 feet thick, are not solid and simple, but contain within them the galleries typical of broch-building—the roof of one being the floor of that above—which circle the tower and are interrupted, each at one point, by a staircase which starts in a sort of lobby in the wall, about 7 feet above ground-level, and rises round half the circumference to a landing near the summit. Each of the horizontal galleries, which are about 5 feet high, has one open end, facing the stair, and a blind end closed by the staircase rising to the gallery above. This intricate structure, which is obviously designed to give access to the top of the tower, has the additional advantages of reducing the total weight of the building, and of providing the builders, while they were at work, with an integral scaffolding. In Orkney and Shetland there was no supply of native timber to supply exterior scaffolding, but the broch-builders needed none, for they had devised a means of building upwards from floor to floor. How they kept their inner wall so straight, and their outer wall so judiciously battered, is admittedly a mystery; but the shipwrights who built the viking longships laid down no lines, they judged by eye alone, and the masons of the Iron Age must have had as strict a vision, and with it a knowledge of their material—an ability to shape and handle stone—as assured as the fulmar's intuitive knowledge of the currents of the air.

The broch of Mousa is almost as perfect in outline as when its builders laid the last stone on its parapet, and the visitor, before leaving the island, should try to imagine how Orkney and Shetland would look if all their ruined brochs—perhaps a hundred in Orkney, and almost as many in Shetland—were still complete. They would certainly present the appearance of a country that had once been occupied by a gifted, energetic, and martial people. But a martial people who made no conquests? So restricted is the broch-builders' area—the islands of the north and the west, and the knuckle-end of Scotland—that their warlike towers, if all remained, would appear to stand as monuments to a people whose elaborate defences failed against a stronger and more mobile enemy.

We return to the Mainland—to the Sumburgh leg—and the road that lies on its east side, and come next to Cunningsburgh, where nowadays, in July, there is a numerously attended and competently managed cattle-show: a lively concourse of well-groomed animals and people whose manners are civil and whose kindliness is manifest. This deserves attention, because Cunningsburgh in the past had a different reputation. Its people were said to be surly, inhospitable, and a menace to any stranger. I have spoken to a man, of middle age, who told me that his father, as a boy, would never venture near Cunningsburgh after dark. It is one of those places where legend has settled Spanish sailors from a wrecked ship, and in the nineteenth century, when crime was hardly known in Shetland, a notorious thief lived there. But the most famous of its stories tells of the traditional warning given,

St. Ninian's Isle, Shetland

in the old Norn of the islands, to visitors who out-stayed their welcome. "*Myrkt i ljora; ljost i lyngi; timi at gestrinn se genginn,*" their host would growl. "Dark in the chimney, light on the heather, and time that guests were gone."—From the evidence of "light on the heather" it seems that a long-suffering host had sat all night, till the fire was out and dawn was brightening, before he grew tired of his visitors; but even so late a curtailment of hospitality was, presumably, resented in Shetland.

By Fladdabister and Easter Quarff the road goes north to Gulberwick, and another memory of saga times. It was in Norway, in 1148, that Earl Rognvald was persuaded to make a voyage to the Holy Land; but he had first to go home, and the King of Norway gave him two small but very fast ships called *Arrow* and *Help*. The Earl and his companions put to sea on a Tuesday evening, and by Wednesday it was blowing hard from the east. They ran before the wind, and by Thursday it blew so hard they could do nothing else but run. Night fell, and through the darkness, with the roaring gale behind them, they saw breakers ahead. They steered for what looked like a beach, and through the new violence of shallow water, to the thunder of breaking waves, the long, light ships were carried ashore, and all aboard were saved though they lost most of their belongings.

Earl Rognvald was in high spirits, cracking jokes and making verses: he was a man, it seems, who responded to danger as to drink—it went to his head—and the shipwreck at Gulberwick is remembered because, in the house where he found shelter and sat drying his clothes before a great fire, his laughter was memorable and the verses he made were good enough to survive repetition. In all the Norse sagas there is no more amiable a man than Rognvald—it was during this enforced visit to Shetland that he helped a poor fisherman to get a good catch on the edge of Sumburgh Roost—and if his canonization owed something to favour, he repaid it by giving an uncommon gaiety to the muster-roll of the saints.

Between Gulberwick and Lerwick, within sight of the capital, there is, on the left-hand side of the road, another broch. It stands on what was once a rocky islet in a small fresh-water loch, and is now a promontory reached by a causeway over a neck of marshy land. The entrance to the broch of Clickhimin—or its substantial remnant—opens in a massive wall that surrounds the islet, and then passes through an unusual feature: a long, ponderously

Old corn-drying kiln in use, Shetland
Esha Ness

built, detached rampart of dressed stone. The broch itself, or what is left of it, stands some 17 feet high, and in addition to the doorway shows two other openings in the wall at higher levels. These are abnormalities in broch-building, and cannot be explained. The over-all appearance of neatness and precision is also a little odd, and one gets the impression of looking at the model of a ruined broch, rather than the ruin itself.

Clickhimin was excavated in the late nineteenth century by a lady whom I suspect of idealism. I think that after excavation she instructed her labourers to rebuild some parts of what had been uncovered—to rebuild them as she believed a broch ought to be built—and, of course, to leave everything tidy. But I am no archaeologist, and I may be doing her an injustice.

4

Lerwick

The appearance of Lerwick, from the Sumburgh road, is both revealing and deceptive. What is seen, very clearly, is the extraordinary growth of the town within the last fifteen years or so; nearly all the visible building is new, and while respectable enough—and indeed praiseworthy as the evidence of municipal energy—is by no means characteristic of Shetland. What is not seen, from this approach, is the singular charm of the town—its unique and sturdy look of a miniature, sea-cousined metropolis—for this, its better part, lies on a pavement that opens at intervals to the harbour, and is as intimate with herring-drifters, Swedish trawlers, and coasting steamers as with its own shop-windows.

Lerwick is not an old town, but Bressay Sound, by which it lies, has a long and varied history. The island of Bressay, six miles long, covers it from the east, and to its sheltered waters have come ships of many different sorts. In Norse times Harald Hardrada lay here before he went to defeat and death, at the hands of Harold Godwinsson, at Stamford Bridge; and two hundred years later, in 1263, old King Hakon Hakonsson waited for better weather on his ill-fated voyage to the Firth of Clyde and the disappointment of hope at the so-called battle of Largs. The English fleet made its first appearance when George Monk, the soldier who became an admiral, commanded ninety-four sail and for some days in 1653, while searching for the redoubtable van Tromp, lay at anchor in Bressay Sound. The Royal Navy came recruiting here, and when Nelson's incomparable genius crowned it with constant victory—at Cape St. Vincent under Jervis, at Aboukir Bay, at Copenhagen and Trafalgar—there were, it has been estimated, some 3,000 Shetlanders serving under the White Ensign: not all as volunteers, of course, but in a navy largely recruited by the press-gang, their lack of an explicit patriotism was of little moment compared with their native aptitude for the sea.

In later years Bressay Sound knew such great ships as the first *Dreadnought*, as *Rodney* and *Barham*, and the indomitable destroyers that Warburton-Lee took through a snowstorm to battle in the Narvik fjord. In the early years of the century it had seen the German High Seas Fleet, and made its sailors welcome; for it had long been accustomed to foreigners. In 1640 it had seen a battle between ten Spanish men-of-war and four Dutchmen, two of which were sunk; and at the beginning of the eighteenth-century French privateers sailed at will among the islands, whose sailors, when they came ashore, "pillaged like gentlemen". But fishermen of one nation or another, in boats of many different sorts and sizes, have been its most faithful visitors, and pre-eminent among them, for a couple of centuries and more, were the Dutch.

Early in the fifteenth century the Dutch discovered, or apparently perfected, the great art of curing herring; and this discovery led the way to a national industry, of major importance, called The Great Fishery. By the middle of the sixteenth century the Dutch busses—fishing-boats of 80 tons or more—were protected against pirates by men-of-war manned and armed for that purpose; and the catch of 2,000 busses was exported to all the countries of northern Europe, throughout the Mediterranean, and as far as Brazil. James I of England—and VI of Scotland—appears to have been the first of our monarchs to forbid foreigners to fish in British waters without a licence, but his veto seems not to have been effective; for a few years later it was reported that 1,500 Dutch herring busses and a smaller fleet of line fishermen were in Shetland waters protected by a fleet of twenty ships of war. Sterner action was taken under Charles I, and after an English fleet had opened fire the Dutchmen agreed to pay £30,000 for the remainder of the year's fishing, and an annual tribute in future.

The Great Fishery was governed by rule and regulation. Fishing did not begin till the 24th June, the feast of St. John the Baptist, but the busses and smaller boats would gather in Bressay Sound some days or weeks before that, and the eager Shetlanders would come to meet them, to barter and drink with their crews. Rude bothies were built to serve the purposes of trade and merry-making, and these informal sheds or huts were the beginning of Lerwick. But the first experiment in architecture did not last very long. Exception was taken to "the great abominatioun and wickednes committit yeirlie be the Hollanderis and cuntrie people, godles and prophane persones repairing to thame at the houssis of Lerwick quilk is a desert place." Drunkenness and bloodshed accompanied the selling of beer, and women who came with the pretext of selling "sokis and utheris necessaris" were guilty of "manifold adultrie and fornicatioun" with the foreigners: or so it was alleged by Sir John Buchanan, Sheriff Principal of Orkney and Shetland, who commanded the houses to be burnt.

But the Great Fishery survived, because it was too valuable to be so easily destroyed, and by the middle of the seventeenth century the fleet that yearly came to Bressay Sound numbered 2,000 busses and more: so many, it was said, that a man could go from shore to shore by stepping from ship to ship. It took war to spoil Dutch industry, and in 1702 a French fleet attacked the Dutch men-of-war off Fair Isle, and then, in Bressay Sound, burnt 150 busses. From then on the Great Fishery declined, but did not wholly die; for in 1878 there were still nearly 400 boats, of one sort or another, engaged in it. What, in this story, is remarkable—other than the long continuance of Dutch enterprise, hardihood, and skill—is the supine indifference, the lack of initiative, of Scotch and English fishermen; who for more than two hundred years let foreigners take home the full harvest of a British sea-bed. But indifference to the wealth of its own waters, and equal indifference to the claims of coastwise fishermen—indifference or invincible ignorance—have long characterized British governments; and only now, after every other European government has protected its own shores, is the insular parliament at Westminster paying some attention to the riches spawned in its domestic sea.

It was not until the early part of the nineteenth century that the Shetlanders began, with any commercial seriousness, to fish their own waters for their own profit. The growth of Lerwick into its present dignity had begun in the previous century, when the growing trade induced by a sheltered harbour brought enterprising merchants to take advantage of it. But a secondary impulse to growth was the absence of roads. A boat rather than a wheeled vehicle had traditionally been the means of conveyance in Shetland, but as the habit of life became more conventional, and among the upper classes a regard for comfort and convenience developed, the lack of roads became obvious, and being obvious was deplored. Road-making, however, would be a long and expensive task; in the meantime it was easier, and cheaper, for a rich family to build a second house: a house for the winter, when travel was impossible. Lerwick had been legitimated, as it were, by the construction of a new fort in the late eighteenth century, and from the middle of that century merchants had recognized it as a place of increasing business and built their houses, gable-end to the sea, and pushed out stone piers to meet their customers' ships. By the 1750s there were some four hundred houses, all above what is now Commercial Street, which was known as "the Shore". Then the gentry moved in, to winter quarters, mostly at the south end of the town, and Lerwick visibly became a capital. A dancing school catered for gaiety and decorum, and gentlewomen amused themselves by knitting stockings fine enough to be drawn through a wedding-ring.

On its seaward side Lerwick now consists of a long, winding, paved street, well furnished with sufficient shops, many of whose windows display the charming, flocculent, and prettily decorated work of Shetland knitters: in the small economy of the islands knitting is a major industry, and its produce fills shop-windows with a gaiety that is also the promise of a singularly light and airy warmth. At its north end the street is busy with crowded quays, and at the other it breaks into uncommon charm where, between old houses that have their foundations in the tide, a minute beach intrudes. Descending steeply into the main street are narrow lanes, where most of the surviving older houses are to be found, and which retain something of the comeliness which was native to the eighteenth century. But even then there was jerry-building, and the Town Council of Lerwick deserves the highest praise for the manner in which it has replaced the casualties and decay of time with little colonies of new houses that adorn a crowded slope with gay colours, and enhance their environment with a vigorously imagined and workmanlike design.

The Town Council is justly proud of its Town Hall, the foundations of which were laid in 1882, when a former Duke of Edinburgh—the second son of Queen Victoria, who was then Admiral Superintendent, Royal Naval Reserve—tapped the first stone and commended an ambitious plan. The building, in the Scottish Baronial style, is indeed of unexpected and impressive size, and its stained glass windows demand respect as well as interest. The old connexion between Holland and Shetland is acknowledged by one that was the gift of the Burgomaster and magistrates of Amsterdam; and another was presented by the contemporary Earl of Morton, whose predecessor in the eighteenth century had sold his heritable grant of the Earldom estates for 60,000 guineas to Sir Lawrence Dundas. Sir Lawrence had made a comfortable fortune as Commissary-General and Contractor to the Army, and George, 16th Earl of Morton, was at one time President of the Royal Society; but in the islands was justifiably remembered as a vandal. The good John Tudor, with an acerbity remarkable in his well-tempered pages, says of his successor's gift to Lerwick that it was believed to be "a sort of Protestant Mass for the dead, to help to get the souls of his ancestors out of Purgatory."

Another notable building in Lerwick is the Anderson Educational Institute, the only Senior Secondary school in Shetland, which was built and endowed, about a hundred years ago, by Arthur Anderson, a native of the islands whose genius led to a remarkable career. Born in 1792, he went to work at the age of eleven as a beach-boy—his duty was to turn the cod-fish laid out to dry—but his father's good sense and the kindliness of his employer let him acquire some education, and prompted him to volunteer for the Navy. He quickly rose to the rank of midshipman, and served in the Baltic as Captain's clerk. Later he found employment with a shipowner in London, whose partner he became; but retained the leisure to intervene, personally and successfully, in a civil war in Portugal, and to found in Shetland a newspaper devoted to the Liberal cause. In 1837 he and his partner Willcox founded the Peninsular Steam Company; and Anderson presented to Queen Victoria—and introduced to fashionable society—some fragile, finely knitted Shetland shawls. In that same year he broke the iniquitous system which held all the local fishermen in a feudal grasp, and established on the island of Vaila the Shetland Fishery Company; and the following year brought to Lerwick a regular mail-service by steamship.

He aided and abetted Cobden and Bright in their campaign against the Corn Laws, and in 1840 he and Willcox secured a government tender for the carriage of mail to India. The service was later extended to China, and the steamship company that supplied it was renamed the Peninsular and Oriental, whose splendid ships, in the course of time, were to impose upon their passengers a discipline almost as rigorous as that of the Royal

Navy. Willcox was the P. and O.'s first chairman, and in 1862 Anderson succeeded him.

He was for some time a Member of Parliament for Orkney and Shetland, and spoke on behalf of postal reform and repeal of the navigation laws. Many years before de Lesseps began to cut the Suez Canal, Anderson had written a proposal for it, and he recommended the arming of merchant vessels in time of war. He pensioned the officers of his shipping company, when pensions for civil employment were hardly known, and founded in Lerwick the Widows' Homes for the wives of fishermen and sailors who had died at sea. This benign and noble man, who lived to the age of seventy-seven, is said to have retained throughout his life a sense of humour undimmed by worldly wisdom or good works; and it is generally agreed that no Shetlander has ever done more for his own people.

The habit of educational endowment, once established, was generously maintained by the late Robert Bruce of Sumburgh, who gave to the county the very handsome Bruce Hostel for Girls; and by the Carnegie Institute, which founded the Carnegie Boys' Hostel. These hostels are of the greatest benefit to children whose parents live in remote parts of the Mainland or in the outer isles; and there is no lack of good material for teachers to shape and nurture. The pity is that so much native talent has to be exported, because there is so little scope for it at home.

Every intelligent Shetlander will complain of this disability, intrinsical to island life. Their brightest wits, their keenest intellects, must travel south, they say; and yet they expose no lack of wit or intellect in Lerwick or Scalloway, in Whalsay or Unst: no lack at all of the ability to argue and debate. But paradox is indigenous. They exhibit it again when they deplore the islands' poverty, and fill your glass with whisky while they search for further instances. They grumble strenuously at the foreigners' invasion of their native seas, and entertain with equal hospitality Germans and Swedes, Norwegians and Dutchmen—and Russians too, when they get the chance. Philosophically they denounce the Welfare State for its undiscriminating charity, and in a more practical mood apply with scrupulous promptitude for the latest social benefit or agricultural subsidy. They have, moreover, the admirable faculty of laughing at themselves.

Until quite recently Lerwick published two weekly papers, but one of them died in 1963. The survivor, *The Shetland Times*, a publication of unusual merit, is thoughtfully edited and concerned with larger topics than those which commonly fill a rural paper. It is well aware of the instabilities in Shetland's economy, and the difficulties entailed by a demand for new standards of living within a traditional pattern of life. It will report at length an academic discussion on the feasibility of maintaining all three native industries of agriculture, fishing, and the production of woollen goods; and question the advantages of concentrating on one or other of them. It will examine the benefits of re-seeding sterile land, and consider a scheme for the apportioning of common grazing and the enlargement of small holdings by the redistribution of crofting tenancies whose absentee crofters are, in the aggregate, as great a nuisance as absentee landlords.

Its contributors are outspokenly critical of existing conditions, and generous with suggestions for improvement. They discuss the findings of a delegation sent to the Faeroes to learn how that remote and sterile archipelago has found in sixty years a prosperity reflected in the doubling of its population from 15,000 to something over 30,000; and among contributory reasons disclose the fact that while the Faeroes receive little direct aid from Denmark, their banks are remarkably liberal in financing new enterprise. Or, with a realistic eye, they examine the parlous state of the island of Yell, and quote the adverse comment of a foreign observer who said that if the people of Yell had more faith in themselves, and would show some initiative, they could make a very fair living from the sea around them: in deep water near their island, said the foreigner, there are plenty of halibut, but none is caught by a Yell fisherman.

The energetic Member for Orkney and Shetland is Jo Grimond,* and Mr. Grimond's well-known views on the nonsensicality—the very mischievous nonsensicality—of concentrating, not only so much of industry, but so much of management, administration, and all national interests in the over-crowded south-eastern corner of England, are amply recorded in the *Shetland Times*. With eloquence and reason Mr. Grimond pleads for a distribution of effort, at once more democratically fair and commercially more sensible, throughout the kingdom; and the editor backs him up with an article about the regeneration of the northern parts of Norway—so remote, so harshly afflicted by boisterous weather, and wasted in war by the efficiency of German malevolence—but now restored by the kindly attention of a government whose

*Jo Grimond, now Baron Grimond of Firth, served as MP for Orkney and Shetland from 1950 to 1983.

servants, with an efficiency equal to their good will, have domesticated so distant a village as Hammerfest, so remote an area as Finmark, in the whole economy of their country.

There is, in Britain, no local newspaper that shows a more realistic, intelligent, and comprehensive awareness of the problems of its own environment; and the *Shetland Times* is only one indication, or proclamation, of an intelligence that must be called endemic. What other county, with a population of less than 20,000, produces a quarterly magazine, with a predominating literary interest, like *The New Shetlander*? This lively, sentimental, but self-critical review is characterized by a passionate interest in boats and the sea, and a stubborn devotion to the Shetland dialect which does not exclude toleration of those who see the dialect as mere anachronism, and devotion to it as a whimsical self-indulgence. The review is decorated by cartoons drawn with much skill and humour, and coloured by a general pessimism that hardly escapes the charge of equanimity.

But the most signal example of Shetland's highly individual will and creative fancy is the annual festival, held in Lerwick, of Up-Helly-Aa. This flaming declaration of viking ancestry and glorification of the Norse heroic spirit is, as I have said already, no ancient rite, but a deliberate metamorphosis of a pagan fire-festival, observed in several parts of Scotland, that marked the end of Yule and saluted, with a distant hope, the sun emerging from winter's bondage. At Burghead on the Moray Firth, not far from Elgin, a blazing tar-barrel, called a *Clavie* and prepared with proper obedience to old precept, is still, on New Year's Eve, carried round the town, and up its main street to a small hill; and something of this sort—but accompanied by guizers, men in carnival dress—was what occurred in Lerwick till 1889. In that year the tar-barrels were banished, and a Norse galley made its first appearance.

Who first proposed this spirited re-creation of what had become a dangerous and a rowdy spree is not certainly known, but there was then living in Lerwick a man of remarkable character, a poet of great local renown, called Haldane Burgess, who wrote much verse in dialect and a tale called *The Viking Path*. He had been a boy of brilliant promise—first in the Glasgow University Bursary Competition in 1886—whose academic career was cruelly halted by blindness. His spirit was undimmed, however, and with patient ingenuity he taught himself many languages, learnt to play the violin, kept himself by journalism and private teaching, and expounded Christian Socialism. A man of natural fervour, he wrote a boisterous poem called *Scranna* which—in Shetland—has been called the best comic poem since *Tam o' Shanter*, and his devotion to his own islands and their Norse hinterland cannot be doubted. I think it probable that Haldane Burgess, seeing through blind eyes a romantic vision, was the man who first proposed the burning of a viking ship. It is to the music of his song that the procession still marches, and his song is a curious compound of Norse glamour and early Socialism. Glamour gilds such a verse as:

"Of yore, our fiery fathers sped upon the Viking Path;
Of yore, their dreaded dragons braved the ocean in its wrath;
And we, their sons, are reaping now their glory's aftermath;
The waves are rolling on.

And Socialism shines naively through the concluding verse:

"Our galley is the People's Right, the dragon of the free,
The Right that, rising in its might, brings tyrants to their knee;
The flag that flies above us is the Love of Liberty;
The waves are rolling on."

But Haldane Burgess—if his was the invention—created something that found a matching spirit in all Shetland, and the festival has lived and grown more elaborate year by year, till now it is a resplendent parade, prepared with sedulous care, and conducted with an impressive dignity that even the wildest spirits never break, though the celebration lasts all night.

The last Tuesday of January is the night of Up-Helly-Aa. The procession is led by the Guizer Jarl and his squad, who escort the Norse galley. The Jarl and his tall followers wear winged helmets and shining armour, they carry axe and shield; and following them come perhaps thirty other squads, a dozen or more men in each, and they are dressed according to their fancy as Red Indians or Cossacks or Cabinet Ministers. All carry torches, the well-drilled column turns and counter-marches, bands play, and from ships in the harbour rockets rise into the riven darkness of the sky. The galley is brought to its journey's determined end, and the guizers in a circle round it sing *The Norseman's Home*. Then their torches are flung into the ship, and flames envelop it. The funeral pyre lights the black streets, and sometimes, it is said, the Aurora Borealis—the Northern Lights, the Merry Dancers—come up from the Polar horizon to expand illumination.

From hall to hall in the waiting town the guizers go to entertain—perhaps with elaborate masque or a rehearsed cabaret performance—and the dancing starts. But curiously, in a town much given to strong potations and the old generosity of the Norse drinking-hall, there is no rowdiness, no ill behaviour. The authority of the Guizer Jarl is absolute, and in the dim of the morning light the dancers go home—if not with undiminished dignity—at least with a nicely preserved circumspection.

Up-Helly-Aa is a living festival, and its overt romanticism flows naturally from a small and secret spring in the strange heart of Shetland.

5

The Shetland Model

On almost every beach in Shetland, pulled well above the high-water mark, the traveller will see three or four small boats built on distinctive and singularly graceful lines. They are double-ended—that is to say, the bow and stern have nearly the same shape—and the gunwale rises at either end with the wing-sweep of an Arctic tern. The over-all length is much longer than the keel—in the proportion of about 3 to 2—and the entry, duplicated at the stern, has the smooth curve of a bird's egg. There is usually a fleet of these boats lying to moorings at the south end of Lerwick's harbour, and on gently moving, green, translucent water they sit with the buoyant assurance of a small gull: of a kittiwake, or that exquisite little bird the grey phalarope.

There are, in Shetland, more boats to head of population than anywhere else in Britain—perhaps as many as in Norway—and their importance in the life of the islands can hardly be over-estimated. Not all of them serve a commercial purpose. Many are still used for inshore fishing, but many have been built for pleasure only, and the competition of local regattas. These fill an emotional need, for the Shetlander is very much a marine creature, and the boat in which he sails on a summer evening is a lively symbol of an heroic past. It is a lineal descendant of the viking longship, and its intermediate ancestor, as bravely handled, was the sixareen: an open fishing-boat. Its name or classification, whatever its size, is the Shetland model, and no account of Shetland can ignore it.

It first came into use, as a commercial fishing-boat, after the Dutch trade declined and many landed proprietors adopted the industry which the Hollanders had abandoned. They bought the boats, they cured and sold the fish. A fisherman could work only for his own laird, or the laird's tenant-in-chief, and all he needed for his labour and his household he had to buy at the laird's shop.

This state of total dependence, and poverty resulting from it, lasted until Arthur Anderson broke the wretched system—or at least opened a gap in it—by starting the Shetland Fishing Company on the island of Vaila.

That was in 1837, and till then the custom had been to import boats from Norway in parts ready-made for assembling. The largest of these boats pulled six oars—hence the word sixareen—and were used for the haaf fishing: that is, the open sea as far as forty miles from land. (*Haaf* is the old Norse or Norn word for the deep sea.) They carried a mast stepped almost amidships, in viking fashion, and a square sail which, in the early days, was used only when running before the wind. The oars were pulled against single thole-pins by means of a grummet of cow-hide called a *humlaband*.

Gradually the Shetlanders took to building their own boats, but continued to build on the Norwegian model. Some refinements were achieved in due course, and here and there a builder became pre-eminent for his skill and the artistry of his eye; for builders worked by hand and eye, and a man's trademark was the suavity of a boat's entry, its sea-kindliness and speed. All the boats were clinker-built, with a great sheer and rake, and flared sides. The sixareens measured about 30 feet over all, with a keel of some 20 feet, and they had to be built with a strength sufficient to bring home a heavy catch through rough seas, but light enough to let six or seven men haul them up a steep shingle-beach. A smaller model was the fourareen, used for inshore fishing, which measured some 20 to 22 feet over all; and a still smaller one was built for saithe fishing in fairly sheltered water.

For the haaf fishing the men lived in bothies built with rough stone walls on the shore, and went home only for the week-end, or *helly*: the holiday time that is celebrated, as an exceptional holiday, at Up-Helly-Aa. They would spend two or three days at sea, probably out of sight of land, in an open boat, and live mainly on oat-bread or oatmeal mixed with cold water and fresh cod's liver; though latterly it was usual to carry an iron pot in which, when set upon stones, a fire could safely be kindled to warm their meal-and-water, or even cook a fish. But this rough life was lived with great verve and spirit, and when half a dozen boats set off together from their shore station, they would always make a race of it to the fishing grounds, bending to their oars and urging their fleet boats through the tumbling sea. Then with their lines baited, feeling for the pluck of a codling, they would watch the changing sky and sometimes have to run before a sudden gale. Exhilaration might go hand-in-hand with danger, for when a boat was running with a full sail her speed might increase till she was "sea-loose"—surfing, that is—with a noise as if "she were being drawn through a beach of pebbles."—So says Charles Sandison in a pamphlet on the sixareens which includes high technical detail with absorbing narrative.

There were two tragical episodes during these days of the haaf fishing in open boats, the first in 1832, the next in 1881. There were, perhaps, as many as five hundred boats at sea in mid-July, 1832, when a sultry day was suddenly broken by a roaring westerly gale that, on land, tore great clods out of old turf-dykes. Many of the boats were on the Atlantic side, and ran home quickly, but others—those that kept afloat—were driven so far to the east that they could see the high hills of Norway. Thirty-one were lost, but some of the crews were saved by Dutch busses. A hundred and five men did not come home from the haaf.

Sandison has preserved an account of the gale of 1881 as it was experienced by a boat fishing some thirty miles north-west of Uyea Isle, which lies off the northern corner of the long Mainland. For nine hours the men had rowed in a calm sea, and on the fishing grounds they shot six lines, and hauling three, unhooked 180 ling. The day was still fine. But suddenly they both saw and heard "the weather coming". It struck them hard, and the sea broke over them. At their mid buoy there were fish on the line that floated it to the surface, but they had well over a ton aboard, and wanted no more. Under a bare mast the boat was already foaming at the bows.

It was half-past nine at night—but a summer night, with little darkness—when they cut their line, and their course home would bring the wind well abaft the beam. They set the square, close-reefed sail, and brought the tack forward to let them sail on a broad reach. There were two men at the halyards, and the skipper sat down to lee with the helm over his shoulder. The other four men kept quiet and still. No one spoke, for the men at the halyards knew what to do.

Sometimes the boat had the wind broad on the beam, but often they had to bear away and run the waves. They tried to avoid the heaviest of the breaking crests, but once, when they had to run clean through the middle of a great surging wave, the sea rose very high astern, so "they pressed her with the sail when the surge came round her, and although the sail was laid down she run in it for a bit like a field of snow, and took water over both sides."

The silent skipper at the helm, watching the tumultuous sea, and the silent men at the halyards raising the sail a couple of feet, lowering it lest they drive under—so they sailed through the roaring summer night—and once she was caught by the tail of a breaking wave and smothered from the mast aft—but still sailed on, and at last made the shelter of Ronas Voe, the long curving inlet under the great bulk of Ronas Hill. They had taken four hours to run home, and Charles Sandison, by plotting the distance they had sailed, discovered their average speed had been 9¼ knots. It seems incredible for a boat with a 28-foot waterline, but Sandison's calculations had been careful and he was sure of his conclusion.

But ten boats failed to return from that gale, and more than sixty men were lost. It was the death-blow to the old style of haaf-fishing, and the open sixareens were gradually replaced by larger, heavily built, decked boats of a sort already in use in the Moray Firth, the Fifies and Zulus. And then, for a generation or longer, Shetland lived and prospered on herring. New markets opened in Germany and Russia, and herring, those elusive fish, abounded. Year after year Lerwick and Bressay Sound were crowded with boats, the harbour a forest of masts, and a migrant population of gutters—bluff, loud-voiced women—and salesmen and curers filled Commercial Street and the echoing lanes above. By the end of the nineteenth century Lerwick was the herring capital of Scotland, and through the early years of the present century the boom continued. Then came recession, and depression; but today one is grateful for a small revival of that great industry. For how good a fish the herring is!

But one needs to go to Lerwick to taste it at its best. To Lerwick in July, when the long journey is immediately repaid at the breakfast table with a pair of freshly kippered, lately caught herring fat with the plankton of the summer sea, coloured by the curer to that exquisite hue which reminds one of dark lamplight on armour painted by Rembrandt's brush, and cooked till the firm white flesh strains plumply away from tenuous bones. There is no flavour so good—unless it be the quite different flavour of fresh herring, of the same quality, fried with a delicate care in

Broch of Mousa, Shetland
(overleaf) *Jarlshof*
Fladdabister

oatmeal. But all fish, newly caught in northern waters, have a native virtue that far surpasses the confectioned dishes of the most sophisticated kitchen: the colder the water the better the fish—the Orkney or Shetland lobster is slightly better than the Hebridean—and a new-caught herring is better than a Dover sole that has lain on ice. One does not, perhaps, associate Shetland and luxury; but nowhere have I eaten, with equal greed and pleasure, such good breakfasts.

As for the gallant sixareens, they died as all things die, but one is consoled for their disappearance by the survival of lineal descendants in the racing models, the regatta boats, that sit as lightly as grey phalaropes on the grass-green water at the south end of Lerwick harbour. They are lovely little craft—as lovely as can be seen anywhere—and in skilful hands they are marvellously seaworthy. But skilful hands are advisable.

Running before the wind in a Shetland model
Boat repairs

6

Scalloway

From Lerwick the traveller should drive to Scalloway. It is a matter of no more than six or seven miles on a climbing road that offers a long view to the north before it turns in a broad loop to the west and south, and approaches the old capital of Shetland. Scalloway is now a sturdy village that shows some recent growth; it is very pleasantly situated, and with a couple of small hotels is an excellent base from which to explore the intricate geography of the parishes that lie in a brown and watery maze to the north-west. Its most obvious features are fish-quays and the ruins of a castle. The fish-quays are more important in an economic context—the curious visitor should walk warily under a cloud of quite incontinent herring-gulls—but the castle is more interesting.

The ruin is tall and gaunt, but not without grace. An oblong block, four storeys high with a garret on top, has a square wing attached to its south-west angle; and turrets are corbelled out from the corners. On the ground floor of the main block is a vaulted passage off which opens a kitchen with a vast fireplace at one end, a well at the other; and a noble hall with nine windows occupies the first floor. On the second floor two chambers, and three on the third: all with fireplaces and good windows. Single rooms occupy the second and third floors of the square wing, each with a fireplace and well lighted; and on the third floor there are doorways that open into little circular privies in the corner turrets. It is, quite clearly, a building planned for noble ease, for a certain splendour rather than harsh dignity, and so lavishly is it lighted that one has to suppose, in him for whom it was built, an eye for a view.

The date of its foundation is 1600, and Andrew Crawford—buried in Tingwall churchyard—built it for Patrick Stewart, that rascally but fastidious Earl whose greed and tyranny reduced the islands to surly poverty, and left to posterity some enchanting monuments. Patrick Stewart and his works reinforce the notion that all good architecture is anti-social, and the memory of Black Pate is justly execrated while his memorials are admired. But it is, perhaps, easier to forgive him than that vandal, the Earl of Morton, who ruled and robbed Orkney and Shetland two hundred years later; for Morton showed respect neither for people nor architecture, but gave leave to a local magnate, Sir Andrew Mitchell, to plunder the gateways and windows of the Stewart Earl's castle to furnish material for a house of his own that Mitchell was building in the western parish of Sandsting.

To the south the upper windows of the castle overlook the green island of Trondra, and Trondra lies above the Siamese twins of West Burra and East Burra, which are joined at their middle parts by a minute isthmus. They lie along the Sumburgh leg of the Mainland, and though pleasant to the view are losing their population. At Hamnavoe, in the northern part of West Burra, there is an admirable natural harbour, close to good fishing grounds, but the islands have no peat, an indifferent water supply, and the literal fact of isolation is increasingly repugnant to the modern mind.

The historical interest of these long, green, narrow islands lies in a tradition that there was once, at Papil on West Burra, a tall-towered church like that on Egilsay in Orkney; and in the two Papil Stones that were found there. The simpler, showing an incised cross, remains on the site; the other, now in the National Museum in Edinburgh, is a splendid example of the fantastically Christianized minds of the island Picts who accepted baptism from Celtic missionaries. A cross whose arms are divided by decorated almonds, and whose shaft stands between cloaked and crosier-bearing churchmen, fills the upper segment of the stone; below that is a beast that looks like a mastiff with a boar's head; and under it are two creatures, part bird and part man, who carry axes and whose heron-beaks are lodged in a human skull. It will seem extravagant to claim a Pictish ancestor for that enigmatic painter Hieronimus Bosch, but the heron-men show a curious family resemblance to some of the creatures in those paintings by Bosch that caught the sombre eye of Philip II of Spain, and now hang in the Prado.

North-west of the two Burras there is a sprawl of islets, and above them the sea thrusts into the Mainland the long, narrow arms called Whiteness Voe, Stromness Voe, Weisdale Voe, and Sandsound Voe. To approach this splintered landscape a minor road from Scalloway runs north along the western side of the little loch of Asta and the larger loch of Tingwall.

7

The Watery West

In Norse times the lochside at Tingwall was the meeting-place of the Shetland Althing, or parliament; and according to tradition it sat on an islet in the loch which is now no more than a peninsula. It may not be necessary to accept this tradition, for there is nothing in the law-books to suggest that Norse legislators had to choose the windiest and least comfortable of places for their deliberation. More probably the islet was used for holmgang: the legal, ritualistic duel which served the purpose of trial by ordeal.

As on the island of Burra there was once a high-towered church here, but on the authority of Arthur Edmonston, a doctor who wrote about Shetland in 1809, they were both "demolished within the last fifteen years, from a principle of barbarous economy, to supply stones at a cheap rate for building the plain presbyterian churches which now occupy their places." It was probably the rich pasture of the district that brought parliament and church-builders here, for this is limestone country, and in early summer the ditches bloom like gardens. But over much of Shetland—which is not yet addicted to the wholesale and abominable use of insecticidal chemical sprays—there is a wonderful roadside florescence that delights the traveller with a natural but ever-decreasing gaiety.

A little way north of the Tingwall loch the main road leads north-westward to pass the long, intrusive voes and bisect the fantastic peninsula that includes the parishes of Sandsting, Walls, and Sandness. It is approximately triangular in shape, with its base to the east and its apex pointing to the west and the island of Papa Stour; and on the map it looks like a jigsaw puzzle of which the pieces have been shaken loose, while on the spot—from any commanding viewpoint, that is—it is a bewilderment of land and water. In grim and storm-beshadowed weather it is a spectacle of utter desolation; but under a brightly blowing sky it has a marvellous and wild appeal.

The road to it offers first a southward view of the green sides of Whiteness Voe, then crosses a neck of land between Stromness Voe and Strom loch: here is a Church of Scotland manse on one of the most delectable sites in all Shetland, commanding a parish where fields grow down to the tide-mark and fish swim within the sounds of harvest.

Then the road, heading north, turns sharply round the narrow top of Weisdale Voe, where the Weisdale burn is said to offer outstandingly good sea-trout fishing. But sea-trout come into many a Shetland burn and voe—to the fisherman they are Shetland's strongest lure, though they themselves are fanciful and frolicsome in their choice of lures, and hard to hold when they have taken—and a greater distinction is the plantation of trees which decorates the lands of the principal proprietor in this neighbourhood.

A tree in Shetland is a great rarity, and its principal enemy is wind. Shetland is subject to frequent and violent gales, and persistent strong winds prevent, by agitation, the rootlets of a tree from securing a strong and nourishing hold on the soil. If one built a wall forty feet high, it would be possible to grow trees of an equal height immediately under its lee. Without shelter, the odds against the growth of even such sturdy creatures as Corsican pine or plane tree are heavy. It is, then, greatly to the credit of the proprietor of Weisdale that he has succeeded in maintaining and increasing a plantation that—though its individual members have a somewhat strained and meagre look—can fairly be called a wood; and if other proprietors had so firm a belief in the benefits of natural shelter, and the aesthetic value of woodlands, there are several parts of Shetland where the hostility of nature and the pessimism of the professional sylviculturist might be overcome. An aesthetic impulse—the wish to improve a harsh prospect—might, with good luck, find economic justification; for a belt of trees does excellent service in drying a wet soil.

On the western side of Weisdale Voe the road turns south for a couple of miles before taking its true westward course through the watery maze of Aithsting, Walls, and Sandness. Sandsound Voe leads into a little inland sea called The Firth, and beyond that there lies, to the north, a riotous confusion of land and loch and intrusive firths. But a minor road, that turns to the south, leads to a greater surprise than any natural wonder can afford. At a place called Stanydale—two and a half miles north-east of the village of Walls—there was recently discovered what C. S. T. Calder, formerly of the Royal Commission on Ancient Monuments, describes with some confidence as a temple. Not indeed a temple of the sort one sees in Sicily or Egypt or southern India, but a massive structure of the neolithic age, built by a people of whom, so far, nothing has been said and nothing seen.

Some attention has been paid to the differences that still exist, or have existed, between Orkney and Shetland, and improbable though it must seem, there is evidence that, so long ago as the late Stone Age, the two archipelagos were inhabited by two different sorts of people. In Shetland there are no chambered cairns of any kind found in Orkney; but of a type of cairn unknown in Orkney twenty-eight examples have been discovered. Uniform in plan—or approximately so—they are shaped like the heel of a boot, or a horse-shoe, with a slight concavity in front and an inner chamber of trefoil form: consisting, that is, of three recesses of nearly equal size. They have been given the name of heel-shaped cairns, and all of them—or all that are known—lie north and west of the loch of Tingwall. There are several in the watery maze of the western peninsula.

Calder says emphatically that "the Orkney cairns are clearly distinct from those of Shetland", and quotes Professor Bryce as saying that the heel-shaped cairn "is not simply a degenerate Orkney or Caithness monument, but is a variety of chamber tomb developed independently in Shetland by people with traditions of their own, who perhaps reached the islands, not by way of the north of Scotland, but directly from south or east."—If that is so, the weather of the sub-Boreal period must have been much more equable and kindly than our present climate, but even allowing the voyagers calm seas, it is difficult to imagine what sort of boats they came in. The heel-shaped cairns were certainly not the work of people who had the tools to build a shapely vessel; but perhaps they could construct a raft of the Kon-tiki kind.

Now the so-called temple at Stanydale is the same shape as these typically Shetland cairns, but considerably bigger. Obviously, says Calder, it is associated "in style and date with the cairns, at least in outward appearance and general technique", but the interior is so different that it must have "served a very different function". The temple is 65 feet long by 45 feet broad, and within walls more than 12 feet thick there is a nearly oval chamber that measures 40 feet by 20 feet. In plan the chamber looks like an egg balanced in a cup too small for it, and the shell of the egg is broken by five intrusions. To find buildings of a similar kind, Calder says one must go to the Mediterranean, where in Malta and Gozo there are like structures; and they "are authoritatively classed as temples".

From Stanydale one returns to the main road, but leaves it again, a mile or two farther on, to go south to the village of Walls, which has a good natural harbour protected by the island of Vaila, where in 1838 Arthur Anderson established his Shetland Fishery Company. But Walls has lost its importance. It was once a port of call for ships from Leith and Aberdeen, and once a port from which Shetland boats went out to fish the Faeroe and Greenland seas. It is a pleasant place, a pretty place, but it has that air of sadness which is native to all places where endeavour has been defeated; a crumbling village is like a miniature of Samarkand or Carthage, though it may inspire the consoling reflexion that its history was certainly less wicked. The seasons of history change, of course, as do the seasons of the year, and natural advantages may bring to deserted ports a return of the prosperity they once enjoyed; but it must be admitted that no such prospect is as yet visible for Walls.

The main road—the road that bisects the peninsula—comes to an end at Sandness and Melby, opposite the island of Papa Stour. Of the parish of Aithsting, that lies north of the road, it is impossible to give a coherent account or describe in any detail its shape or scenery. The land is too fragmented, the water too discursive. An excellent County Council has built roads to serve, as it seems, almost every house in the peninsula, and some are still unmarked on the map, and not all are adequately signposted. The motorist may lose his way, and be rewarded beyond expectation by coastal views of a rude majesty broken here and there by small idyllic beaches that lie serenely under the frowning aspect of adjacent cliffs, or the shining innocence of little hill-lochs reflecting a brilliant sky against dark hill-slopes scarred by the black trenches of the peat-diggers. Curlew and golden plover, whimbrel and wheatear, and about the shore innumerable gulls, populate enormous vacancies, and broken walls betray the extent of a vanished population.

Longest of the voes that reach into the jigsaw parish of Aithsting are Brindister, narrow and sheltered, running into curiously patterned shallows; and Aith, much broader, that stretches from Papa Little to the village of Aith on the neck of the peninsula. Between them is the rock-walled island of Vementry, with a good heel-shaped cairn in it; and elsewhere in the peninsula are ruined brochs. However inhospitable much of this land may seem, it has nurtured a population for two and a half thousand years.

8

Papa Stour and Foula

The road that bisects the watery peninsula comes to an end at Sandness and Melby, opposite the island of Papa Stour, which is separated from the Mainland by a channel not much more than a mile across, but less innocent than it looks. The name of the island records an early settlement by Christian monks or missionaries, perhaps from the church that sent its messengers to St. Ninian's Isle; perhaps from Columba's Iona; or possibly from some northern group of Pictish converts.

It is interesting that the other two *Papa* islands in Shetland lie nearby: Papa Little at the head of Aith Voe, some ten miles to the east; and Papa, by West Burra, about twenty-four miles to the south-east. South again from Papa is St. Ninian's Isle. All the known or named settlements of the Celtic church, that is—whether mission-stations or hermitaries—lie in the southern half of the west side of Shetland, and may be coeval. Perhaps a little fleet of coracles put out from the Isle of Whithorn or Iona—trusting in God and the Atlantic—and by southerly winds and a westerly drift were cast ashore on these bare islets, and there their Christian passengers may have remained, contented with the landfall to which God and the benignity of the tides had directed them.

Papa Stour, deeply indented by three large voes and numerously bitten by lesser geos, measures about three miles from west to east and less than that from north to south. John Tudor, the Victorian traveller, writes of it with Victorian enthusiasm. He begins his chapter with the stout assertion: "There are caves and caves, but probably none in the British Isles which excel those this little isle can show in weird, fantastic outline and rich colouring combined." He describes a circumnavigation of the island from Melby to its south side and round to the west: to

Kirk Sands and Clingarie Geo, past Gorsendie Geo and Shepherd's Geo to Hamnavoe. Here, for winter fishing, there used to be a fishermen's booth and a curing station; in Olas Voe, on the other side of the island and pointing north, the Dutchmen had a booth; and in Housa Voe, nearest the Mainland, the herring-fishers mended their nets. But there is no trace of such industry nowadays.

What remain, however, are the caves that excited Tudor's imagination and roused him to rare enthusiasm. A little way beyond Hamnavoe "You come to Francie's Hole, one of the show caves, and though not very large, in the writer's opinion the most beautiful one of all. You enter through a perfectly arched entrance cut in the face of a cliff of perhaps forty feet or so in height, and can almost fancy you are in a cave in fairyland, so exquisite is the colouring of the roof and sides, and so pellucid is the water. What the length, breadth, or height may be the writer cannot say, so overpowered with the beauty of the place was he, that he utterly forgot to estimate them. The rock forming the sides and the roof, apparently porphyritic, is partly green from sea-weed or slime, and partly red of many shades, and in places glistens like mica. The roof is studded with bosses of a deep rich purple, like the bloom on a grape, and resembling in form and regularity what are to be seen on the roofs of cathedral crypts and cloisters. Several caves branch off on the left, and at the head is a beautiful pink beach, at the top of which are alcoves or recesses like stalls in a church."

Tudor continues his voyage to Brei Geo, where "the rocks assume the most fantastic forms, as often as not resembling ruined castles"; to Christie's Hole where pigeons roost and cormorants drop from their filthy nests; and so to Eshy Wick, and the islets of Fugla and Lyra Skerry. Fugla, as its name declares, has always been a home for many sea-birds, and Lyra for the nocturnal *lyrie* or Manx shearwater: the Skerry is caverned and cross-caverned by long, high-arched tunnels through which the Atlantic tides roar with a frightening speed. Just north of it is the tall, impressive column of rock called the Stack of Snalda, on whose summit an eagle used to nest, and from here are visible, some three or four miles to seaward, the broken waves that mark the dangerous Ve Skerries, a peril to ships but a sanctuary for Arctic terns.

Tudor's voyage continued, past the arch of the Horn of Papa, to the Hole of Bordie, a tunnel half a mile long through the headland of Bordie, the northern exit of which is studded with *baas*, or submerged rocks. His powers of admiration, however, had been exhausted by the western cliffs, and of the north shore he has little to say, though its names—Shelma Wick and Lamba Ness, Bottomless Geo and Doun Hellier—are as wild and romantic, or sinister it may be, as any of the others. But near the entrance to Housa Voe another isolated stack, with some show or sign of a ruined house on top, revived his interest, and he tells its story.

Its name is Frau Stack, or the Maiden's Stack, and it is said that a gentleman once imprisoned his daughter in that inaccessible dwelling in order that "she might be shut and secluded from the Company of Men". But alas for the poor gentleman's paternal care! For "tho a Maiden when put in, yet she was found with Child when brought out, notwithstanding of her being so closely kept." There are, it appears, other isolated pinnacles with the same name, both in Shetland and on the coast of Norway; memorials, every one of them, to men's long endeavour to impose their will on women, and their ancestral failure.

"Papa Stour," says Tudor, "is wonderfully fertile for Shetland on its east and south-east sides," but "want of fuel is the great drawback, and peat has to be boated either from Sandness or Papa Little. Many families have in consequence emigrated in the last ten years to New Zealand." The population fell from 351 in 1871 to 253 in 1881; and has been falling ever since.

I went there in the summer of 1963 with an official of the County Council who was looking at abandoned crofts and common grazing unused because of depopulation, with the benign hope of apportioning vacant land so as to make the remaining crofters self-sufficient. There is, in Shetland, a peculiar affection for Papa Stour, and a corresponding dismay at the thought of its being abandoned. It has, indeed, a sort of generous charm—an attraction separable from the splendour of its cliffs—for it is small enough to be visibly an island, yet large enough to dispel any sensation of confinement, and much of its soil is kindly. But the poverty that Tudor noted was still apparent, and to repair the lack of peat there had been pitiful attempts to cut fuel from the sandy turf of the island: turf that looked as if it would hardly smoulder in a gale of wind.

It has, moreover, a basic disadvantage other than its lack of peat, and that is the nature of the mile-wide channel that divides it from the Mainland. It is swiftly tidal, and can be rough.

It was rough, or roughish, when we went out in the morning, and by mid-afternoon the sea was running high, with white-hooded waves from shore to shore. Our boat was the island ferry, a Shetland model with a sufficient engine and a boatman of superlative skill. Though the channel, at its narrowest, is not much more than a mile, the voyage was a lot longer because, with a strong tide running, the shortest distance between two points is not necessarily—or very often—a straight line. It was, indeed, long enough to demonstrate the necessary art of boat-handling in such a waterway; for with an untutored man at the tiller we would certainly have filled, whereas we sailed dry between or over great tumbling ridges, and near the Mainland shore, where the wind and the tide were viciously opposed, the boatman throttled back his engine with so exact a judgment that we slid through a wild confusion of broken water on the strong power of the tide alone, and divided the waves with quiet assurance.—A very pretty lesson in seamanship, but a reminder that an island community, though it may live without doctor or parson, cannot exist without a good boatman.

It is well to remember this prime necessity when, from any commanding position on this side of the Mainland, one looks westward and sees the gaunt, forbidding silhouette of Foula.

Some years ago a memorable film called *The Edge of the World* was made there, and for a vast number of people Foula became a symbol of loneliness. Every winter its symbolism is revived by Scottish newspapers which, from mid-December till some time in March, report at intervals that Foula has had no communication with the Mainland of Shetland for three, four, or five weeks; and the islanders' supply of flour and paraffin, tea and tobacco, is running short. It lies twenty-seven miles west of Scalloway, or rather more than twenty miles from the village of Walls. But those twenty miles are open to westerly gales and the surge and swell of the whole Atlantic.

On a fine day Foula's great cliffs can be seen from Orkney, and from the Atlantic it is visible long before the Mainland of Shetland can be seen. The grim height of the Sneug stands 1,370 feet above the sea, and the awesome Kame, its neighbouring cliff, is 1,220 feet high: 84 feet taller than St. John's Head in Hoy, and only 5 feet less than the dreadful cliff of Soay in the St. Kilda group.

When Tacitus reported that Agricola's fleet, in Orkney waters, had seen legendary Thule on the horizon, it may well have been the stark sides of Foula; though it must be admitted that there are other claimants for that distinction.

The island is over three miles long, from north to south, and something more than two miles from east to west. There is only one landing-place, on the east side under a dark and very steep hill: a landing-place, not a harbour, for though a jetty has been built, Ham Voe is open to the sea and the post-boat has to be hauled up in davits and pulled inland over the jetty for safety. Nor is the island a fertile place. There is a broad belt of cultivated land, or land that could be cultivated, under the eastern slope of its hills, but more than half of it is high, sour moorland that holds the clouds. Yet for three hundred years, and probably much longer, its people have been warmly attached to their comfortless home, and sturdily reluctant to leave it.

In 1701 a minister of the Church of Scotland, John Brand, published a small book describing his recent visit to Orkney and Shetland as one of an ecclesiastical commission of inquiry. He was a credulous man, much given to the posturing, narrow-minded, bitterly religious enthusiasm which, since the Reformation, had kept all Scotland in a state of sterile conflict; and much of what he says cannot be trusted. But he has an interesting passage on Foula.

"Remarkable are the Dangers," he says, "which many in these Isles do undergo in climbing the Rocks for Fowls and Eggs, especially in *Foula*, where the Inhabitants in the Summer time do most live by this kind of Provision, and are judged to be the best climbers of Rocks in all this Country, for some of them will fasten a Stake or Knife, as some say, in the ground on the top of the Rock, to which they ty a small Rope or Cord, and so they will come down the face of the Rock with this in their hand, 60, 70, or 80 Fathoms, and do return bringing up Eggs and Fowls with them; but indeed very many of them lose their lives; yea, it is observed that few old Men are to be seen there, they being so cut off before they arrive at old Age; Many of them are weary of the dangers and hazards they daily incur, yet neither will they leave the place, nor give over these perilous attempts, all the sad instances of their Friends and Neighbours Perishing and death cannot have this influence to deter and affright them from undergoing the like hazards: At so small a rate do they value their lives, that for a few Fowls and Eggs they will endanger them, whereas they might have as good and a much safer living elsewhere."

They were stubbornly attached to their own way of life, and when Brand was in Shetland they had some reason for their attachment. They must have been largely immune from the alien discipline of life on the Mainland, and their relative freedom was supported by the rich harvest they won from the surrounding seas. There were cod in abundance on the Foula Banks, and mackerel, shoals of haddock, saithe, halibut, prolific ling—accounted most valuable of all—on fishing-grounds within thirty miles of the island. The men were famous oarsmen, tireless at sea, and great dancers when winter evenings found them ashore. They had their own dance, the Foula Reel, which went to the tune of *The Shaalds of Foula*; "Up wi' da lines an link it awa, awa, ta da shaalds o Foula."—The *shaalds* were the shoals where they fished.—A visitor in the latter part of the eighteenth century, George Low, reported that these dancing people were "much at their ease, decently clothed, and of a cheerful, inquisitive character. Indeed I met no peasantry in Shetland to equal them. Their frank, free disposition, simple primitive manners, render them a very amiable people."

As lately as 1880 Foula had a population of 267, and seven sixareens fished from the island. But numbers dwindled from then on: there were 222 in 1901, and half a century later only 70, most of them old. Today they are fewer still, and the average of their age is higher. Their living vanished when steam-trawlers appeared on their fishing-grounds; the trawlers swept their livelihood away, and now they are waiting till their surviving boatmen are too old to face that hazardous little voyage to Walls.* And when their boatmen retire, the island will be evacuated, and left as a sanctuary for the myriad sea-birds that first gave it the name of Fowl Isle.

In the early part of the eighteenth century, when all Shetland was ravaged by the "Mortal Pox"—a virulent epidemic of small-pox—Foula was almost depopulated, and replenished from the Mainland. But there is no imaginable inducement to re-colonize it now, and when the little houses stand empty the Foula Reel will be forgotten in the howling of an Atlantic gale, and the bonxie will be left victor over all his human neighbours. The bonxie himself was at one time very near extermination.

*See note on page 163

Bonxie is the Shetland name for the Great Skua, a large, dark brown, heavily built rascal of a gull that lives by piracy and will not hesitate to attack a gannet. In Tudor's time, some eighty years ago, they bred nowhere in Britain except Foula and Unst, and on Foula there were perhaps fifteen pairs. The Victorian egg-collector was largely responsible for their rarity. Now they are numerous—they were carefully protected, as few human islanders are—and I have seen half a dozen of them following a ship out of Bressay Sound; others, full of fish, afloat on the Pentland Firth.

Their ordinary flight is slow and looks sluggish, but they are marvellously swift and agile when they go into the attack, take a gannet by the wing-tip or menace a black-backed gull, till the victim vomits up the last fish it has caught, and the bonxie dives again to catch it. On land they are pompous, and walk like an over-fed, old-fashioned German recruit, lifting their webbed feet high and ponderously, as if goose-stepping in heavy boots; but they can be alarming too, and in the nesting season will meet intruders—dogs or men—in head-on attack, though they rarely strike. Tudor says that if the young are taken from the nest they are easily reared and become very tame.

Powerful though he is, the bonxie is not immune from assault. His much smaller, hawk-like cousin the Arctic skua, which also nests on Foula, shows no fear of him. In Orkney and Shetland the Arctic skua is engagingly called Scootie-allan, and I have seen a pair of them harry and drive away a humiliated bonxie as if he were a heavy bomber engaged by agile Spitfires.

Commercial Street, Lerwick

YOUR
MURPHY
DEALERS
HANDCUT
TAILORING
H
Hepworths

SF 313 S

9

Tingwall to Nesting

To resume a northward journey it is necessary to return to the east shore of the Mainland and the axial road a little way north of the loch of Tingwall; where, in succession, Dales Voe, Lax Firth, Wadbister Voe, and Cat Firth let the North Sea deep into the land.

On the southern horn of Dales Voe, on the very tip of the horn called Kebister Ness, there is a little eminence that may be of volcanic origin, known as Luggie's Knowe. It was named after a fisherman of the seventeenth century who, when the weather made seafaring uncomfortable, would fish here in a cleft of the rock from which he was able to catch cod or ling at will. It was also said of him that when at sea he could catch fish ready boiled or fried; and in consequence of this ability he was burnt as a wizard in Scalloway.

A. T. Cluness, author of a fairly recent handbook on Shetland, makes the ingenious suggestion that Luggie had discovered, on Kebister Ness, a hot spring of the sort common in Iceland. He may, that is, have demonstrated his ability to boil a fish without lighting a fire, and so uncommon a faculty could easily be magnified, by jealous gossip, till he was credited with a magic art. It is a plausible explanation, though it does not account for the disappearance of the hot spring.

A long, low-lying peninsula, culminating in Hawks Ness and the ruins of a broch, separates Dales Voe from Lax Firth, at the head of which a very small lochan called the Strand that used to be famous for its sea-trout. *Lax* means salmon, and wherever it is found in a place-name there is the assurance of a long tradition of game-fishing; but I do not know if the Strand maintains its reputation. If it does, I am doubly sorry for my ignorance.

Wadbister Voe and Cat Firth make a little inland sea which, on a fine day, offers a charming, brightly coloured scene, but the land

Victoria Pier, Lerwick, until 1976 the main island terminal

is poor and here again the population has declined. The road skirts the loch of Girlsta where, in saga times, a young woman on her way to Iceland is said to have been drowned; but the legend is obscure. West of the road lies a flat and open reach of the pleasant parish of Tingwall, and hereabout—or a little farther on—I remember once meeting a woman who was the epitome of a Shetland legend much sturdier than the shadowy tale of the young woman drowned in Girlsta.

She on the road was by no means young, but she walked at a light infantry pace, and on her back was a woven basket laden heavily with peats, and in her hands a pair of knitting needles that flashed in the sun. She was knitting as she walked, with the fantastic speed that only the fingers of Shetland women could show till electronic machines began to catch them up—she was walking at a hundred and sixty paces to the minute, and on her back was a small mountain of peats—but her old brown face was serene, and neither her knitting nor her cargo prevented her from answering with warm enthusiasm when vacuously I said to her, "What a fine day it is!"—"Hid is dat, boy!" she replied, and was away down the road like the Rifle Brigade, with another stocking knitted before the next corner.

Or so it seemed, for she was truly an heroic figure, and the most remarkable thing about her was the lightness—the gaiety and ease—with which she carried her share of the Shetland woman's immemorial burden of toil. The wives of fighting men and seafaring men have always had to bear a double load—of loneliness when their husbands are away, and of added work when they come home again—and the Shetland women have shown the favour and good heart, with which they accepted toil, by the deftness of their spinning, the grace of their knitting, and the unwearying speed of their speech and movement. As with the formidable women of the Icelandic sagas, it is useless to argue with them, impossible to compete with them, and no well-brought-up Shetlander would try.

Just beyond Girlsta there is a minor road, bending to the east, which leads to the complex geography of Nesting.—A kindly visitor from the south, seeing a signpost that read *Nesting*, asked if he might add a notice *Do Not Disturb*. But like all the parish names that end in "ting" it is merely a reminder that a local parliament once met here.—South Nesting is another bewilderment of small, well-kept roads insufficiently marked, and because the coast-line is wildly improbable it is as easy to lose one's way here as in the watery peninsula on the west. And again it may be unexpectedly rewarding.

Between South Nesting and North Nesting there is a broad bay, and along its shore have lately been uncovered the small remains of a large number of neolithic houses of a sort—like the heel-shaped cairns—that do not appear in Orkney. This is not the only part of Shetland in which they have been found. There are other colonies or clusters near Sumburgh; south-east of the village of Walls; and north of Muckle Roe. But enough sites have been identified about the Bay of Nesting—nearly a score, though they have not yet been thoroughly excavated—to make it seem probable that all this district was well populated in the late Stone Age; and what has been found, where excavation has been completed, fortifies a belief that neolithic people lived in tolerable comfort.

Unlike the village sites at Skarabrae and Rinyo in Orkney, the houses here are separate, individual dwellings, the surface indication being a stout bank, grass covered, that surrounds an oval hollow. The walls are very thick, with a filling of rubble between built revetments, and they stand on a slope to permit drainage. There is evidence that the occupants enclosed fields within drystone dykes, and such artifacts as have been found seem to be agricultural rather than warlike; there are no defensive buildings. Barley was cultivated, cattle and sheep were pastured, and the Stone Age farmers enjoyed the companionship of dogs. Let it be remembered, too, that their weather was better than ours.

In contrast to these remnants of a distant age, during which life may have been relatively peaceful, there is, on the Noup Head of Nesting north of the bay, the memory of a savage occurrence at the tail-end of the sixteenth century, when Christian doctrine had lately been reaffirmed by the Scotch Reformers.—Harry Colville, the parish minister of Orphir in Orkney, had been suborned, as it seems, by Earl Patrick Stewart to assist him in depriving four brothers, of the name of Sinclair, of their rightful inheritance. The four brothers resented a gross injustice, and let their resentment be known. Whereupon Parson Colville fled from the menace of their looks and words, and took refuge in the manse of Nesting. But the four brothers followed him, hunted him to his death on the Noup, and one of them, not yet content, cut open his chest, tore out his heart, and drank the bad parson's blood. That happened on the 9th July, 1596, and in some curious by-way of justice one Gilbert Pacock, a servant of Earl Patrick, was found guilty of complicity in the murder, and a month later was beheaded at the Mercat Cross of Edinburgh.

From the loch of Girlsta the axial road marches by Sand Water, at the top of which there is a good side-road to Weisdale, and proceeds grimly northward into the desolate valley of the Lang Kaim, which is five miles long. Nowadays the road is good, and even though the traveller is benighted he need little fear meeting the trolls that used to await a tardy wayfarer here. Peat-cutters or peat-gatherers may be encountered, who now travel by motor-car to the smooth, gleaming-dark trenches they cut so neatly in the moor, and the bright black turf is no longer carried in panniers on a train of Shetland ponies, but more commodiously by motor-lorry.

Near the middle of the Lang Kaim is a little loch called Petta Water. This means the Picts' loch, and it may have added to the ghostly reputation of the valley. In the popular mind the Picts were the inhabitants of all those inexplicable ruins called "Piccy hooses"—people who lived underground or in stony chambers—and between them and the "peerie folk", the wee folk, who occupied haunted knowes, there was certainly a supposed relationship. But the peerie folk were harmless people, even helpful at times, and the worst they did was to put a cow off milking, or invite some reckless wayfarer into a knowe where they might keep him dancing for a year or more. Trolls, on the other hand—those wicked immigrants from the Norwegian forests—were rowdy and destructive spirits. Supernatural creatures have their own characteristics, and trolls and peerie folk should not be confused.

The parish of Nesting has its northern boundary near Petta Water, and beyond it are Lunnasting on the one hand, Delting on the other. At the little loch of Voe there is a road to the right, which leads to Dury Voe and Lunnasting, and there are several reasons for taking this eastern fork before continuing the northward journey.

10

Lunnasting

The eastward road, from the loch of Voe, reaches—after little more than a couple of miles—a bridge across the Laxo burn, which empties into Laxo Voe, the inner corner of Dury Voe; and no one who cares about sea-trout can cross that bridge in haste, or linger without reverence and an eager hope that the burn will rise, with rain on the sour hill that feeds it, to meet a spring tide from the voe that's pulsating with noble fish.

There are forty places where you can fish for sea-trout in Shetland, and to my sorrow I know few of them. But I have often fished the Laxo burn—by grace of its proprietor, who is Shetland's Lord-Lieutenant—and such is the pleasure I have got from it that I propose to speak a little of its rewards and difficulties, because in other places, of which I know almost nothing, the rewards may be comparable and the difficulties cannot be less; and to a fisherman the sea-trout of Shetland are a lure beyond compare.

Immediately above the little bridge there is a long, dark, narrow pool whose banks are built of a quivering peat that betrays the lightest footfall to any fish waiting there for another freshet. You must approach on your knees, as if in prayer, and cast from a distance. No lure but a fly is permitted, though a worm—reluctantly it must be admitted—would always be more deadly. Day after day, though great fish break the narrow surface, you may cast in vain, and when at last a new-run trout of some four or five pounds takes your fly, the odds are you will lose it; for your flies must be small, and the mouth of a trout freshly come from the sea is very tender. But if you can retain him, what joy to see him splash and leap and run, what anxiety when he bores or sulks in the undercut of a peaty bank!

A little way above the bridge pool, under a high side, is a

half-circle of black water always rimmed with foam, and into this also you must cast from a distance. Here you may see fish lunging and plunging, and for fifteen minutes none will acknowledge your fly except, perhaps, by invisible curiosity. But leave it for half an hour, return and cast again, and the second or third cast may be taken with a sudden, decisive grasp, your rod will bend and your reel purr with satisfaction—and the fight is on.

Peat-dark is the burn, and a few hundred yards above the foamy pool is an angle in the narrow stream with a placid surface though the wind may snort and bellow on the hillside above. Casting into a ripple that broke the black mirror of the pool I once took a five and a half pounder there—it had little room to play, but surged indignantly up and down—and I almost lost a boot in the soft peat as I netted him.

But below the bridge lies a tidal pool, with rock above and a sandy, grass-grown shoal beyond, that gives, when the tide is high, the best sport of all. For when it's full a fish has room to run, and a trout of three or four pounds, with all the strength of sea-feeding in its muscle, will leap and run like—oh, but there's nothing except another sea-trout to compare it with. And even when there are no big fish in the pool there may be many finnoch—some call them finnoch, some herling—of up to a pound in weight, and a pluck at your fly will be succeeded by a dancing progress over swirling, tidal water by something that's like the talented offspring of a strong brown trout which mated with a flying-fish. These smaller fish are very beautiful, bright as burnished steel and exquisitely shaped. The larger ones combine, very happily, a look of intrinsic power with the shape of speed, and when new-run are also steel-bright or polished silver. But after two or three days in a pool above the bridge they are stained by the dark water.

The burn meanders down to a shallow beach and the sea in a box-shaped voe. Again and again have I waded and fished in vain from the beach while great fish, sea-trout and grilse, were dancing thirty yards away—sometimes almost brushing my boots—and in the distance, on either shore, others leapt in some mysterious marine ballet. But once, from a boat, I found a marvellously good substitute for the lordly ones that would not take. There was a shoal of mackerel in the voe—mackerel, as it happened, of twice the common size—and to catch them, on a trout-rod, was superlative though short-lived sport. Any sort of large, gaudy lure, such as a Terror or an out-size Alexandra, attracted them, and when they took they went off like a torpedo, no holding them, but after once sounding deeply and running twice, for thirty yards or more, they came in obediently enough.

There is fishing in Shetland—wading in voes or casting with nervous precision into narrow burns—that paints a lustre on all one's memories of that grim and splendid archipelago; and the habit of fishing entices one into places of strange and desolate beauty. Once, I remember, I walked to a small loch that lies steeply above the Laxo burn, and while idly fishing for little brownies I was enchanted by the singular concourse of birds I saw. To the east, against a low hill-side, there were no fewer than seven ravens, all talking hoarsely; on the loch were three pairs of red-throated divers, and a single male who made unsuccessful efforts to break up those happy marriages; and on the shore from which I waded I counted eleven wheatears. But no other birds, of any sort, were visible.

Before branching to the Laxo bridge the road points east and then turns north past Vidlin Voe—where one can wade and fish very agreeably—to a long, spindly peninsula that points to the northern isles of Yell and Fetlar. Where the peninsula is very pinched and narrow, the large, gaunt, and now empty mansion called Lunna House—dating in part from the seventeenth century—stands high in a position of lonely grandeur. From it there are views of large variety and oceanic extent, and in the foreground stands a monument to some early proprietor's exalted fancy: a wall protects the slope of a green height crowned by what may have been meant for a gazebo or belvedere. Above the beach is a little abandoned church, almost smothered by a plane-tree, and on the slope of the hill the remains of a minute pre-Reformation chapel. But history of a more recent sort has also touched Lunna.

When Germany invaded Norway in 1940, the initial success of German arms was quickly followed by the birth of Norwegian resistance, and within a few months angry and determined men began to make their escape—some in perilously small boats—in order to carry on the war from oversea. Shetland was their nearest landfall, and the old traffic of viking days was resumed. That, however, was only the beginning. The next step was to devise means by which some of the escapers could return to Norway without advertising their return; their purpose being to make themselves obnoxious to the German occupants of their country, and keep the escape route open. To this end a small organization came into being under two officers whose imagination was not unduly hindered by military convention, and they established their headquarters at Lunna House. A few British N.C.Os., of the imperturbable, all-purpose sort, and about forty Norwegian sailors arrived; a couple of sturdy Norwegian fishing-boats were acquired; and in the stables, barns, and out-houses at Lunna a miscellaneous collection of weapons and ammunition, explosive and incendiary material, was assembled. The organization grew—as all military organizations do—and Lunna became the centre from which a small but useful offensive was maintained.

One of the original pair of imaginative officers was David Howarth, who described the hazardous and improbable operations of the Lunna force in an admirable book called *The Shetland Bus*. The name is a testimonial to the reliability of the service provided: Norwegians who found life intolerable under German rule, and resolved to escape, took the Shetland bus to Lunna, and freedom.

11

Delting and a Suit at Law

From Lunna's narrow peninsula one returns to the round loch of Voe, and a short way beyond it the road forks again. The right-hand of the fork traverses the northern part of the parish of Delting and leads to Mossbank, from where a ferry crosses to Ulsta in the island of Yell. This parish, much of which is fertile, once supported a large population, but like other parts of Shetland suffered—as did, in grosser measure, the northern Highlands of Scotland—from the discovery, in the first half of the nineteenth century, that big sheep-runs were more profitable to a landowner than a host of subsistence farmers. The consequence was the removal of small tenants from the land to make room for a shepherd and his flock. The land was over-populated, and the standard of living deplorably low. But human beings have irrational, strong emotions, and a peasantry long settled, in even the most meagre holdings that have the benison of the sky and the ever-changing sea, cannot be turned off their land without the infliction of wounds that are slow to heal. Though economy says *Go* the heart cries out to *Stay*, and here as in so many other green and growing fragments of the Highlands and islands of Scotland there is a sense of sorrow and defeat; though cold reason will support the evictions and say, with perfect truth, that no one within living memory would have accepted the rack-ribbed conditions of life that prevailed when the outer fronds and fingers of Shetland were loud and bustling with people.

Cutting the base of this part of Delting is a little glen called Skella Dale which long retained two traditions of a sort that is native to picturesque poverty. Some way down the dale is a large, conical mound that is, or was, known as the Thieves' Howe; and its reputation was twofold. Sheep-stealing and cattle-rustling were common in its vicinity—a manifest advertisement of the richness of neighbouring pasture—and also it was a fairy knowe: one of those hillocks, that is, into which benighted travellers, especially if they were musically gifted, might be lured to entertain and play for the peerie folk who lived there. Within the knowe hours were not measured as at Greenwich, and it might be that a couple of years went by, as if in the passage of a single night, before the kidnapped wayfarer returned to his family.—Thus were the iron circumstances of poverty relieved: by an imagined dalliance with fairies, and the more realistic adventure of sheep-stealing.

Sometimes it happens that outer events impinge upon, and produce sudden, violent change in a countryside where life has been almost static for centuries, and Delting, with other parts of Orkney and Shetland, submitted to a drastic alteration in its normal activities, and in its old appearance, when war broke out in 1939. On the western side of this, its northern part, lies the long inlet of Sullom Voe—eight miles of it, the longest voe in Shetland—where the Royal Air Force came to write a paragraph in history that was fantastically different from old tales of poverty, trolls, and lifting a lamb or two. Coastal Command established a great station here from which, in the most desperate years of the war, it maintained watch and ward over the wintry North Sea between Shetland and Norway, and westward from Shetland to Iceland and the Denmark Strait.

It was a hard and bitter service, and in the Royal Air Force Sullom was not a popular station. But the pilots and their navigators who lived in the large hutted camp beside its cold waters were a cheerfully heroic company who maintained their patrols against the enmity of wild weather, and guarded with constant effort the northern approaches to our vital Atlantic sea-lanes. I remember being storm-stayed there, in the early weeks of 1941, waiting for passage to Iceland in a Sunderland flying-boat, and under a biting hail-storm watching, in the midst of wind-blown activity, the emergence from a nearby hut of a pilot, a navigator, and the booted, hooded, muffled figure of a gallant Bishop of the Episcopal Church of Scotland: Bishop Deane, of Aberdeen and Orkney, who was about to embark in a sturdy, slow-flying, stern-propelled Walrus for some other bleak island shore. "Hullo, hullo!" he shouted in his high, churchly voice. "What uncommon fun we have!"—It would be a gross and sentimental misreading of stern facts to pretend that such was the daily spirit of life at Sullom Voe, but with surprising frequency it coated, as if with a bright varnish, the roughness of danger and discomfort.

The road to Sullom Voe leads nowhere else. The axial road bends westward and lies along the northern shore of Olna Firth; and where it first opens a view of the firth, reveals what might be some displaced portion of a Norwegian landscape. This Atlantic inlet bends and broadens between its opposing walls, and at its inner end stands a little group of houses and warehouses of particular interest. They belong to a family called Adie, of much value to Shetland. Nowadays its industry is knitting and weaving, and its handwoven tweeds are characterized by charm and softness and a novelty of design that—so far as I have seen it—has succeeded marvellously well in marrying a modern desire for bright colours to the dignity of a traditional craft. Persian carpets are more intricate, but Shetland tweeds are comforting as well as gay.

Towards the end of the nineteenth century the Adies owned a fleet of fishing-boats, and sailing smacks that traded coastwise and to the Faeroes. Then, when profit from the sea began to dwindle, they set up their looms, brought weavers to Olna Firth—or taught young men to become weavers—and opened a new industry that found new markets. If a few other families had shown such enterprise and shrewdness, and set their faculties to work in their own country, the state of Shetland would be happier than it is; but only rarely do men of uncommon gifts and exceptional energy find scope for them at home. Talent, as a rule, is foot-loose.

Olna Firth opens to the west and is guarded from the Atlantic by the almost circular island of Muckle Roe. Reaching to the north from the seaward end of Olna Firth is a sheltered inlet called Busta Voe, on the far side of which stands a big house surrounded by trees. So rare a sight is this in Shetland that the traveller's eye is caught immediately, and the traveller's attention may be held for an appreciable time by a strange and sinister story of the family that once lived at Busta.

When Lerwick was still a village, Busta Voe was busy with Dutch traders who set up their booths on its sheltered beaches, and in the eighteenth century the Hall of Busta was the home of Thomas Gifford, landed proprietor and rich merchant, a man of dominating importance in the islands, whose curious motto was

"Spare when ye have nought." He had plenty, and his abilities were not limited to trade and the management of his estate. He wrote *An Historical Description of the Zetland Isles*, and enjoyed a reputation for hospitality that was commensurate with his wealth.

He had, moreover, a formidable wife who cherished the distinction of being the daughter of a baronet: the only titled man in the islands. Lady Busta, as she was known, had a sublime sense of her own importance, ruled her husband, and domineered over her family and all her neighbours, the poorest of whom were well paid for the acknowledgment of her greatness; for she was generous in her charity. Generous, too, in her fecundity: she bore fourteen children within twenty years.

High fortune seemed to bless the family until, in 1740, the red menace of smallpox struck hard and cruelly. In his diary that year Thomas Gifford wrote: "5, Wednesday. Poor Betty and Franky took the bed yesterday morning. 10, Monday. The pox out. Betty and Francie very bad. The pox riseth very slow. 12, Wednesday. The bairns are worse. This day is the 9th with them. 13, Thursday The bairns very bad all day. . . ."

Only two died of the smallpox, but not all the others made full recovery, and three more were dead before long. The family survived this diminishment, however, and the big house was still well filled. There also lived in it a tutor, the Rev. John Frisken, a cousin of the Giffords, whose father was the parish minister of Delting, and Barbara Pitcairn, a pretty and attractive girl but a poor relation. The Rev. John may have been an excellent tutor, but he seems to have drunk too much, and to have been incapable of carrying his drink. It is recorded that he fell on the table, at a marriage, and cut himself on a broken bottle; and in a neighbour's house he complained of not being given enough to drink, and praised the generosity of another host, who had given him so much that he was unable to leave.

On the 13th May, 1748, four sons of Gifford of Busta, with the Rev. John and a farm grieve, were returning by boat from Hillswick, where they had been shooting seals. The weather was fine, and the sea calm. The boat was at the mouth of Busta Voe when suddenly it was stopped by some unknown and unseen agency. The oarsmen pulled with all their strength, and could not move it. They backed, and tried to turn, but the boat was held fast. The young men grew frightened, and the Rev. John, kneeling on the bottom boards, began to pray. The others followed suit. Then they took to the oars again, the boat moved, and from the sea below came three creatures that looked like seals, and slowly swam away.

That was the story they took home, and however badly they had been frightened, four of them forgot their fear by the following day. The 14th dawned calm and bright, and in the afternoon they decided to row across to Wethersta on the east side of the voe, where Andrew Gifford their uncle lived: three of the brothers, the Rev. John, and with them they took the faithful grieve. But one of the brothers, Hay, refused to join them, and took horse to ride round the head of the voe. Andrew Gifford's household was apparently of a jovial temper, for the party did not break up till nearly midnight, when the Busta party went down to their boat. Hay, though still reluctant, went with them, for his horse had run away. They put to sea, in fine, calm weather, for a little voyage of no more than a mile; and none was ever seen again alive.

On Sunday—again a bright, windless day—the search began, and the empty boat was found with John Gifford's hat and stick in it. Every family in the parish came out to search the shores, and every boat to drag the voe. John's body was recovered, and the grieve's; but none of the others.

John was the oldest of the family, and when his body was carried ashore, where many stood waiting and watching, Barbara Pitcairn came down from the house, and knelt beside him. She undid his coat, and from an inner pocket took a paper that she hid in her dress.

The death of his four sons left Busta without a male heir; or so it seemed till Barbara Pitcairn announced that she was John's widow—married in secret by the hard-drinking tutor—and, moreover, with child. Old Lady Busta, despite her grief, could not contain her rage. Indignant at her son's *mésalliance*, she refused to recognize her poor relation's altered status, and it is said that she took the paper which proved Barbara's story, and burnt it. If this is true, it was an expensive gesture.

Six months later Barbara Pitcairn bore a male child, who in the course of time won his grandparents' affection; though Lady Busta never forgave Barbara, who lived out the rest of her lonely life in Lerwick. But the boy, Gideon, grew up, and despite his apparent illegitimacy was acknowledged heir to the Busta estate. He succeeded in 1760, he married, he enjoyed his wealth, and like his grandfather grew famous for his lavish hospitality. Then, in 1805, an elderly cousin, Andrew Gifford of Ollaberry, whose reputation was none too good, opened a correspondence with the initial purpose, as it appears, of extortion. Gideon refused his demands, and died in 1812 at the age of sixty-four; Andrew Gifford having predeceased him by a couple of years. But their quarrel survived them, and was inherited by their sons, each of whom was named Arthur.

For twenty years it was inactive, but in 1832 Arthur of Ollaberry, being a great-grandson of Thomas Gifford of Busta, began a legal process to prove himself heir to the estate, and dislodge Arthur of Busta by establishing the illegitimacy of his father Gideon. The jury gave a verdict in favour of Busta, and Ollaberry appealed. The Court of Session found in favour of Ollaberry, and Busta appealed. The Lord Justice Clerk heard his appeal, but upheld the previous decision, and Arthur of Busta found himself liable for expenses amounting to £40,000. The estate was crippled, and Arthur of Ollaberry appeared satisfied with his revenge: for though entitled to such lands as were not included in old Thomas of Busta's will, he made no effort to take possession, but presently went to live in Canada.

Some ninety years had passed since four young Giffords, their drunken tutor and a faithful grieve, were drowned mysteriously in the calm waters of Busta Voe; and Ollaberry's pointless hostility seems almost as inexplicable as the three water-beasts, with the appearance of seals, which swam away from the doomed boat. But monsters, born of the mind, still spawn as thickly in the law courts as in mythology.

South of Busta the road leads to a bridge which spans a narrow sound and gives access to the circular island of Muckle Roe, which has, on its western side, very handsome high red cliffs; but of which I can claim no great knowledge. Once, however, not many years ago, I walked round its eastern shore in bright summer weather and found the whole populace making hay with that sort of communal, genial energy which, in our mechanical and directed age, seems like an afterglow from some brightly imagined season of a past beatitude. Was there ever a time when laughter went with labour, and the fruits of labour were tossed in the sun for the labourer's own benefit? I seemed to catch a glimpse of such a time —that afternoon in Muckle Roe—and certainly it was a scene that would have engaged the heart and mind of William Morris.

12

Northmaven and North Roe

Muckle Roe is a terminus from which one can only return, to resume the journey where the axial road approaches a geological freak called Mavis Grind.

To the east, at the head of Sullom Voe, the water deepens suddenly to something between 20 and 25 fathoms; and this finger of the North Sea is separated from an inlet on St. Magnus Bay, which belongs to the Atlantic, by a steep-faced isthmus measuring no more than 50 or 60 yards across. "Grind" means gate, and "mavis"—no relation to the bird—a narrow isthmus.

Beyond the gate is Northmaven, a scenically splendid tract of rough and varied country that lies in the shape of two erratically drawn triangles; beyond Northmaven, and separated from it by the broader isthmus between Ronas Voe and Colla Firth, is North Roe, dominated by Ronas Hill; and beyond North Roe the green, fertile, but very lonely northern tip of the Mainland of Shetland.

The main road bisects that part of Northmaven which forms its right-hand triangle, and east of the road, looking over Yell Sound, is Ollaberry Bay, a pleasant, small, sheltered corner—when the wind is in the west—with a delightful view of islets in the Sound and a slightly uneasy memory of the malignant Gifford who once lived there. But the major or dominating part of the parish lies west of the road and faces the Atlantic over a rampart of cliffs which, nowhere very high, are sculptured with a fantastic wildness.

A couple of miles north of Mavis Grind is Mangaster Voe, into which runs a burn that looks interesting to a fisherman, and between Mangaster Voe and Ura Firth—within a matter of five miles or so—are at least a score of small lochs, some of which, with access to the sea, might well be worth fishing. It is a matter of regret to me that I have never explored and made trial of these waters, for I feel that a little patience and a certain amount of rough walking could be well rewarded. Some of the lochans will hold nothing better than little dark-skinned brownies, but even on them there may be the pleasure of seeing a pair of red-throated divers.

On the outer side of Ura Firth, at Hillswick, there is a well-known tourist hotel; and its popularity is proof, if further proof were needed, of the perceptive eye of John Tudor. This is what he wrote some eighty years ago: "When, as must come sooner or later, proper accommodation shall have been erected throughout the length and breadth of Shetland for the travellers in search of the beautiful, who will flock northwards as soon as the country shall be better known, there will be no spot in all Hjaltland, which in its manifold attractions will be so popular as 'Grey Hillswick'. To the painter, the geologist, and the mineralogist, Hillswick will afford such a centre from which to follow out their respective pursuits as will be hard to find elsewhere on British soil."

Much has changed since Tudor's time, and we no longer write with such Victorian enthusiasm. The view that he admired remains the same, however—and that means that it varies from splendour to savagery, from idyllic grace to sombre melancholy, and in its nearer aspect the ocean-bed erupts into strange pinnacles of stone to amplify the bizarre, the unpredictable fashioning of the cliff-wall. On a fine day St. Magnus Bay stretches in glinting blue to Papa Stour, and Foula rises like a giant's fortress on the horizon. But in grey, westerly weather the sea breaks white and fountains over the fearful stone fangs—gaunt stacks which, on occasion, can strangely look like a ship under sail—that are called The Drongs.

For an afternoon's walking, over easy ground, there is, perhaps, no part of Shetland that repays a little energy with more agreeable and essentially Shetlandic scenery than Esha Ness, the western extremity of the parish. In the sea to the south, a mile away, is the tall, water-worn arch of Dore Holm, and one of the several small lochans on the peninsula is said to have been the home, in more credulous days, of the dreaded *Nuggle*, or water-horse; a monster which carried to instant death anyone rash enough to mount it. There is a ruined broch, and the echoing Hole of Scraada, into which the ocean pours through a narrow tunnel. Near the southern corner of the peninsula is a lighthouse, and at the northern corner the Grind of the Navir: a huge window in the

Norse-type watermill with radar towers on distant hill
Pier House, Symblister, Whalsay

rock that the force of the Atlantic has opened. Here, within a few miles, is a natural, exhilarating magnificence; and if the Hole of Scraada echoes with a sinister menace, its note of gloom may well be contradicted by the nearby sweetly plaintive conversation of a pair of golden plover.

This part of Northmaven is separated from North Roe by the long scimitar of Ronas Voe—where, some three hundred years ago, a Dutch man-of-war was captured, after a bloody fight, by two English frigates—and north of the voe rises Ronas Hill, bare and ruddy brown, to a height of nearly 1,500 feet. There is little beyond it but an almost empty land, that once was populous, and another score of small lochs; but it is worth driving to Burra Voe and the end of the road. There is a curious feeling of coming to a full-stop, and the satisfaction of finding a shop there. Manifestly remote—and almost sensationally far from anywhere else—the place has the robustness befitting a frontier. But a fishing-boat in the voe, when I was last there, was a sad reminder that Fethaland, the ultimate promontory to the north, was once a stirring place when the noble sixareens went out to the haaf fishing. As many as thirty boats fished from here, and their crews, in the season, lived ashore in huts or bothies.

There is no road to the Point of Fethaland, which is a green finger pointing to a little dangerous group of rocks and islets: Gruney and The Club, Fladda, Turla, and the Ramna Stacks. The birds which gave their name to the Ramna Stacks were ravens, and the raven—*Corvus corax*, the old aristocrat of the crow family—is a fine, bold, sagacious bird. I do not know if it still nests on the Stacks—birds are subject to change and calamity—but if it survives, it is a noble sentinel for the uttermost fragments of the Mainland of Shetland.

Scalloway, Shetland

13

Bressay and Noss

Of those lesser islands which lie west of the Mainland, something has been said; but there are larger islands on the east, as well as many little ones, and for some discussion of them it will be convenient to return to the south and again make, or pretend, a journey from south to north.

Mousa has been described, and north of it are Bressay and Noss. Beyond them is Whalsay, with the Out Skerries to the north-east. The long island of Yell reaches beyond the northern point of the Mainland, and Fetlar lies east of it. Northernmost of all is Unst.

Bressay, lying close to the capital, is the useful, suburban island which provides Lerwick with a sheltered harbour. About six miles long and some two and a half miles broad, it is dominated by a hill, the Ward of Bressay, 740 feet in height, which in the darkest months of winter blinds the morning sun till an unseemly hour. The Ward slants gradually to the south and the precipitous rock of the Ord Head, a sheer cliff more than 500 feet high. The southern cliffs are very fine and terminate in the Bard Head, a promontory in which is a great cavern called the Orkneyman's Cave. Who the Orkneyman was is not known. Perhaps a refugee from the press-gang, or possibly the master of a small ship who recklessly took shelter there to avoid a French privateer.

In the latter years of the nineteenth century there was a pony farm on Bressay, owned by the contemporary Marquis of Londonderry, where Shetland ponies were bred for the Seaham Colliery in Durham. The mares were pastured on Bressay, the stallions segregated on the lesser island of Noss. It was a profitable trade, for in 1878, at a sale at Seaham Harbour, the average price was £25. A hundred years before a pony cost between five and fifty shillings, and in the earlier years of this century the price again was low: in the 1930s a mare with foal at foot could have been bought for £5 or £6. But recently the Shetland pony has become more valuable, and a new market has been found in the United States, where it is bought, not for labour underground, but for children's pleasure. Its price has sometimes risen above the Seaham average, and children who have acquired a pony may have had to stiffen their nerves as well as learn equitation. For the Sheltie is a proud and independent little beast: dainty, strong, and attractive, but not always perfectly docile.

On the north side of the island, near the head of the Voe of Cullingsburgh, and touching the site of a vanished broch, are the remains of what is said—perhaps doubtfully—to have been a cruciform church: the only one in Shetland. In it is a memorial stone to the Dutch captain of the ship *Amboina*, who after harrying Portuguese galleons off the coast of Mozambique, loaded a cargo of Persian silk in Surat, north of Bombay, and set sail for home on the 19th February, 1636. Violent gales off the Cape of Good Hope delayed him; the death from disease of twenty-nine sailors hindered the working of the ship; which did not arrive in Bressay Sound till the 26th August. And poor Captain Claes Bruyn died on the following day.

A much older stone, now in the National Museum of Antiquities in Edinburgh, was also found here. Known as the Bressay Stone, it is elaborately carved on both sides. Above a Celtic cross two sea-monsters—possibly whales—appear to be either consuming or vomiting a man—Jonah, perhaps—while below them are a mounted man between priests; what may be a horse; and possibly a pig. On the other side are priests with croziers, combatant beasts, and more Celtic ornament. It is incised with Ogham characters which have been variously translated. The inscription possibly commemorates the daughter of a Faeroe viking who may have been called Naddod and is said to have discovered Iceland in 861; but if that is so, the stone is older than the inscription.

The north shore of the island was settled in very early times, for there are mounds and standing stones that date from prehistory; though that is a loose term for an island that has very little recorded history.

East of Bressay, a cable's length away, is the Isle of Noss, a bird sanctuary whose majestic cliffs are dominated by the Noup, which is just under 600 feet high. Here is a metropolis of sea-fowl: herring-gulls and kittiwakes, guillemots and razorbills in sable feathers, bonxies in the grass above, solemn fulmars and clownish puffins, a lately established colony of gannets, tysties (or black guillemots) with scarlet feet and mouth, and rock-pigeon to add a blur of blue to the general pallor of the populace.

The cliffs have their names: on either side of the Noup are The Cletters, Whiggie Geo, and the Rump; Rumble Wick, Holm of Noss, and Feadda Ness. The Holm is a stack, 160 feet high, manifestly too steep to climb. In the seventeenth century, however, it was climbed—for the reward of a cow. The bold cragsman drove a couple of stakes into the green turf of its summit, hauled a string across the water-gap of 60 or 70 feet, and established a rope-railway strong enough to carry a wooden cradle able to accommodate a man and a small Shetland sheep. The top of the Holm measures about 500 feet by 170 feet, and gave summer pasture for a dozen sheep. The railway was used till the latter part of the nineteenth century, when the cliff-top field was abandoned because of a changing economy or a growing indolence. There is a melancholy addition to the story, for the solitary cragsman who drove in the stakes—the only man ever to have climbed the Holm—fell to his death while making the descent. One can only hope that his widow got the cow.

14

Whalsay and the Skerries

Some ten miles north of Bressay is Whalsay, and five or six miles north-east of Whalsay the miniature archipelago of the Out Skerries. These are most admirable islands, the abode of hardy, industrious, and skilful fishermen who, in despite of the severe disadvantages of living so far from a market, not only take a rich harvest from the tempestuous meadows of the sea, but are capable of enjoying life with the generous freedom of their Norse ancestors. I heard lately the story of a Whalsay wedding, to which all the Whalsay folk and some of their neighbours were invited, and on the depth of the whisky drunk a lifeboat could have been launched; if such extraneous assistance were ever needed in Whalsay, which is unlikely.

The island, to be precise, measures some five and a half miles in length by about two and a half miles in breadth. It contains seven or eight small lochs, and rises to its maximum height in the Ward of Clett, which is 400 feet high or thereabout. It is surrounded by lesser islets, reefs and shoals and skerries, that create good spawning ground for haddock and other pelagic fish, and dissuade ruinous great trawlers from scraping and bankrupting the sea's bottom, as they do in too many coastal areas.

There are, in the island, sufficient relics, of the usual sort, of prehistoric or very early occupation to prove its settlement in remote ages, and provoke yet again—as so often in these islands—speculation about the skills and temperament of our distant predecessors. Were they reckless adventurers, trusting themselves in frail craft to the mercy of the sea and unknown gods, or consummate masters of wind and tide who in soft-skinned coracles could navigate with the certainty of migrating birds? Or was there, for longer periods than scientists are willing to admit, a benign, halcyon climate in the north?

Dated within fairly recent times—no farther from us, that is, than the early years of the nineteenth century—there is, in Whalsay, a distinguished monument to the arrogant eccentricity of which Shetland lairds were then capable. Tudor takes note of what he calls "the present house of Symbister", near to an older house with a walled garden, above Symbister Bay at the southern end of the east coast, and records, with a note of awe in his sentence, that it was reputed to have cost £30,000. He was, apparently, unaware of the reason for this extravagant expenditure; but the reason was cogent. He who built the house was the head of a distinguished family in Shetland, and he had on the Mainland a mansion sufficient for his needs; but also he had an heir, and heirs presumptive, of whom he disapproved. So rather than bequeath his fortune to unworthy successors—or successors with whom he had quarrelled—he spent it on a structure as vain and meaningless as a Pharaoh's pyramid. He was a man of character; though not, perhaps, of a wholly amiable character.

Whalsay is called "a bonny isle", and indeed it lacks any aspect of bleakness or undue harshness; but what characterizes it far more than any scenic aspect is the redoubtable character of its inhabitants. A passenger in the little inter-island ship, the *Earl of Zetland** may well be surprised to watch the unloading there of milk from Lerwick. Most manifestly there is on the island abundant pasture for cows, but no cows are kept, and milk is imported. "But why?" asks the inquiring passenger. "It takes a great deal of work, and a great deal of care and trouble, to keep a couple of cows," is the reply, "and for a few quarts of milk it isn't worth the effort. It's easier, and cheaper in the long run, to buy milk in Lerwick, for our business isn't farming, it's fishing. It's fishing that's our interest, and there's not a boy on the island that wants to be a farmer. They want to go to sea."

Exaggerate the temper of Whalsay and you approach the temper of the Out Skerries. This cluster of minute islands is, by repute, one of the richest parts of Shetland, and their riches are earned by continuous association with the unpredictable sea and an acquired dominance over all its traps and perils. Sail to them from the Mainland—I went there, a year or two ago, in a sixty-year-old fishing-boat from somewhere in South Nesting—and over a sea that mysteriously swells and sinks again, and draws great tidal convolutions on its troubled surface, you slowly approach a line

The island is now served by a car ferry from Laxo.

of harshly broken cliffs that nowhere seem to offer shelter or an entrance.

Then, quite suddenly, a narrow, rocky channel opens—you turn hard a-port and over pale green water, through which a great sunken rock most dangerously peers, you go slowly in to a land-locked natural harbour—and on either side is a cluster of small, trim, brightly painted cottages, all as neat and tidy as an exhibition of Ideal Homes, and surrounded by little garden-plots of growing fields. Behind them the land rises to cliff-top heights, before them it descends to leaf-green, deep lagoons; and on a fine summer day the view—the whole aspect of that small community—is idyllic. But a winter storm can drastically change the scene.

On Housay, the largest of the three little islands—the others are Bruray and Grunay—I went into a doll's-house supermarket—a miniature but most compendious shop—the most brightly clean, scrupulously ordered small shop I have ever seen. On its shelves there was an astonishing array of all those packaged goods, from bathroom adjuncts and the products of our commercial alchemists to tropic fruits and Pacific salmon, with which advertisement has made us familiar; and through a window a sheltered bay shone like a pool of sapphires in the sun. "But come here in January, in a January gale," said the girl in the shop—and a very attractive girl she was—"and you'll see nothing but spray lashing over us, as if you were on the under-side of a wave, and it breaking over you."

But there, in that intimate association with the roughness of the sea, a small community lives in apparent contentment, for its population of about 120 has not diminished with the years; and so far from living on grudging terms with its environment, it has created for itself an orderly comfort that, in a modern assessment, is not without a degree of elegance.

The Out Skerries have, too, their own romantic story, and possibly a fortune under their cliffs. In 1664 a Dutch East Indiaman, the *Carmelan*, was wrecked there on an eastward voyage from Amsterdam, and striking a cliff was lost with all hands but four who, aloft on the foremast, were thrown ashore when the mast broke. The *Carmelan* carried 3,000,000 guilders and several chests of coined gold, some of which were salvaged by the rascally Earl of Morton who held the islands at that time, but the rest of that vast treasure has never been retrieved. The ship, most certainly, was broken to pieces, but its treasure-chests may have been lodged in some corner of the cliffs or rocky coign of the sea-bottom. A few scattered coins have been found, as tantalizing evidence of their existence.

If the bulk of the treasure is ever recovered, I hope the people of Whalsay and the Out Skerries will be its beneficiaries. My last view of them was of some two dozen men and boys, in a fleet of a dozen little boats—Shetland models of the prettiest sort—going out through great rising and falling, heavily dancing seas to an evening's inshore fishing; and I felt, without yielding to sentimentality, that they deserved a richer haul than cod and haddock. Or would riches absorb and spoil their virtue?

15

Yell, Fetlar, Unst

Yell is the problem-child of the archipelago. It is a large island, 17 miles long by 6 or 7 broad in its thickest part, and more than any other it has suffered from depopulation and depression of spirit. There was a time when its people numbered about 2,700; in 1962 when, at the instigation of something between a sense of urgency and a feeling of desperation, a conference was summoned to consider its plight and debate plans for its rehabilitation, its population was less than 1,200, young people were still leaving, and unemployment was high.

The conference was remarkable for some very plain speaking. "Yell is perilously near disintegrating," said the Shetland Development Officer, and explained the consequence of further, unchecked depopulation; it would become impossible to provide essential services and "the social fabric" would break down. The island's difficulties were due, in part, to its strictly egalitarian society, which made it difficult for anyone to come forward and offer his leadership. Its people had been criticized for lack of initiative and lack of faith in themselves; but an egalitarian society did not encourage the sort of initiative they needed, and lack of faith was largely due to lack of capital.

The resources of the island were closely examined, and realistically discussed: agriculture was on a crofting level, fishing had been neglected, knitting could be developed, and some commercial future might be found for the abundance of peat with which the island was overloaded. The island was without electricity, and for the common comfort of electric light and power there was a clamorous demand. The County Council, it was recognized, had done much to improve the island roads, and a water scheme was under way. But better piers were needed, larger housing grants, and some sort of subsidy to offset freight charges. To revive a fishing industry it might be necessary to provide a training-school—so long had the sea been neglected—but the new popularity of shell-fish appeared to offer new rewards from nearby waters.

A sense of apathy was widely admitted; and yet seemed to be contradicted by the liveliness of discussion, and the fact that the conference gave birth to a very sensible report and some practical recommendations for what was described as "a holding operation" until long-term planning could be brought into being. It was recognized, however, that the island's future largely depended on the goodwill of the Scottish Office, and there were those who admitted a pessimistic view of Government policy. It is common, indeed, among Shetland observers of the political scene to look south and discern, both in London and Edinburgh, little regard for the outermost parts of Britain: little interest in them, knowledge of them, or sympathy with their disabilities.

The report confessed that "Yell's economy is at present so fragmented and indeterminate that radical improvement will require agreement among the development agencies as to the relative significance of their various fields of action." There was no dominating, overriding problem to be solved, but a whole complex of problems, arising from Yell's place in time and geography, that had produced a general malaise rather than any single, crippling injury. "While the main process in Britain has been development from an agricultural to an industrial and affluent society, the changes in Yell have amounted to little more than a heightening of human aspirations. An island community in a peripheral situation, it entered the twentieth century as an economic outsider. Today it finds itself in an alien climate."

The people of Yell—and their neighbours—were well aware, however, that another Atlantic archipelago, some two hundred miles to the north-west, lived in a very favourable climate of its own creation; and the publication of the Yell report was soon followed, in May, 1963, by the report of a delegation which the Shetland County Council had sent to study conditions in the Faeroe Islands. In 1839 a Faeroe man had come to Shetland to learn the art of fish-curing, and Shetlanders had taught the Faeroese the craft of deep-line fishing for cod. Since then the Faeroes had come up in the world, their population had shown a prodigious increase, and the more northerly archipelago was alive with enterprise and manifestly prosperous, though nature had given it a harsh and stormy environment, a sterile soil. What was the reason for so large a disparity between Thorshavn and Lerwick, between Suderö and Yell?

A vital difference was immediately apparent to the visiting delegates: the Faeroese "possess unlimited confidence in their future. The young folk stay on and the man of means is not afraid to risk his capital in local investment." Obvious, too, was the fact that the Faeroese had concentrated all their energy on the one industry of fishing; there was no diversity of interest, no fragmented economy. And while out-of-work Shetlanders could always fall back on unemployment pay and national assistance, the fully employed Faeroe man could rely on his local bank to give him credit for the building of new enterprise.

Apart from its insistence on the need for expert analysis and over-all planning of Shetland's economy, the Faeroe report offered two suggestions of unusual interest. It recommended the establishment of a Folk High School, of the Danish sort, and a new pattern for vocational education. The Folk High Schools that the good Bishop Grundtvig established in Denmark in the mid-nineteenth century were certainly responsible for much of that country's spiritual revival and commercial growth; and the Faeroese recognize the value of the school, of the Grundtvig sort, which they have established in Thorshavn. As for vocational or technical education, a soundly devised system is clearly an instrument of great potential worth in the development of an island economy, and might be so shaped that it would help to keep young people in their native place by giving them, or creating for them, the sort of employment for which they had been trained: it would have to be part and parcel, that is, of the over-all plan.

A third suggestion in the report was that consideration be given to the need for a sizeable centre of population—at least 1,000 people—in the north of Shetland, another in the west. In the Faeroes "only centres of this kind have shown appreciable growth".—As London has drained into its unwieldy conurbation too much of England's manpower, so in a miniature way has Lerwick drained Shetland; and a contrary centre of attraction should be found. But is Yell the place for it?

It is a long rectangle in shape, almost cut in two near its middle by the voe of Mid Yell on the east and the long inlet of Whale

Firth on the other side. Much of its coastal part is agreeable enough, but the interior is dull and dark, and the road from Ulsta in the south-east to Gutcher, and the Unst ferry, can seem interminable and leave in the traveller's mind an everlasting dislike of peat. The interior is not, in fact, one large peat-bog, but it is difficult to rid one's mind of that impression. With unlimited capital, of course, it could be transformed within a few years. On the long, dark island of Lewis there are now patches of brilliant green where peat-moor has been reseeded—ploughed, fertilized, and sown with grass, that is—and the Yell moors are no more inhospitable than those of Lewis. But where is the capital to come from?

The southern half of the island is served by a ring-road, and from the south and west sides there are fine views of the island-studded waters of Yell Sound. Whale Firth was popularly supposed to give occasional shelter to German submarines in the Kaiser's war, and in few places could they have lain with a greater assurance of being unnoticed; for north of the Firth there is no road on the west side of the island, and the crofting lands of Lumbister are uninhabited. Lumbister, immediately beyond Whale Firth, is said to be the most attractive part of Yell, a green and pleasant land with a foreground of great cliffs opening into deep caves and broken arches, a background of good fishing-lochs, but roofless cottages for a melancholy reminder of livelier days. On the other side, facing east, Mid Yell has an excellent natural harbour, sheltered from all sides, but lacking a sufficient pier.

The north end of the island is reputed to have a certain charm—half genial, half wild—and there is testimony to its attraction in a journal kept by a traveller who, in 1832, must have held the awed attention of its natives. His name was Edward Charlton, he was a doctor of medicine, and when he walked abroad he was equipped for any adventure. "On my shoulder," he wrote, "was a double-barrelled gun and ammunition, the other shoulder was frequently balanced by my heavy German rifle, while on the one side hung my game bag, and on the other a huge tin case, into which I stowed away shells, plants or sea-weeds, and in various pockets were to be found numerous smaller boxes as safe receptacles for insects or for finer and more delicate shells. As I was on an island composed almost entirely of gneiss, I seldom took out my hammer, except when on an excursion I had discovered some fine garnets or felspar crystals, for these were almost the only minerals afforded by the rocks of the island of Yell."

With his rifle he shot seals, with his gun he brought down starlings. He found roasted starlings palatable. He was a Roman Catholic and deplored the religious habits he found in Yell: "Neglected by the Presbyterian ministers, the poor Shetlanders have taken refuge in the arms of the Wesleyan missionaries; and the Methodists now outnumber in these remote islands the followers of the Church of Scotland." But walking to the ruins of an old chapel on Papil Ness he found there a halfpenny of George III, the thank-offering of some fisherman who had been in danger, and consoled himself with the reflection that "to this day the Shetlander, when in danger, invokes the assistance of the Virgin and St. Magnus; to this day do they, as in the time of Brand, make pilgrimages in the dark hour of night, to pray amid the ruins of the deserted chapels."

Charlton also noted that "the land shells, chiefly the *helix arbust.*, that occur about the ruins of the old chapels, are looked upon with great veneration by the Shetlander, and are much employed for the cure of disease." He was a sympathetic traveller: a more sympathetic and reliable critic than George Buchanan, the sixteenth-century Latinist and perhaps the worst of Scottish historians, who described poor Yell as "so uncouth a place that no creature can live therein, except such as are born there."

Fetlar, on the other hand, has never lacked champions. It is, perhaps, a fifth of the size of Yell, it lies east of Mid Yell, and has been described as the Garden of Shetland. It wears today, unhappily, something of the look of a deserted or half-tended garden, but the archaeologist may still find the reward of some delightful puzzles there.

At the top of Hamara Field, for example, in the north-western corner of the island, the *Inventory of Monuments* describes a semi-circular enclosure of large serpentine stones, some thirty yards across, with an apparent opening in the northern arc. The largest of the stones, which are set singly but in parts make—or appear to have made—a distinct wall, are between 3 and 4 feet high, about 4 feet broad; and in the centre are three earth-fast stones.

In the middle of the island, between Vord Hill and Skutes Water, are the Fiddler's Crus: three rings of small stones, set edge to edge at the corners—or so it seems—of an isosceles triangle. The diameter of the rings varies from 42 feet to 53 feet. "No satisfactory suggestion as to the period or purpose of these curious constructions can be offered," says the *Inventory*; and aggravates the puzzle by pointing out that one of the circles has some resemblance to a nearby structure called Haltadans, some 200 yards north of Skutes Water.

This consists of an outer ring of weathered serpentine stones, with a diameter of some 36 feet, and within it a low, concentric, earth-bank. Two earth-fast stones lie at the centre. The name Haltadans means a lame or limping dance, and the popular explanation of the stones is—or used to be—that they were dancing trolls who were petrified because they went on dancing till they were surprised by the rising sun. The two stones in the middle are, of course, the fiddler and his wife.

Also bewildering are the remains of a substantial stone dyke that once divided the island into roughly equal halves. Its northern end is on the cliffs above a geo called Muckle Funziegord, and here, on barren ground, its course can be clearly seen. For a mile or so it runs west of Vord Hill, and reappears south of Skutes Water. Its name, Funzie Girt—pronounced Finny Girt—means the Finns' dyke, and according to a once popular rumour the Finns, those powerful magicians, built it in a single night.

The ruins of two or three brochs, dilapidated cairns, and mysterious mounds may also be observed; and there can be no doubt that Fetlar's fertile soil was discovered and appreciated in ancient times. But the island lacks a good harbour. It would be inconvenient to live there, but the visitor will find it picturesque and charming.

About the head of the Wick of Tresta there is geniality in the landscape, and the little loch of Papil Water remembers in its name some small enclave of Celtic priests. In the nearby district of Houbie was the home of a famous Edwardian surgeon, Sir William Watson Cheyne, and the opposing peninsula of Lamb Hoga rises to a long and noble shape that may recall a name of great consequence in Queen Victoria's time. To John Tudor, approaching it from the south-west, it looked like one of Landseer's lions in Trafalgar Square; though from a slightly different point of view it changed into a benign, Egyptian sphinx. Beyond it, to the north-west, the house of the late proprietor, Sir Arthur Nicolson, presents a curious and distinctive landmark; and if the visitor sees some good-looking Shetland ponies, they may be the product of some experiments in breeding undertaken by one of Sir Arthur's predecessors.

The cliffs of the east coast, rugged and splendidly erratic, though not very high, show white in places, sable-dark in others; and between Hesta Head and The Tind is a rocky point with the handsome name of Heilinabretta. It was here that a Danish ship called *Vandela*—though some say she was Dutch—was wrecked in the eighteenth century. She was carrying more than £20,000 in silver coinage, much of which was recovered, and the early process of salvage appears to have been fortuitous; for a story survives of one of the first discoverers of the fortune which the lost ship held.

He was a local man who had gone down to fish from the rocks, and when, in the dark of evening, he returned home, his wife asked what he had caught. To which he replied by emptying his basket and pouring on the kitchen floor a flood of silver. "See's du dat?" he said. "If it wisna fur dee, I could marry a leddy noo."

North of Fetlar, and reaching beyond the farthest part of Yell, is the large island of Unst: 12 miles long and 4 or 5 miles broad. Its distinction of being the northernmost land in Great Britain is fortified by the intrinsic interest of much that lies within its stormy boundaries. There is, for a start, the ruin of Muness castle in the south-eastern corner of the island: a handsome building closely related to Scalloway Castle, Noltland in Westray, and the Earl's Palace in Kirkwall. In plan it is oblong, some 73 feet long by 26 feet broad, with circular towers at diagonally opposite corners, and on the other corners there were turrets on corbels projecting from the floor-level of the third storey. This storey was demolished to make an enclosing wall, but otherwise the whole structure of the castle remains. "The architectural detail shows a greater sense of design than is found in any other secular building in the islands, with the exception of the Earl's Palace in Kirkwall": so says the *Inventory*, and to that I would add Scalloway Castle. Ruins though they are—broken and defaced and deeply scoured by time—both Muness and Scalloway preserve, with an heroic obstinacy, something of the elegance that was inherent in the design to which they were built. No matter what other purposes they may have served, they were intended to give pleasure to the eye: to an instructed and judicious eye.

In the south-west wall of Muness there is a gap where the main door once opened, and above it, within a moulded border, a panel on which is inscribed in Gothic letters: LIST ZE TO KNAW YIS BULDING QUHA BEGAN LAURENCE THE BRUCE HE WAS THAT WORTHY MAN QUHA ERNESTLY HIS AIRIS AND OFSPRING PRAYIS TO HELP AND NOT TO HURT THIS VARK ALUAYIS.

The date is added—"The zeir of God 1598"—and the inscription acquires a greater interest than at first appears when it is realized that Laurence Bruce, the chief magistrate in Shetland, was nearly related to Earl Patrick Stewart. Laurence's father, John Bruce of Cultmalindy in Perthshire, married Euphemia Elphinstone, who had been the mistress of King James V and borne to him a son Robert, who became Earl of Orkney and Patrick's father. Dr. Douglas Simpson, whom I quoted in my description of Noltland, therefore concludes: "Nothing is more likely than that Earl Patrick should have lent his own master mason to Laurence Bruce for building Muness."

According to a legend long preserved in verses of the local Norn the castle was burnt in the seventeenth century by someone called Hakki of Dikkeram, otherwise unknown. A young Bruce is said to have abducted a girl called Helga, after killing her father; but did not live to enjoy the reward of enterprise. Helga let herself down a rope from an upper room of the castle—but who imprisoned her? That is not recorded—and with her adventurous friend put to sea in a small boat; where a storm engulfed them both. Whether these two legends are connected is not known, though Hakki's incendiarism would be a neat response to Helga's abduction and the murder of her father. It is said, too, that in the eighteenth century the castle was sacked and burnt by French privateers; but again the story is of doubtful truth.

Muness and Scalloway in Shetland, and in Orkney the Palace at Birsay, Noltland Castle, the Earl's Palace in Kirkwall, and the reconstructed Bishop's Palace—what a rage for building there was in the sixteenth century! Much of it was done by forced labour, and though Shetland, in that respect, seems to have suffered less than Orkney, there were complaints against Laurence Bruce for his misuse of the power vested in him, and with Muness for evidence it may not be unfair to see in him a shadow or smaller edition of Black Pate.

The *Inventory* records the ruins of seven churches or chapels in the island, and according to Tudor there was, in his time, the

Last of the hand-gutters, Lerwick
Modern fish-processing factory, Scalloway
(overleaf) *Whiteness* and *Muckle Roe Brig*

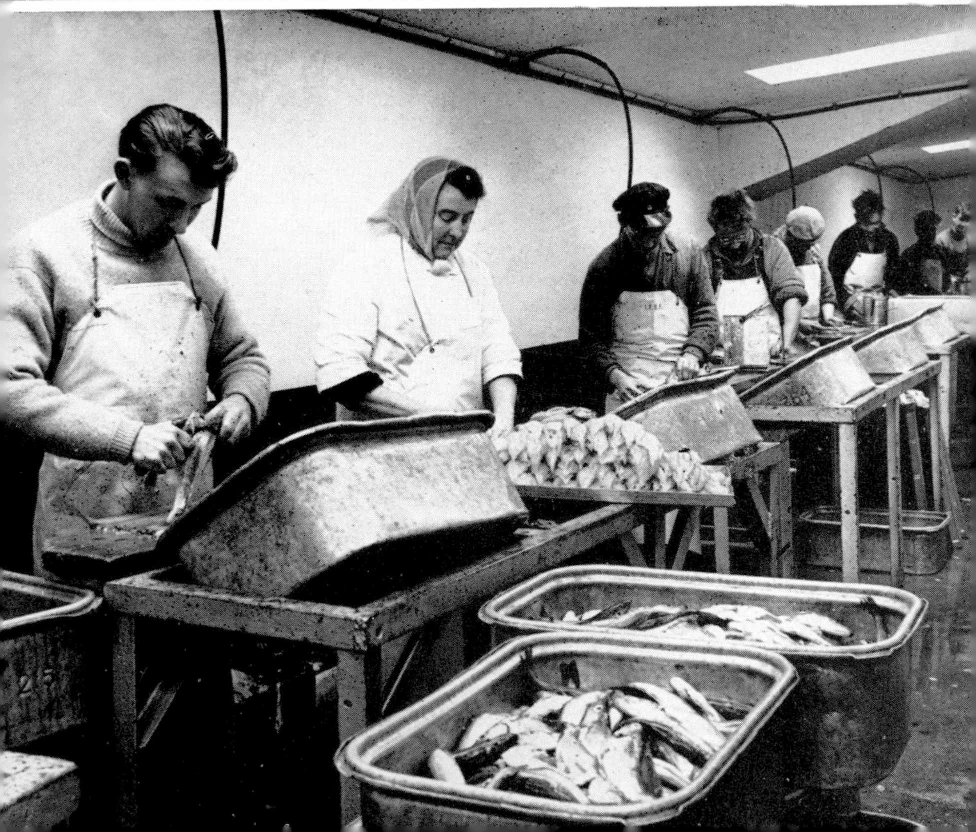

memory of twenty-two or twenty-three, with another on the little island of Uyea. One of those described by Tudor was dedicated to St. Sunniva, who in the tenth century is said to have sailed from Ireland to Norway in a ship full of virgins, who in Norway perished in a cave. Though one may feel doubtful about Sunniva, one can hardly fail to be impressed by the early piety of both Orkney and Shetland: from South Ronaldsay to Unst there was no lack of churches.

Brochs and cairns—but all much dilapidated—can also be found, and at Uyea Breck and by the Loch of Bordastubble are tall Standing Stones, with lesser ones elsewhere. Of minor antiquity but more interest are two badly weathered tombstones in the graveyard by the roofless, twelfth-century church at Lunda Wick which commemorate Segebad Detken, a merchant of Bremen who "carried on business in this country for fifty-two years" and died in 1573; and "the worthy and well-born Hinrick Segelcken", also a burgess of Bremen, who died in 1585.—Two prosperous and respected fish-merchants, it may be presumed.

The present population of Unst lives mainly on the south and east; at Uyea Sound, Balta Sound, Harold's Wick and Norwick. The island of Uyea, now deserted, lies in the bight of the south end, and from the pier the north-going road bisects the island as far as the deep inlet of Balta Sound. East of Uyea Sound rises Gallow Hill, and little more than a mile north of the pier the road passes the ruin of Gletna Kirk, which legend says was never completed, because as fast as the masons built its walls, so prompt were the trolls to pull them down. Past the Loch of Watlee the road rises over the bare slope of Coldback Hill, and the view enlarges to include the sheltered water—empty now, but once populous—of Balta Sound, and beyond it the high moors called Crussa Field and the Heogs, on which are ancient cairns and the vestiges of a stone circle. Inland from the Sound, and a little south of it, are quarries that were the site of a brief industry.

The geology of Shetland is more complex than that of Orkney, and in Unst the western flank, under the long ridge of Valla Field, is mainly a coarse-grained gneiss, while east of the ridge are various schists and masses of gabbro and serpentine. In the serpentine mass there are veins of chromate of iron, and at the north-east corner of Harold's Wick a pale green vein of talc. The chromate of iron was discovered in the nineteenth century, and quarried in several places in the eastern half of the island.

(previous page) *Shetland crofts* and *Modern-style ploughing at Asta Annual Shetland pony sale*
Skerries. Shetland

In the last days of sail Balta Sound was a busy place, a centre of the herring curing industry, and in summer presented a recurrent scene of splendid and picturesque activity as the fishing fleet, filling the narrow bay with its dark brown sails, jockeyed for position as in some vast, heroic regatta, and headed for the dancing sea beyond the enclosing isle of Balta. In 1907 nearly 800 Scottish luggers were engaged in the fishing, and several score of big Swedish ketches as well.

The evolution of the Scotch fishing-boat did not become decisive until about 1855, when the beamy, open boat with a very raked stern called a *Scaffie* was gradually superseded by the half-decked or fully decked *Fifie*. The Fifie grew larger—up to 45 tons or so—and in turn gave way to the *Zulu*, so called because the first one was launched in 1879, from Lossiemouth, during the Zulu War. The stern of the Zulu had the great rake of the Scaffie, but a straight stem like a Fifie and a deep fore-foot to give it a grip to windward. These were noble boats, and when reaching in a hard breeze their speed was remarkable.

Balta Sound is empty and peaceful now, but here and there about the shores of Orkney and Shetland can still be seen the heavy, rotting timbers of a dead Zulu. It is worth while, perhaps, to stand and muse a little beside the mouldering stiffness of its great stem, or under the rake of its rotting stern, and try to imagine it in life, creaking and thundering through a rolling sea under its tall, straining, tawny canvas. And then to conjure up a picture of six or seven hundred of them, in the brightners of a summer evening, beating stiffly out to sea in the hurly-burly days of Balta, when the salt air was richly perfumed by the curing sheds.—I remember watching a Zulu, one of the last survivors, from a railway carriage on the Highland Line where it skirts the coast from Helmsdale to Golspie. There was a strong easterly or north-easterly breeze and my recollection is that the Zulu, under full sail, kept pace with the train for at least ten minutes. I admit, however, that the Highland Line was never renowned for speed.

North of the Sound is Buness where a notable family, the Edmonstons of Buness, lived busily. Arthur Edmonston, sometime a surgeon in the army, wrote a history and excellent description of island life, and his youngest brother Lawrence—twenty years his junior—who died in 1879 at the age of eighty-four, was an ornithologist who first recorded the Glaucous, Ivory, and Iceland gulls as regular British visitors, if not precisely

British species. His eldest son, Thomas, became Professor of Botany in the University of Glasgow before he was twenty; published the first complete Flora of the islands; and was accidentally killed, while still a youth, in the South Pacific. His cousin, another Thomas, compiled a glossary of the Orkney and Shetland dialects; Dr. Henry Saxby, a son-in-law of Lawrence, published in 1874 *The Birds of Shetland*; and his daughter also wrote much on island life. In a literary way Buness was almost as busy as Balta Sound.

To the north lies Harold's Wick, so called in the belief that King Harald Fairhair, on his historic voyage to subdue piracy in the west, first landed here. North again is Norwick, on the shore of which is a great rock-cup, called Saxi's Kettle, in which the sea tosses and grumbles though the bay is calm; and inland from it a larger, deeper vault called Saxi's Haa. Saxi was a giant, in some unchronicled period of history, who lived on the hill called Saxa Vord. Westward over Burra Firth lived Herman, another giant, on Hermaness Hill, who with a ship's mast for a fishing-rod caught a whale, and asked Saxi to let him boil it in his kettle. Saxi said, "Yes, if you'll give me half your fish." Herman thought the price excessive, and from angry words the giants advanced to throwing stones. The rock that Herman threw can still be seen on the west side of Saxa Vord, and a skerry called Saxi's Baa, on the opposite shore, is what Saxi threw.

I have taken this story from Mr. A. T. Cluness's book on Shetland, and he explains why the giants never got to grips with each other, but contented themselves with throwing stones. There was water between them, a stream to be crossed, and giants hated to get their feet wet. Why? Because, says Mr. Cluness—presumably with Antaeus in mind—they fetched their strength from contact with the earth. He tells of another giant, Siggi, who lived not far away, and was mocked by his wife when she saw him carrying a great rock that he meant to use as a stepping-stone to a reef where he wanted to fish. He turned to pursue and punish her for her rude laughter, but slipped and fell, and died of his fall. But the rock he was carrying can still be seen.—Were they German giants, asks Mr. Cluness, these vulnerable monsters with Teutonic names? Before the Norsemen came there were certainly Saxon raids upon our eastern coasts, and there may have been short-lived Saxon settlements. Or perhaps fear of the invaders spurred invention.

Here, in the northernmost part of Unst, there is truly magnificent scenery, and the ultimate gesture of Britannic geology is one of sheer grandeur. A radar station now projects its mast and antennae from the hill, but the cliffs are not diminished, and from Saxa Vord one looks across the huge cleft of Burra Firth to Hermaness, that seems a true giant's stronghold and faces the Atlantic over frowning cliffs. It is, in fact, a bird sanctuary, and the bird to which it primarily assures safety is that ponderous rascal the Bonxie or Great Skua. Some eighty years ago, when the Bonxie was in danger of going the way of the Great Auk, he had no home but here and the isle of Foula. But now he has become almost a multitude, and can be seen as far south as the Pentland Firth. A rascal he is, but no one should complain of the Bonxie unless he is prepared to make war on that cold-eyed ruffian the Great Black-backed gull.

Looking down from Burra Firth one sees the long, calm canal of the Loch of Cliff, and south of that is a valley that opens into lesser lochs, so that Unst appears to be an island that barely held itself together in the earth's last great convulsion. It was the violence attending its birth that gave it most of its fine scenery, but the grace of creation has added much that is gentle and genial and wears sunshine as naturally as it stands up to storm. Hermaness, the giant's stronghold, breeds a race of delicate rare moths as well as bonxies, and the dullest of fields breaks into vibrant gaiety under a stampede of Shetland ponies.

But finally, from Saxa Vord, one must look to the north—or, to be accurate, the north-west. There, in the white flurry of a breaking sea, is a wild group of holms and skerries: Rumblings and Tipta, Out Stack, Little Flugga and Muckle Flugga. Muckle Flugga, crowned with the white column of a lighthouse, is the dominating islet—rough and fierce as a cock's comb hugely carved in stone—and the fine, resounding names of the west coast of Unst seem to lead ear and imagination north to it: Hagdales Nest and Orknagable, The Stacks of Poindie and Tonga Stack—Grunka Hellier, Bluescudda Kame, and the Kame of Flouravoug—it is an orchestra of wild imagination, and imagination is what Shetland needs to stay alive.

Muckle Flugga may be the signpost, for Muckle Flugga points to the Faeroes, and the Faeroese have shown what can be made from sterile soil and stormy seas by people who believe in their own land, their own virtue, and their own ability.

PART THREE

MODERN ISLANDS

1

A Tide of Confidence

The years that followed the Second World War saw a flurry of minor improvements in living conditions in Orkney and Shetland as crofters and fishermen began to modernize their houses, adding kitchens and bathrooms, and piping in water from the nearest spring. In the more progressive areas scores of wind-driven electricity-generating sets appeared and the gales that kept the fishermen ashore in winter at least supplied them with a cheap source of light. These examples of private initiative, however remarkable they may have been, were but forerunners of large scale improvements carried out in both groups of islands as the Government sought to extend to the remote areas of Britain the amenities so long enjoyed in the cities. Council houses were built and water and drainage schemes brought improved sanitation while the overhead power lines of the North of Scotland Hydro-Electric Board spreading out from their diesel-driven stations at Kirkwall and Lerwick soon brought the marvels of electricity to all but the most remote communities.

In spite of these improvements the most marked trend of the postwar period was a steady decline in population as hundreds of people sought a new life on the British mainland or overseas. In Orkney depopulation was caused largely by increasing mechanization on the farms—an unfortunate result of greater prosperity. In Shetland, on the other hand, the situation was far more serious since many people had lost faith in their islands being convinced that continued decline was inevitable. A symptom of Shetland's malaise was the stress placed on secondary education which was seen as the passport to a good job outside Shetland. The lack of opportunity at home was reflected in the scores of young people who lined the rails of the passenger vessel, *St. Clair*, as she left Lerwick on her twice weekly trip to Aberdeen. Young men and women who should have been the backbone of their communities were forced to go and live in a city just to have a job. Fortunately a remarkable change took place as confidence returned to Shetland and, as in Faeroe, the key to success was seen to lie in the development of the traditional industries of fishing, crofting and knitting each of which went through a period of restructuring and growth in the early 1960s.

One aspect of Shetland's economic revival was the rebuilding of the fishing fleet—an acceleration of a trend which had begun as far back as 1946. The old Zulus and Fifies, built in the age of sail, had become worn out after half a century of fishing in stormy northern seas and they were replaced by modern wooden vessels built in yards along the north-east coast of Scotland. The new boats were generally between seventy and eighty feet long and were powered by compact diesel engines. They were equipped with driftnets for the herring season in summer while for the remainder of the year they fished with seine nets for haddock, cod and whiting. Before long over two score of these fine vessels were owned by Shetland fishermen most of them based at the islands of Burra and Whalsay.

The changes in the fish processing sector of the industry were even more remarkable as the practice of consigning for British fresh fish markets was replaced by the new technique of quick freezing. The first locally-owned processing plant opened its doors in 1960 and by 1971 there were fourteen factories of this type at several parts of the Mainland as well as in the islands of Burra, Whalsay, Yell and Out Skerries. The Highlands and Islands Development Board, set up in 1965, played a great part in the expansion of Shetland's fish-processing industry and under their fisheries promotion scheme encouraged the revival of the fishing industry in islands such as Unst and Yell where it was in danger of dying out.

Marketing within the United Kingdom was still a headache for local producers. Small firms found it difficult to maintain a steady through-put and fulfil their contracts when bad weather interrupted supplies and added to this was the perennial problem of high freight charges between Shetland and Aberdeen. It was a businessman in Scalloway who found a solution to the problem when he realized that a virtually unlimited market for white fish fillets existed in the USA and in co-operation with a Danish shipping company he arranged for cargo vessels to call regularly at Scalloway. The first cargo was shipped in 1967 and in 1971 a record 4,500 tons of frozen fish were shipped in refrigerated cargo vessels to ports in Massachusetts.

While fishermen and fish processors were turning their attention to the sea, Shetland's crofters were taking a long hard look at their land and considering how it could be made more productive. Vacant crofts were allocated to those who were willing to work them and gradually viable units evolved. They were made still larger as crofters exercised their right to apportion their share of the common grazings for improvement. This was another of the remarkable developments of the 1960s as thousands of acres of hill and moorland formerly covered in heather, rushes and coarse grasses were sweetened with lime and reseeded with better strains of grass and clover. With improved pasture crofters and farmers found it possible to increase their stocks of sheep and cattle until by 1970 the islands supported over 7,000 cattle and over 260,000 ewes and lambs. Each autumn 40,000 lambs were shipped to Aberdeen on the first stage of their journey to mainland slaughterhouses whence their carcases were distributed all over Britain to satisfy the growing demand for Shetland lamb.

The knitwear industry—the third strand in Shetland's traditional economy—also went through a period of unprecedented growth in the 1960s. Established firms had full order books and new firms set up small factories in rural areas offering full-time work at reasonable rates of pay to young women in these districts. Traditional methods of production could not keep pace with demand and mechanization became imperative. The housewife however was unable to work under factory hours and conditions and for her a compromise was found in the hand flat machine—a device sufficiently compact to be installed in her kitchen or living room. It was still a cottage industry in which the whole family could participate in their spare time although some women, and men too, made knitting at home a full-time occupation.

By 1969 when it had a record turnover of almost £1,500,000 the industry was supporting over 2,000 home knitters working regularly and perhaps 1,000 working less regularly for 35 local merchants most of whom also operated a knitting unit with up to 50 full-time employees. The bulk of the produce consisted of plain woollen sweaters which were exported to France and other European countries but there was still a considerable trade in hand-knitted garments incorporating the traditional Fair Isle and Shetland patterns. The latter were sold to merchants in Lerwick or sent by post to private customers in all parts of the United Kingdom.

Apart from these developments in the three basic industries a host of lesser ventures started—new projects that would not have been possible a few years earlier—such as mink farming and stone polishing at Whiteness while at Weisdale, Shetland Silvercraft found a keen demand for their brooches and ornaments based on ancient Celtic and Scandinavian designs. They started in a small way and prospered to the admiration of all—each in its own way was symbolic of Shetland's modern economic revival.

The 1960s were good years for Orkney too with a steady growth in the island's vital farming industry. In 1969 Orkney exported 20,000 beef cattle which brought £1,800,000 into the islands and 30,000 sheep which were worth £210,000. Three million gallons of milk earned over £58,000 for Orkney's farmers while 25 million eggs realized a further £28,600. As in Shetland a large number of smaller projects sprang up some of them assisted by loans and grants from the HIDB. One of the most remarkable of these developments was the establishment of Sykes Robertson (Electronics) Ltd which began in Sanday in 1967 without any government assistance at all. Among its earliest successes was the sale of language laboratories to schools in Stromness and Hong Kong—a truly remarkable feat for a small firm of this kind. Boatbuilding also experienced a revival especially at Stromness and in the island of Burray. One of the Stromness yards, that of J. T. Anderson, was chosen by the HIDB to build the 50 feet long trawler, *Kildinguie*, the first vessel to be built under the Board's Fisheries Development scheme. Orkney's own shellfish industry made rapid progress in the 1960s encouraged by Orkney Fishermen's Society which had been reconstituted in 1961. A different kind of venture was started at Stronsay with the formation of a co-operative which processed white fish for export to the USA.

In spite of all the skills acquired by seamen and the many aids to navigation that science has introduced the sea is still a force to be reckoned with and it still exacts its toll of human lives with monotonous regularity. No episode in recent years has brought more grief to the northern isles than an event that took place in March 1969 after the Liberian ship, *Irene*, got into difficulties in appalling conditions south-east of South Ronaldsay.

Heedless of the danger to their own lives and impelled only by the knowledge that other men were in danger the crew of Longhope lifeboat left the warmth of their homes and put out into the storm-tossed waters of the Pentland Firth. Where it happened we shall never know but somewhere along that exposed stretch of coastline a wave bigger than its neighbours whipped up by the tides and a Force 10 gale picked up the lifeboat like a child's toy and turned it right over, whereby eight brave men lost their lives.

The *Irene* ran aground at Grim Ness on the eastern side of South Ronaldsay and all her crew were rescued by breeches-buoy. Her master came in for a considerable amount of criticism when the full story leaked out of how the ship had left the Firth of Forth with insufficient fuel for the trip to Norway and how the master had thought he was within a hundred miles of the Norwegian coast when in fact he was within a few miles of the Pentland Skerries. But from Longhope there came no recrimination. A ship had been reported in distress and the lifeboatmen had put to sea as usual to save the crew if they could. They died in response to an ideal and in upholding a reputation that for generations has set their island apart. Within a few weeks from the shores around Longhope another crew had volunteered to man another boat.

However unpredictable tragedies like this may be they have long been accepted as part of life in the northern isles. As winter gave way to spring and the chill easterlies dried the sodden fields, farmers prepared for the new season's growth and inshore fishermen repainted their boats and overhauled their lines and their creels. Before long the perennial problems of bad weather, high freight charges and disappointing returns for fish and livestock again came to dominate the conversations of the islesfolk.

There was much to talk about in the late 1960s. Local government was about to be reorganized and a Royal Commission had been set up under the chairmanship of Lord Wheatley. In 1969 the report was published and among its recommendations was the proposal that Orkney and Shetland should be merged in a large Highlands region stretching southwards as far as the Mull of Kintyre. This suggestion caused disquiet in Orkney and created a furore in Shetland not from blind patriotism or from opposition to change but from the deeply held conviction that the suggestion was impracticable. The distance involved was colossal—indeed it was pointed out that the southern extremity of the proposed region would be as near the south-east coast of England as it was to Shetland. Again it was explained that Shetland's economic ties and links of communication are with Aberdeen and these cannot be swept away overnight. Three members of the commission, however, disagreed with the majority and proposed special first-tier status for Orkney as well as for Shetland. The white paper was published in 1971 and with considerable relief it was noted that in the coming reorganization Shetland and Orkney would each form a special island authority.

No sooner was one problem solved than another began to cause mounting concern in both Orkney and Shetland—Britain's application to join the European Economic Community. Greatest cause for worry was the threat to the islands' fisheries if the twelve mile limit should be abolished and continental fishing vessels be allowed to fish almost up to the shore. Unlike some continental countries Britain has long enforced rigid restrictions to avoid overfishing with the result that some of the richest fishing grounds that remain in the North Sea lie around the Northern Isles. The British government seemed totally unconcerned about the dangers inherent in the EEC's common fisheries policy. Of course in Britain as a whole the fishing industry is of minor significance but in a place like Shetland fishing is the most important industry—a point which is not fully appreciated at Westminster.

The dangers of overfishing had already become apparent to local fishermen when, in 1965, a large fleet of Norwegian purse seiners descended on the herring shoals east of Shetland and in the next few years carried out a ruthless exploitation of the stock which led eventually to the near extinction of the North Sea herring and a total ban on herring fishing.

But not even these worries concerning the future of the fishing industry could stop the tide of confidence that still flowed strongly in the northern isles. The effects of economic success were soon to be reflected in the population statistics. By 1961 the population of Shetland had dropped to 17,483 and it was to drop still further by 1966 but the census of 1971 produced a figure of 17,567 proving that the downward trend of more than a hundred years had been reversed. The question now was how far the population could rise. It seemed that Shetland could continue to develop her resources indefinitely with a steady increase in population. The need to attract incoming workers was tackled by the county council when they embarked on a building programme with sectional timber houses imported from Norway. These were set up in what were considered fairly large schemes of ten or a dozen houses at places like Scalloway and Whalsay where more workers were urgently required. Then in 1971 oil was discovered east of Shetland and plans for cautious growth were thrown to the winds as Shetland and Orkney to a lesser extent were caught up in the nation's race to get the oil ashore.

2

The Coming of Oil

Dazzled by the success of their own modest achievements in the 1960s, the people of Orkney and Shetland had tended to ignore developments at the other end of the kingdom and the steady northwards march of the oil rigs. The first signs of the coming oil boom were the seismic survey vessels that interrupted their research programmes and slipped into northern voes and harbours to shelter from storms or to take on stores. Passers-by tended to dismiss them at first as just another type of survey vessel engaged in some obscure branch of fisheries research. But these vessels were different—they were not interested in the shoals of fish or even in the minute life of the upper layers—their interest lay in the rock strata far below the sea bed and in the folds, unconformities and other geological structures that could conceivably contain oil.

After the seismic survey vessels came the oil rigs working under a veil of secrecy, their drills biting ever deeper into the floor of the North Sea. As they advanced northwards they recorded some minor successes off the Scottish coast and then one day in 1971, while drilling east of Shetland, the diamond-studded bit of Shell's rig *Staflo* penetrated the huge reservoir of oil and gas to which the company gave the name Brent after a species of Arctic goose. Almost immediately Shetland assumed a new importance and businessmen and entrepreneurs who until then had had only the vaguest notion of the islands' geographical position packed their bags and booked their passages north to stake their claim to a share of the expected bonanza.

First to feel the impact of oil were Shetland's harbours some of which found a new role as service bases from which cement, chemicals and other supplies could be shipped out to the oil rigs, while Sumburgh airstrip at the southern tip of Shetland found a new importance as the airfield nearest the oil reservoirs of the northern

North Sea. This was just the beginning of Shetland's involvement with oil since it soon became clear from the magnitude of subsequent discoveries that Shetland would play a central role in the extraction of the oil and that a large storage complex would be required somewhere in the islands.

Inevitably there were those who were opposed to oil-related developments who, if they had been able to, would have prevented oil being landed in Shetland. They dreaded the effects of industrialization on a predominantly fishing and crofting community and feared that the islanders might be outnumbered eventually by strangers. With the latter, it was feared, would come all the evils that have so long plagued Britain's cities including drug addiction, vandalism, theft and even murder. Children would no longer be able to play out of doors without causing their parents concern and even social functions would have to stop since village halls would be unable to cope. Environmentalists feared the loss of amenities through industrial developments in some of the most attractive parts of Shetland's coastline and dreaded the effect that an oil spill would have on seabirds and marine life. It was also suggested that people would forsake the traditional industries for the promise, at least in the short term, of more highly paid jobs with the oil industry.

Zetland County Council was entirely unprepared for major oil-related developments. So little had happened in Shetland between the end of the Second World War and the reawakening of the 1960s that Shetland did not even have a Development Plan. Nevertheless the council acted with amazing speed and an Interim Development Plan was quickly drawn up, the most important of its proposals being the zoning of a large tract of land around Sullom Voe for major oil-related developments. At the same time the council was determined to prevent a proliferation of installations and stated its intention to guide potential developers towards the establishment of one industrial complex in the Sullom Voe area.

The area around Sullom Voe was the obvious place for developments of this type. The voe itself is a large sea inlet deep enough to take all but the largest oil tankers and with a broad belt of reasonably flat land along its eastern shore much of it lying derelict since the Second World War when it was used as a base by the Royal Air Force. But no matter how obvious its merits might be from a casual inspection the whole area had to be subjected to a rigorous examination and this was the remit given to a London firm appointed consulting engineers to the county council.

Developments at Sullom Voe were delayed by a bitter dispute that occupied most of 1973. An Edinburgh-based firm of financiers had foreseen the potential of Sullom Voe and had entered into agreements with landowners in the area. Having purchased or secured the option to purchase large tracts of land they produced their own plan to provide the facilities required by the oil industry. The outcome was protracted legislation at Westminster until with the passing of the Zetland County Council Act of 1974 the council was granted practically all the powers originally sought. These included the right to exercise jurisdiction as ports and harbour authority over the whole of Sullom Voe, to acquire land for oil-related developments, to issue or refuse licences to dredge and licences to construct works within the three mile territorial limit, to take shares in commercial undertakings and finally to establish a Reserve Fund. These were exceptional powers for a small local authority and their granting was a clear indication of Shetland's important new role in the extraction of North Sea oil.

With legislation safely behind them Zetland County Council and their successors under the reorganization of local government—the Shetland Islands Council—could begin to put their plans into practice. The consultants' reports were now ready, covering every aspect of the proposed developments at Sullom Voe from constructional and navigational considerations to social and environmental implications. During the next few years the eyes of the nation were focused on Sullom Voe where out of a once quiet inlet and a bare headland was created, at a cost of £850 million, an entirely new port destined to become the largest oil terminal in Europe with a storage capacity for 70 million tons of oil a year. Near the peak of its construction in 1979 no fewer than 5,000 men were employed on the site, all of whom had to be housed, fed and kept healthy and provided with recreational facilities during their leisure hours. While most of them were housed in two large labour camps nearby, several hundred were accommodated in two redundant passenger liners anchored in Garths Voe, an inlet at the head of Sullom Voe. Only a small proportion of the labour force was made up of Shetlanders—most came from England and Scotland while quite a few came from Northern Ireland.

Gradually the terminal took shape, the acres of peat bog and green pasture being replaced with concrete and tarmacadam while thousands of tons of wood, steel and aluminium went into the construction of the sheds and workshops and the many other types of building required in the operation of a large oil terminal. Most conspicuous are the large power station, the oil storage tanks on Calback Ness and the loading jetties which project like long probing fingers into Sullom Voe.

As work on the terminal proceeded, interrupted at times by industrial disputes and Shetland's weather, the oil companies turned their attention to another integral part of the project—the laying of two massive pipelines which link Sullom Voe to the major oilfields of the East Shetland Basin. During this part of the operation they came into direct conflict with local fishermen who resented this intrusion into what had been until then their undisputed territory. Between Shetland and the oilfields lie long ridges of hard rock including the wide expanse of the Pobie Bank but between those ridges there are narrow channels of sand and mud where pipelines can be laid and buried. Unfortunately these small strips of soft bottom, so coveted by the oilmen, are also the very areas where fishermen are enabled to tow their seines and trawls.

The laying of the pipelines marked the lowest ebb in the relations between fishermen and oilmen. The two pipelines come close together near the north end of the Pobie Bank and cross the rich fishing grounds that lie east of Unst. They turn shorewards south of Fetlar and then their routes diverge slightly as the Brent pipeline runs towards its landfall at Firths Voe and the Ninian line follows a more southerly route to come ashore near Lunna. In this way much of the good fishing grounds off Unst and south of Fetlar have been destroyed.

Much of the inconvenience to fishermen could have been avoided by commonsense and stricter control over the contractors employed to lay the pipelines. All sorts of debris ranging from old safety helmets to broken hawsers were dumped indiscriminately without thought for the men who would follow with their fine-twined trawls. It is galling for the crew of a fishing boat to tow their gear for several hours over what was known to be clear bottom to heave up and find the catch gone and the net torn or destroyed with a lump of jagged metal enmeshed in what remains of the gear. The oil industry operates a scheme whereby fishermen are given compensation when it can be proved that damage to fishing gear is caused directly or indirectly by oil-related activities but in few cases does the sum awarded provide adequate compensation for the loss of valuable nets and fishing time.

Another difficulty encountered by the fishermen was the problem

Yell Ferry, Shetland, replaced in 1973 by a modern car ferry
The North Harbour at Lerwick showing a ro-ro terminal with MV St. Clair

of deep anchor holes left in the sea bed after the passage of the lay barges. These vessels are hauled slowly ahead on hawsers attached to heavy anchors which are constantly lifted and repositioned. When the anchors are lifted out of the mud they leave craters surrounded by mounds of clay and boulders that had been buried for centuries. It has been suggested that in time natural forces will restore the sea bed to its former state but that is little comfort to a fisherman who has to make a living today.

In spite of so much friction between fishermen and oilmen the former have frequently been grateful for the facilities provided by the new industry. Several fishermen owe their lives to the skill of a helicopter crew who lifted them when ill or injured from the deck of their fishing vessel and carried them quickly to land to receive medical attention. In other cases fishermen having got into difficulty through stress of weather have been rescued by helicopter, the most memorable incident occurring in December 1977 when the Aberdeen trawler, *Elinor Viking*, ran aground on the dreaded Ve Skerries that lie west of Papa Stour. Aith lifeboat slipped her moorings and headed out through St. Magnus Bay, her crew eager to make the rescue attempt in spite of all the dangers involved. Considering the state of the weather and the position of the wreck in the midst of so many submerged rocks and breaking shoals it is doubtful if they could have succeeded. Fortunately help was available at Sumburgh Airport in the shape of a British Airways helicopter which proceeded to the Ve Skerries and quickly located the stricken vessel. Showing great skill and a total disregard for their own safety the crew winched the trawlermen to safety.

While the Sullom Voe oil terminal is by far the largest project in the islands it is only one of several oil-related schemes that have already been completed. Sumburgh Airport has been entirely reconstructed; one of the most important developments there being the provision of a new east-west runway straddling the peninsula from Atlantic to North Sea. This has greatly improved the service to the public through removing the dependence on a single runway which was frequently unusable on account of cross winds. Not so long ago an aircraft standing on the runway at Sumburgh was a sight seen only twice or three times a day. By 1975 there was constant activity as chartered Viscounts brought in hordes of oil workers to be flown to their rigs by helicopter while the sleek private jets of oil executives competed for parking space with the Viscounts and HS 148s of British Airways and the small but dependable Islanders that are operated by Loganair.

A new type of vessel for Shetland – the 70,000-ton oil tanker, Donovania, *approaching Sullom Voe in October 1978*
The oil terminal at Sullom Voe

Lerwick Harbour, too, has been transformed under the impact of oil-related developments especially the north part of the harbour, an area virtually unused since the days of the herring boom. The old rotting timber jetties, a reminder of former activity, have gone and in their place have come modern quays with silos and warehouses and now there is a constant coming and going of smart cargo vessels and the more clumsy oil supply vessels. At Holmsgarth there is a development of a different kind for here no fewer than six old herring stations have been swept away to make room for the new roll-on-roll-off terminal which with its hydraulic ramps, large transit sheds and offices now serves as the island base for the car ferry, *St. Clair*, which plies between Lerwick and Aberdeen.

Outside of Lerwick only one supply base has been built specifically for the oil industry. This is at Sandwick where the old pier at Broonies Taing is now swallowed up in Hudson's service base. Over at Scalloway some oil rig servicing was carried out in 1972 when Esso carried out exploratory drilling west of Shetland and Scalloway may yet play a role when the more difficult Atlantic oilfields come to be exploited. In the meantime work is underway at Scalloway on a new harbour designed solely for the fishing fleet with the aim of providing better facilities and safe mooring which the present pier cannot offer.

Orkney too plays an important role in the extraction of oil with the Occidental group's terminal on the island of Flotta being linked by 138 miles of pipeline to the Piper and Claymore fields. Orkney is fortunate in being able to confine its oil-related developments to one small island unlike Shetland where three inter-related projects are situated one at either end and one in the centre of the Mainland. Orkney's roads have not suffered to the same extent from heavy traffic as have Shetland's nor is Orkney's landscape scarred to the same extent that Shetland's is by the enormous quarries from which has come the vast amount of rock infill demanded by the various construction sites.

Orkney County Council, too, in the early days of the oil era effected private legislation which gave them powers to act as harbour authority and to control industrial development and land use. As in Shetland's case a cardinal part of the Orkney County Council Act is the authority to set up a Reserve Fund based on disturbance payments from the oil consortium and which is now growing steadily through a levy on oil through-put.

The benefits that oil brought to the northern isles were undeniable—there was full employment and for the first time ever wages were as high or higher than those elsewhere in Britain. At the same time oil brought many disadvantages which tended to be ignored by the rest of the country—the crime rate rose as did the incidence of road accidents while the high rate of inflation aggravated by the affluence of one sector of the community was a serious problem for those who were not engaged in oil-related work. Again, a large section of the islands' business community not only received no benefit from oil but were positively harmed by it. Not surprisingly, those adverse effects were more pronounced in Shetland than in Orkney, solely because of the difference in the scale of their oil involvement.

Shetland's essential services came under severe pressure due to the combined effects of extra work and staff shortages. Hospitals were under-manned and the Police force was stretched to the limit at a time when increasing demand was being put on its staff. Neither should one overlook the problems faced by small firms, employing a handful of people, to whom the loss of one key man was an insurmountable obstacle. Several small shops were forced to close down and the bakery trade lost no fewer than eleven men between 1976 and 1978. Shetland Islands Council had its own problems which were particularly noticeable in the Construction Department since the wages which the council was allowed to pay its employees could not compare with those that could be earned in oil-related jobs and the most obvious effect of staffing problems in this sector was the deterioration of surfaces on all but the important new roads such as the one between Lerwick and Sullom Voe.

Of Shetland's indigenous industries fishing suffered least of all from the oil construction boom. The weakest link in this sector was the fish processing sector which suffered a great loss of labour as workers were lured away to the construction sites by the prospect of higher wages. To add to the problems of the fish processors in the late 1970s the weakness of the US dollar, with its inevitable effect on exchange rates, made the American market less attractive and forced some merchants to seek new markets in France and Italy. Worst affected in the early years of the oil boom was the knitwear industry which used to depend largely on women who knitted at home on a part-time basis to earn a modest addition to the family income. For the first time in Shetland oil brought numerous openings for girls including well-paid office jobs while in the construction camps at Sullom Voe there was a keen demand for cleaners and canteen staff.

As a result of these changes in the pattern of employment the knitwear industry became a mere shadow of what it was before the discovery of oil. The situation got worse as the construction phase neared its peak but in the early 1980s the pace of construction slowed down and workers who had been paid off again sought employment outside the oil industry. Once again there was an upsurge of interest in the traditional industries the difference this time being that Shetland Islands Council had several millions of pounds to invest in the local economy from its astute deals with the oil companies.

Shetland Islands Council is pinning its hopes for the future on the Reserve Fund into which revenue will flow during the life of the oil terminal from rents and tonnage dues and from profits gained by the catering, towage and other companies in which the council has an interest. Already considerable sums of money have been invested in the fishing and fish processing industries while smaller sums have gone to knitwear manufacturers. Under a Ten Year Plan for agriculture grants and loans are available to crofters and farmers with special incentives to raise the quality of the local breeds of sheep and cattle.

Late in 1978 oil from the East Shetland Basin began to flow through the pipelines and tankers began to call at Sullom Voe bringing with them more problems for the two island authorities. Early on the morning of 1st January 1979 while the *Esso Bernicia* was being berthed at Calback Ness a fire broke out in one of the attendant tugs forcing it to cast off the towline whereby the tanker, out of control, collided with the jetty, rupturing her hull and fuel tanks and allowing over 1,000 tons of thick bunker fuel to spill into Sullom Voe. Before booms could be deployed much of it had been carried by the wind and tide out into Yell Sound. A day or two later a mechanical fault in the containing booms resulted in the remainder of the oil escaping into Yell Sound. The swift currents plastered it all along the western shores of Yell and along parts of the coastline of Northmavine.

While oil remains afloat it is theoretically possible to treat it with dispersants but oil on the beaches is another matter. In this case council employees had to resort to shovels and plastic rubbish bags as the only way of dealing with the problem. As Mr. Jo Grimond, the islands' MP remarked, this was "hardly an example of the white heat of technological revolution having gripped the oil salvage industry". In fact the oil companies and the Shetland Islands Council were entirely unprepared for an accident of this nature. While a great deal of discussion had centred on the possibility of a spillage of crude oil anywhere off Shetland no one had given much thought to the possibility of a spillage of bunker fuel with the result that there was no chemical dispersant available to treat it.

Within a few days the full horror of the *Esso Bernicia* incident dawned on the people of Shetland when dead and dying seabirds in their hundreds were cast up on the beaches of Yell Sound and Sullom Voe. These sheltered waters attract wintering flocks of eider ducks, guillemots and razorbills besides the more common species of gull. While all of these suffered from the spill, most concern was reserved for the rare great northern diver, no fewer than 170 of them being found dead in the aftermath of the tragedy.

The months of January and February 1979 were exceptionally severe in Shetland the hills being covered in snow for most of the time. As usual the sheep made their way to the shore to feed on the mounds of seaweed cast up during the winter's storms but on this occasion they found many beaches so badly polluted that their legs became stuck in the thick black cover of oil. Some were drowned when the tide rose while others had their fleeces and bellies badly contaminated as they struggled to escape.

A few weeks after the incident at Sullom Voe, badly oiled seabirds were picked up in other parts of Shetland and in Orkney too. It was suspected at first that these had also suffered from the spillage at Sullom Voe but gradually it became clear that the islands were facing a new threat as tankers on their way to Sullom Voe discharged their oily ballast water into the sea. The problem stemmed from the fact that the Sullom Voe terminal had begun operating before its ballast treatment plant was ready and rather than keep their ballast on board with the inevitable restriction on their payload, some masters found a way round the difficulty by simply pumping out their dirty ballast water as they neared their destination.

As the threat to Shetland's wildlife continued and more than 6,000 dead seabirds were collected from the beaches, Shetland Islands Council and the oil companies were bombarded with protests from people in all walks of life. None were more insistent than the people of North Ronaldsay because of the threat posed not only to their seabirds but also to their special breed of sheep which graze exclusively on the beaches and the grassy banks outside the island's perimeter wall. A petition circulated in Shetland attracted over 3,600 signatures in two weeks. It called for the closure of the oil terminal until the treatment plant should be ready.

As it turned out closure of Sullom Voe was not considered necessary. After a review of the measures taken hurriedly by the oil companies, Shetland Islands Council and the Government it was agreed that these should be sufficient to stop the illegal discharge of ballast water off Shetland. The new measures include the tightening of regulations regarding tanker routes, surveillance from the air and safeguards against pollution to be written into agreements made with both the purchaser and the carrier of oil from Sullom Voe. However painful this experience may have been it may be the means of preventing a greater tragedy provided that the lessons have been fully learned by all concerned in the running of Shetland's oil terminal.

3

Shaping the Future

In spite of the prosperity brought by North Sea oil there is a growing realization that the boom cannot last indefinitely, that it is merely another chapter in the islands' history like the great days of the herring boom and the disruption of two World Wars. Some day the oil will stop flowing and the isles will be left with the land and the sea and the old indigenous industries that have sustained them so long. In Shetland the future is seen to rest solidly on a restructured fishing industry provided that several difficulties can be resolved. The main problem is undoubtedly overfishing since the grounds are being fished to saturation point by fleets from many European countries. To add to the problem, conservatory measures taken by other northern nations have resulted in the closure of many grounds to Britain's distant and middle water fleets thus forcing trawlers from the Humber to seek their share of the already overfished stocks around Orkney and Shetland. If Britain could follow the example of Iceland, Canada and the USA and extend her own limits out to 200 miles there would be no problem since there is enough fish around Britain for the entire British fleet. Unfortunately Britain is expected to share these stocks with other members of the Common Market and there is clearly not enough fish to go round.

The negotiations that preceded Britain's entry into the EEC were far from satisfactory for her inshore fishermen. As the debate over fishing rights dragged on a compromise was reached and incorporated in the 1972 Brussels Treaty of Accession whereby the inner six mile limit would continue to be reserved for British fishermen until 1982 when the whole question would be reviewed. In effect this was not a solution but a convenient shelving of the problem for ten years. These terms did not satisfy the people of Shetland who in the national referendum voted by a big majority against Britain joining the EEC.

Unfortunately their voice was swamped in the overwhelming national majority in favour of joining.

Much of the concern of local fishermen stems from the growing menace of industrial fishing—the practice of taking fish of any size or species for reduction to fish meal which is used in the feeding of livestock. Industrial fishing can be highly remunerative and it forms by far the most important sector of the fishing industry in Denmark. Since quality is of secondary importance and the catch is neither cleaned, sorted nor packed in ice a small crew of three or four men is adequate on a vessel that would require from six to ten hands if fishing for the fresh fish market. The success of a trip depends solely on how quickly the hold can be filled and how quickly the vessel can return to port where the catch is unloaded by mechanical means directly into the fish meal factory.

Within recent years Scandinavian vessels having depleted the fish stocks in their own coastal waters have extended their activities to the area around Orkney and Shetland most of them trawling with small-meshed nets for the tiny fish known as Norway pout. Unfortunately these are seldom found in distinct shoals but are usually mixed with more important species such as cod and haddock which feed on them and with the fry of edible species which are taken in large quantities along with the less valuable Norway pout. Under pressure from local fishermen the British government recently established a 'pout box'—an area east of Orkney where industrial fishing is banned. While recognizing that this is a step in the right direction many fishermen would like to see the 'box' extended northwards to protect the fish stocks east of Shetland while similar measures west of the islands would safeguard the fishing grounds that lie north of Foula.

On a wider scale the two island authorities have each drawn up plans for a regional fisheries scheme intended as part of the final EEC fisheries agreement which came into force in 1983. Basically the local plans involve a licensing system to control fishing effort with preference being given to local boats. Already the two schemes have attracted favourable comment from EEC officials but still the British government seems more reluctant to give them its support. While recognizing the importance of fishing to countries such as Iceland and Faeroe, government ministers are unwilling to admit that a parallel situation exists in remote parts of the UK where in the virtual absence of other resources the people have to look to the sea for their livelihood. How important fishing is to Shetland can be seen from the statistics for 1978 when the value of all kinds of fish landed in the islands and in United Kingdom mainland ports by Shetland vessels was almost £6 million.

Farming remains of vital importance to both groups of islands although the nature of the industry in Orkney is totally different from that of Shetland. In Shetland, with its vast areas of hill pasture and small pockets of arable land, the emphasis is still solidly on the rearing of sheep and every year around 50,000 lambs are sold, most of them being shipped out for slaughter on the mainland. The low price paid for wool has long been a cause for concern to Shetland crofters. Shetland is not covered by the British Wool Marketing Board, local producers having decided many years ago to opt out of the scheme in case the reputation of the islands' high quality wool should be impaired and the price reduced. Unfortunately this decision worked to Shetland's disadvantage with the result that locally produced wool is often difficult to sell in spite of the worldwide demand for Shetland knitwear.

Part of the problem lies in the fact that there is no definite relationship between Shetland wool and Shetland knitwear. All attempts to have the name 'Shetland' reserved for knitwear produced in the islands have failed and the name is applied merely to a type of garment which can be produced legally anywhere in the world. There is only one small woolmill in Shetland so that practically all of the wool clip is sent south to be spun on the mainland where it is inextricably mixed with wool from mainland producers. The yarn that returns to Shetland is merely a blend of wool containing only a small proportion of the raw wool sent originally. There is little doubt that in the restructuring of the knitwear industry that must come in the aftermath of the oil construction phase careful consideration will have to be given to the future role of Shetland wool and the damage that is being done to the local industry by the indiscriminate use of the name 'Shetland'.

An important attempt to make a better utilization of Shetland sheep has been made at Reawick where, in the old farm steading of Stump, lambs are slaughtered and their carcases frozen before shipment. As a by-product of this operation large quantities of skins are preserved in salt for later processing in what would otherwise be a slack period of the year. The end product is high quality sheepskin rugs which find a ready demand from summer visitors.

In Orkney with its much better pasture, cattle take predominance over sheep. Over 25,000 cattle are exported annually and milk production exceeds three million gallons per year a large surplus being processed in the North of Scotland Milk Marketing Board's creamery to produce the well-known Orkney butter and cheese. Sheep, too, play an important though subsidiary role in the farming economy and around 30,000 lambs are sent out each autumn. Pig production has declined considerably in recent years as has the production of eggs and poultry.

The opening of the abattoir at Hatston in 1983 was a landmark for Orkney farmers. First proposed in 1978 by Orkney Islands Council it was built by the council with help from the Highlands and Islands Development Board. Through-put has risen rapidly and the marketing of Orkney Meat as a branded product in mainland supermarkets has proved attractive to consumers.

Agriculture is by far the most important of Orkney's industries bringing an estimated £10,000,000 into the islands each year. Next in importance, at least in monetary terms, is distilling with an output valued at over £3.5 million in 1978. Third most important is tourism which now contributes an estimated £1.7 million to the islands' economy offering part-time employment to a large number of farmers and others through their self-catering and bed and breakfast accommodation. A heartening trend in recent years is the growth of small manufacturing firms, one of the most successful being that of Mr. J. R. Robertson of Stromness which produces the now well-known Orkney fudge and employs fifty people.

The greatest obstacle that people in Orkney and Shetland have to face is the high cost of transport which adds appreciably to the cost of living and creates problems for farmers, fishermen and manufacturers alike. In April 1979 freight on a ton of hay from Aberdeen to Lerwick had risen to £50 while the cost of bringing in a tractor had risen to £152. The high cost of travel is another problem for local businessmen and acts as a deterrent to the growth of the tourist industry. Holidaymakers have to think twice before visiting the northern isles when they can fly to America or to a Mediterranean resort for far less than the cost of a flight to Orkney or Shetland.

At the same time it must be pointed out that the islands now enjoy a first-class system of communications both internally and with the Scottish mainland. In 1971 the North of Scotland, Orkney and Shetland Shipping Company was taken over by P & O, the company founded long ago by Shetlander, Arthur Anderson, and in 1975 the name was changed to P & O Ferries (Orkney and Shetland Services). Within the last few years their fleet of crane-loading passenger-cargo vessels have been replaced by modern roll-on-roll-off ferries on their main routes. Flagship of the fleet is the 4,857-ton car ferry, *St. Clair*, which runs at least twice weekly between Aberdeen and Lerwick. Orkney is served by the new motor vessel, *St. Ola*, which operates across the Pentland Firth between Scrabster and Stromness. P & O, however, no longer have a monopoly of this route. In summer the motor vessel, Souter's Lass, operates on the much shorter crossing between John o'Groats and Burwick in South Ronaldsay.

Shetland's inter-island services have also been revolutionized with the introduction of four car ferries on the most important routes. The first of these vessels, the car ferry, *Fivla*, was introduced to the Yell Sound crossing in May 1973 being followed soon afterwards by an identical vessel on the Blue Mull Sound crossing between Yell and Unst. Gradually the old North Isles vessel, *Earl of Zetland*, found herself with less and less to do and soon she was serving only Whalsay. On 23rd February 1975 she completed her last run and without fuss or ceremony a long era in transport came to an end. The *Earl of Zetland* left Lerwick a few days later to begin a new career in the search for North Sea oil.

The outer isles of Orkney are served by the ships of the Orkney Islands Shipping Company the *Orcadia* and the *Islander* running regularly between Kirkwall and the North Isles. The former has a capacity for over 300 passengers while the latter is a small cargo vessel with accommodation for 12 passengers. The South Isles are served by a converted roll-on-roll-off vessel similar to those in use in Shetland but equipped with a crane since there are at present no roll-off facilities in Orkney's South Isles. In addition a small ferry runs regularly between Stromness and the north end of Hoy while the passenger vessel, *Clytus*, serves the island of Shapinsay, while in summer a motor vessel runs from Kirkwall to the North Isles. Communications between the Mainland of Shetland and the remote isles of Foula and Fair Isle are subject to frequent interruptions due to bad weather. These islands are hampered by the lack of safe anchorages and in the former case the small mail boat has to be lifted out of the water at the end of each trip to Walls. Fair Isle has a slipway where the *Good Shepherd* is hauled ashore after each trip to Grutness.

Another important innovation in both Orkney and Shetland is the air service provided by Loganair whose small Islander aircraft now link the main isles of Orkney with Kirkwall Airport while in Shetland from their base at Sumburgh they operate a service to new runways at Tingwall, Whalsay and Unst and provide chartered flights to small landing strips at Fair Isle, Foula and Papa Stour.

Another valuable function provided by Loganair is the air ambulance service whereby patients can be transferred quickly to Aberdeen when specialist treatment is required. Many scores of islanders have already benefited from this service and some owe their lives to it.

In spite of the warnings of the pessimists the essential character of Orkney and Shetland has not been impaired by the coming of oil. Industrialization has been limited to a few localities in Shetland and to one island in Orkney with the result that most of the area is still unspoiled and residents and visitors can enjoy the peace and quiet that have been a feature of the islands for so long. A serious threat to Orkney's environment came in 1977 with plans for open-cast uranium mining on a major scale. A few years earlier a geological survey had revealed the presence of uranium ore in the sandstone rocks between Stromness and Yesnaby. To carry the investigations a stage further the South of Scotland Electricity Board and the North of Scotland Hydro-Electric Board applied for planning permission to drill a series of bore holes in the three most promising areas of the tract of land now known as 'the uranium corridor'.

Neither the two boards nor the Planning Department of Orkney Islands Council were prepared for the volume of protest that came from all parts of the islands and the skilful campaign mounted against the proposal by Orkney Heritage Society. Cars, houses and business premises were plastered with "No Uranium" posters while 600 letters and a petition containing 6,000 signatures were delivered to the council offices protesting against the drilling application. The school joined in the campaign and on 7th February 1977, when the Planning Committee met to discuss the application, 400 people marched through the narrow streets of Kirkwall to stand in silent protest outside the council buildings. In the face of such a determined show of opposition the committee decided unanimously against the planning application.

Orkney Islands Council went a stage further and incorporated in the Structure Plan for the islands a clause which states that uranium mining will not be permitted in Orkney. Inevitably this decision has come under fire from some politicians and others who argue that in the national interest drilling should be allowed to proceed. The EEC is known to resent the Orcadians' attitude since it is part of the community's policy that all sources of uranium within member countries should be exploited thus lessening the present dependence on uranium from Russia and other parts of the world.

On 20th March 1979 the two electricity boards stated their case before a Recorder at the Scottish Office's examination in public of certain aspects of Orkney's Structure Plan. The people of Orkney were represented by Orkney Heritage Society under their chairman Mrs. Marjory Linklater who summarized the fears of the entire community. Foremost in most people's minds is the safety aspect—the fear that mining operations will lead to contamination as radioactive waste material is spread far and wide by the wind. Many people emphasize the devastating effect that such operations will have on the landscape and point out that while open-cast uranium mining may be tolerable in the vast uninhabited wastes of Australia or Russia it is certainly not so in a small land mass like Orkney.

Orkney Farmers' Union expressed their concern at the effect on the islands' farming industry if mining were allowed to proceed. Many acres of good farm land on the West Mainland would be destroyed while farmers in all parts of Orkney would suffer a loss of income through consumer resistance to the islands' beef, lamb, butter and cheese. A detailed submission by Stromness Community Council supporting Orkney Islands Council's stand against uranium ended with the words "Orkney is a unique community which could be totally destroyed by all that is involved in uranium mining".

A unique community—that puts it in a nutshell and the phrase is as true of Shetland as it is of Orkney. Both groups exhibit a distinctiveness which is rare in these days of standardization and super power blocks. This is seen in the strength of the islands' traditions whether it be Kirkwall's Ba Game or Lerwick's Up-Helly-Aa. It is seen in the columns of the local newspapers and in the vitality of the programmes put out by Radio Orkney and Radio Shetland.

It is this distinctiveness that gives inspiration to the pen of George Mackay Brown, a native of Stromness, whose genius is recognized far beyond the shores of Orkney, who has been given literary prizes and substantial awards from the Arts Council and who was awarded the O.B.E. in 1974. In his poetry George Mackay Brown combines a keen sense of past ages with a deep understanding of life today in a way that seems to ignore completely the intervening centuries and suggests the timelessness of the Orkney scene. He describes the lives of Celtic priests and of their Norse successors as they struggled to derive from an unwilling soil and an unruly sea the means of sustenance which in spite of all the trappings of modern society is still the chief aim of island living today. This theme comes to the surface in his books of poetry, *Loaves and Fishes* and *The Year of the Whale* and in his books of short stories, *A Calendar of Love* and *A Time to*

Keep. Nowhere is it better seen than in *An Orkney Tapestry* where in the sermon of the old priest he describes the coming of spring which was as important an event one thousand years ago as it is today.

The plough has broken the lingering snow.
Fields are seeded and harrowed.
Tar is bright
On the net, the oar, the stone, the shed.
But only a few sour fish
Smoked over peats
Lie between the crust and the last ale
And thin hands droop around the table.
Days are dreicher than January.
A dead lamb is dropped in the thaw.
Yet now we are glad
For all things turn to the sun.
Our hands reach across light to shoal and sheaf.
A lamb flutters across the hill.
We are glad, we give thanks
That the Christ of loaves and fishes shared our labour,
His hammer beat ploughs,
He hauled a loaded net from the outswirls of the ebb.
The girls and widows
Magnify God with Mary in the coldness of March.
(Now lambs come fast in the lee of the dyke.)
We fishermen, crofters, women give thanks
For now the child roots in the womb of his mother,
All summer and autumn harbours there.
And poor and white
Will open omnipotent eyes to a dazzle of snow.
In this grey hungry time between plough and quernstones,
We praise thee, Lord of Lent,
For all the years brightness, snow and lamb and bread.*

Shetland has no equivalent of George Mackay Brown but it has a large number of minor poets led by the redoubtable Rhoda Bulter. It has two magazines, the monthly, *Shetland Life*, and the quarterly, *The New Shetlander*. Together they serve as a forum for local poets and prose writers. *The New Shetlander* was founded in 1946 and it has been kept alive for many years by the brothers, John and Laurence Graham, who can be justly proud of the contribution they have made to Shetland culture. They have given encouragement to many young writers and it is worth noting that a regular contributor

* From *An Orkney Tapestry* © George Mackay Brown 1969, published by Victor Gollancz Ltd

to the magazine in its early years was a then little known poet from Orkney—George Mackay Brown.

Another symbol of the islands' uniqueness is the new political awareness and the interest in the future status of both groups. The mid 1970s saw a reappraisal of the place held by Orkney and Shetland within the United Kingdom and a comparison between the attitudes of Britain and of Scandinavian countries to their remote communities. In particular a comparison was made with the situation in Faeroe which remains part of the Danish state with two representatives in the Danish parliament while it has its own parliament for internal affairs, its own language and its own flag. Orkney and Shetland, on the other hand, while enjoying the privileges of special island regions share a member of parliament and in spite of historical and cultural differences do not even have the status of the Isle of Man.

The debate was sparked off partly by the recognition given to Orkney and Shetland in the reorganization of local government and partly by the coming of oil, the new importance of the islands and the successful promotion of legislation to control oil-related developments. Another important factor was the rise of the Scottish National Party with its demands for an independent Scotland—a move that many islanders viewed with alarm. While the islands have long accepted their place in Scotland as part of the United Kingdom their place in an independent Scotland is something entirely different and cannot be accepted automatically.

There is however no clear concensus of opinion regarding the political status best suited to Orkney and Shetland. While some people advocate the retention of links with Westminster others seek special island status similar to that accorded to the Isle of Man. At the same time the SNP also has its supporters and its candidate did remarkably well in the 1974 general election. Shetlanders are taking the issue of devolution more seriously than their counterparts in Orkney as is shown in the formation of the Shetland Movement whose members represent all shades of political opinion but who are united in their desire to achieve greater autonomy for Shetland.

No one can predict how far this new political awareness will develop or which of the options open to the islands will in the end be adopted. But no matter what the future may hold the Northern Isles will always be a distinctive part of the country and as in two World Wars and during the present oil boom will always play a vital role in the affairs of the British nation.

BIBLIOGRAPHY

The bibliography of Orkney and Shetland is numerous. In the Orkney Room of the County Library in Kirkwall there are some 5,000 items relating to the islands. I have not read a fiftieth part of them. Much of what I have written here is the accumulation of knowledge casually garnered in the course of what is now a fairly long life. But for the benefit of those who may want to know more about the two archipelagos, I append a short list of books that can be classed as essential; or useful, informative, diverting, and stimulating.

The essential books are these:

(I) *The Orkneyinga Saga*. The latest translation, equipped with the most scholarly notes, is by Alexander Burt Taylor.

(II) *Inventory of the Ancient Monuments of Orkney and Shetland:* the Twelfth Report of the Royal Commission on the Ancient Monuments of Scotland: in 3 volumes—Report and Introduction; Inventory of Orkney; Inventory of Shetland.

(III) *A History of Orkney*, by J. Storer Clouston.

Of the others—the useful and informative, the stimulating and interesting—I suggest these, though I do not offer them in any designed order of precedence and importance.

The Orkneys and Shetland, by J. R. Tudor.

Merchant Lairds of Long Ago by Hugh Marwick.

The Orkney Norn, by Hugh Marwick.

Kirkwall in the Orkneys, by B. H. Hossask.

The Cathedral and Royal Burgh of Kirkwall, by John Mooney.

Kirkwall Charters, by John Mooney.

Noltland Castle by W. Douglas Simpson.

History of the Orkney Islands by the Rev. Dr. Barry.

The 1st and 2nd Statistical Accounts of Orkney and Shetland, by various authors.

The General Grievances and Oppressions of the Isles of Orkney and Shetland, by J. Mackenzie.

Notes on Orkney and Shetland by A. Peterkin.

The Northern Isles, edited by F. T. Wainwright.
The Problem of the Picts, edited by F. T. Wainwright.
Shetland Life under Earl Patrick, by Gordon Donaldson.
Reminiscences of an Orkney Parish, by John Firth.
Autobiography, by Edwin Muir.
An Account of the Islands of Orkney, by James Wallace.
A Brief Description of Orkney, Zetland, and Caithness, by John Brand.
The Shetland Bus, by David Howarth.
Skara Brae, by V. Gordon Childe.
The Orcadian Sketch-book, by Walter T. Dennison.
The Sixareen, by Charles Sandison.
Orkney by Hugh Marwick.
The Shetland Isles, by A. T. Cluness.
Viking Society Publications, consisting of
(*a*) *Orkney and Shetland Records.*
(*b*) *Saga Book.*
(*c*) *Old Lore Miscellany.*
Glossary of Orkney and Shetland Dialects, by T. Edmonston.
Footprints of the Creator by Hugh Miller.
The North Sea Pilot: The Faeroes, Shetlands, and Orkneys.
Orcades by Murdoch Mackenzie.
The New Shetlander, a magazine.
The Orcadian both of which are weekly
The Shetland Times newspapers.
County Survey of Orkney, by R. E. and B. L. C. Moira.

ADDITIONAL RECENT PUBLICATIONS

Orkney, by P. Bailey (1971)
Orkney, by R. Miller (1976)
Birds and Mammals of Orkney, by W. Groundwater (1974)
An Orkney Tapestry, by G. M. Brown (1969)
A Spell for Green Corn, by G. M. Brown (1970)
Winterfold, by G. M. Brown (1976)
Selected Poems, by G. M. Brown (1977)
George Mackay Brown, by A. Bold (1978)
Shetland, by J. R. Nicolson, third edition (1979)
Shetland and Oil, by J. R. Nicolson (1975)

Traditional Life in Shetland, by J. R. Nicolson (1978)
The Windswept Isles, by E. Balneaves (1977)
The Shetland Way of Oil, edited by J. Button (1976)
Shetland Fishing Saga, by C. A. Goodlad (1971)
Island Governments, by R. Gronneberg (1977)
Island Futures, edited by R. Gronneberg (1978)
The Making of Modern Shetland, by H. D. Smith (1977)
A Guide to Shetland Birds, by B. Tulloch and F. Hunter (1970)
Northwards by Sea, by G. Donaldson (1966)
The Northern Isles, by A. Fenton (1978)
Air Road to the Isles, by E. E. Fresson (1967)
Orkney and Shetland: An Archaeological Guide, by L. Laing (1974)
The Folklore of Orkney and Shetland, by E. W. Marwick (1975)

INDEX

Index

By Eric Linklater

NOVELS
Whitemaa's Saga
Poet's Pub
Juan in America
The Men of Ness
Magnus Merriman
Ripeness Is All
Juan in China
The Sailor's Holiday
The Impregnable Women
Judas
Private Angelo
A Spell for Old Bones
Mr. Byculla
Laxdale Hall
The House of Gair
The Faithful Ally
The Dark of Summer
Position at Noon
The Merry Muse
Roll of Honour
Husband of Delilah
A Man over Forty
A Terrible Freedom

FOR CHILDREN
The Wind on the Moon
The Pirates in the Deep Green Sea
Karina with Love

SHORT STORIES
God Likes Them Plain
Sealskin Trousers
A Sociable Plover

AUTOBIOGRAPHY
The Man on my Back
A Year of Space
Fanfare for a Tin Hat

BIOGRAPHY
Ben Jonson and King James
Mary Queen of Scots
Robert the Bruce

ESSAYS
The Lion and the Unicorn
The Art of Adventure
The Ultimate Viking
Edinburgh

HISTORY
The Campaign in Italy
The Prince of the Heather
The Voyage of the Challenger
The Conquest of England
The Survival of Scotland
The Royal House of Scotland

CRIME
The Corpse on Clapham Common

VERSE
A Dragon Laughed

PLAYS
The Devil's in the News
Crisis in Heaven
To Meet the Macgregors
Love in Albania
The Mortimer Touch
Breakspear in Gascony

CONVERSATIONS
The Cornerstones
The Raft *and* Socrates Asks Why
The Great Ship *and* Rabela Replies

PAMPHLETS
The Northern Garrisons
The Defence of Calais
The Highland Division
Our Men in Korea